TA-TA, GRANDMA

– *a novel* –

JEFFERY WRIGHT

Ta-Ta, Grandma
Copyright 2016 by Jeffery Wright

Edited by: Sherry Hinman

Front Cover: Picture of a cricket ball decorated with a hibiscus bloom, representing power and passion.

No part of this publication may be reproduced, distributed, or transmitted in any form or by any means, including photocopying, recording, or other electronic or mechanical methods, without the prior written permission of the publisher, except in the case of brief quotations embodied in critical reviews and certain other noncommercial uses permitted by copyright law.

Wholesale discounts for book orders are available through Ingram Distributors.

Tellwell Talent
www.tellwell.ca

ISBN
Paperback: 978-1-988186-66-5
E-Book: 978-1-988186-67-2

Horatio and Myra

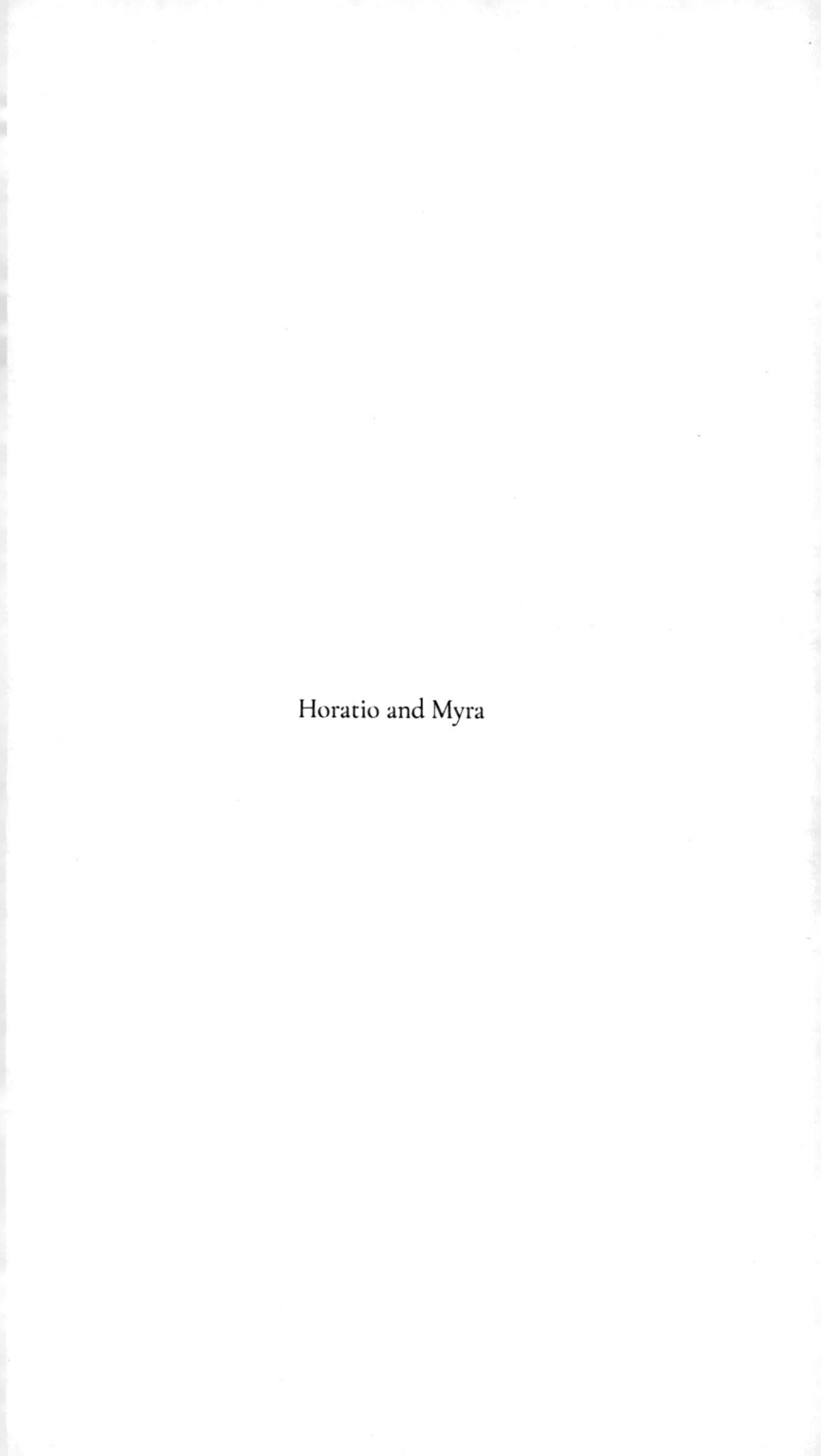

On warm, quiet afternoons, when the wind snoozed and the trees stood still, Flinty Augustus Magnum lay on a bench in his Grandma's garden and listened to the rhythms of Bob Marley and the Wailers' small lyrical axe, swung from radios around Spring Valley District, chopping down big lies and transforming corruption into justice.

TABLE OF CONTENTS

CHAPTER 1:
Blossom Returns — 1

CHAPTER 2:
Gwendolyn: The Lie Factory — 17

CHAPTER 3:
Name's Bond: James Bond — 25

CHAPTER 4:
Hurricane Flash — 39

CHAPTER 5:
From Cricket to Books — 59

CHAPTER 6:
A Grilling at Lunch — 75

CHAPTER 7:
My Name's Mr. Malick Tabangi — 93

CHAPTER 8:
Under the Spell of Joshua's Rod — 115

CHAPTER 9:
Father and Son in a Storm — 139

CHAPTER 10:
The Tonic Wine — 149

CHAPTER 11:
Rasta Binzy — 157

CHAPTER 12:
Waltz of the Unbloomed Hibiscus — 167

CHAPTER 13:
A Matador at the Wicket — 187

CHAPTER 14:
For the Love of Country — 197

CHAPTER 15:
Fallen Into Darkness — 213

CHAPTER 16:
Waking Up — 225

CHAPTER 17:
A Tranquil Afternoon — 241

CHAPTER 18:
Oh, Hello, Mr. Tabangi! — 251

CHAPTER 19:
Musketeers' Farewell   257

CHAPTER 20:
Mr. Magnum, Sit Down   261

CHAPTER 21:
Detective Fitzbright   267

CHAPTER 22:
Hutch's Secret   273

CHAPTER 23:
On the Edge of a Hurricane   281

CHAPTER 24:
Ta-ta, Grandma   291

GLOSSARY   311

ABOUT THE AUTHOR
Jeffery Wright   315

ACKNOWLEDGEMENTS   317

Omar, Pierre and Caroline

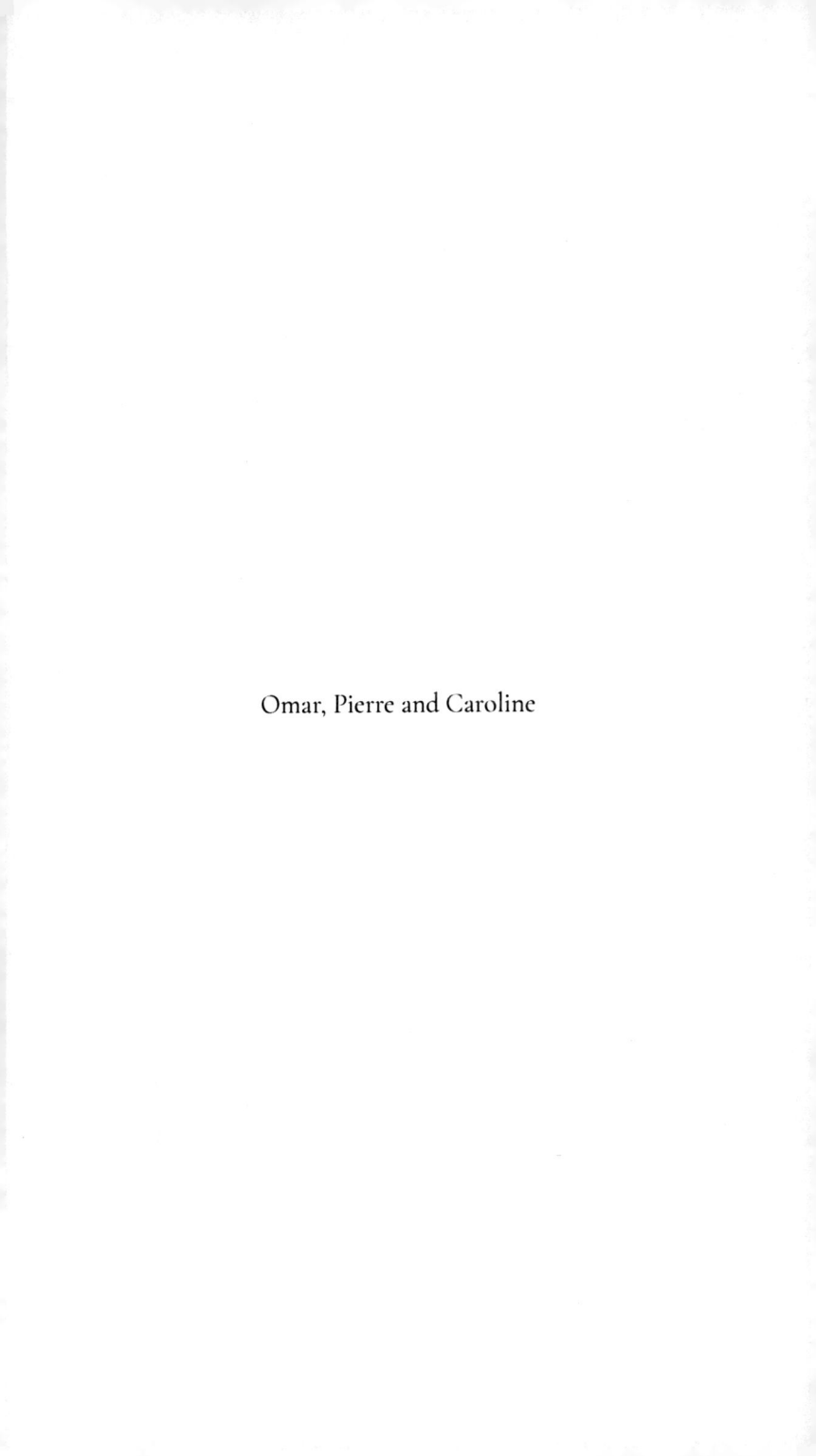

CHAPTER 1:
Blossom Returns

Mother's bright eyes gazed at me through the window of the old grey Morris Oxford, as it pulled up in front of the gate. She was returning from Canada after seven years. As the door swung open, she sprinted from the vehicle toward me with the speed of Donald Quarrie winning the 200-metre Olympic gold medal in Montreal a year earlier. She grabbed my head, pulled it down toward her chest, and rocked our bodies from side to side. Then she pushed me away and gazed at my face before crushing my head again to her chest. I could hardly breathe.

She shuffled her feet to the joyful rhythms of her heart; then, looking up to the blue mid-afternoon sky, she let go a long, pent-up sigh. "Thank you, Lord, for allowing me to hold my sons again." Then, just as suddenly, the dam that was filled with the awful complaints from Grandma's letters to her overflowed and flooded my ears, almost washing me off my feet. She moved her palms slowly over my body, searching for mounds of healed flesh from the accidents and dangerous adventures Grandma had written to her about. "The cricket bat caused this fat bump in your head?" she asked as her index fingers lingered on the hairy patch of healed flesh.

"That was a year ago," I answered, grinning.

"Flinty, which finger did the electrical fire burn at school? Which hand did you break chopping down trees after watching karate movies? What were you doing all the way in Johnson Town to fall off your bike and almost kill yourself?"

Her voice grew angrier with each question that came at me like sharpened darts. She allowed me no time to answer, so I kept quiet. She held my shoulders again and stared at me, amazed that I was still alive. I realized that Grandmother's letters chronicling my bad behaviour had put her on edge for the past seven years.

"You are so tall, but what made you so crazy?" she asked.

"He is almost six feet now," Grandpa Hutchinson—we just called him Hutch—chimed in, beaming at her.

"Oh, Ma, you are making a big deal of it. I have always done these things; you only noticed them because you read about them in letters." I lied because as soon as she left, I had found new freedom to do the things I could not do when she was around.

"I will never leave you boys again, you hear me? Never!" she promised. Then she turned to her youngest son. "Little Hutch, why were you in so much fights at school?"

"The boys dem won't stop bothe-rin' me," said Little Hutch.

Mother patted his head lightly and, within minutes, my two brothers—Brenton and Little Hutch; two cousins—Reggae-Slim and Max; and I—five boys and my mother—were crowded into Grandma's bedroom, listening to her dramatized, line-by-line details of my seven years of unruly behaviour. According to Grandma, because I was the oldest, whatever I did influenced the others. So I was the source of all their awful conduct.

Grandma sat on her old Victorian bed with the four tall, black, wooden posts almost touching the ceiling, as if she was on stage in a one-woman show; all eyes were on her as she began her monologue. Her hands moved slowly through the air, caressing it to conspire with her mouth to make sure her stories came with flair. "Blossom," she began, "every single Thursday evening after school, since Flinty turned 13, he's sneaked off to karate movies," she complained. I gazed at her and then at my mother, wondering what was coming next.

"He gambled on domino games and bingo for beer, drinking alcohol in his school uniform at Berti's Bar. Gambling has gotten so bad at the bar, many children gamble off their tuition money. Two years ago, when parents complained, the police raided it with guns drawn. Some of the schoolboys had to jump through the window to escape. Gwendolyn swears that Flinty was there and he denied it, but I would rather put my money on Gwen than Flinty." Gwendolyn was Spring Valley's chief gossip queen. "Sometimes, he comes home from school drunk, staggering around like a rabid dog." Grandma shook her head in disgust, jiggling her red head wrap.

"That's another one of Gwendolyn's lies," I shouted. "I was not drunk; I had a stomach ache," I said, but all eyes were on the one-woman show.

"You know Alfred—Angie's father—he caught your son in her bedroom on top of his daughter. Imagine that? And I found a half-used pack of condoms in his pocket three years ago, when he was only 14, saying he was safekeeping it for Mookie. You know Miss Tula's son from up the road? The two of them are bench and ass; best friends needing each other to cover up their slackness." Grandma's voice rose higher and her eyes opened wider as her accusing words filled the room.

"Ma, all of Grandma's stories are Gwen's lies," I said, trying again. Everyone ignored me.

Grandma was handing off to my mother the seven-year burden I had heaped on her back, like an exhausted night watchman delivering a frightening overnight report to his morning replacement. Grandma was ending her terrified graveyard shift and felt lucky because there were many scrapes and bruises, but no deaths, during her watch. To my surprise, the bad report she was delivering did not seem to ruffle Mother. She listened quietly throughout and at one point reached out, took my hands and just stared at me, her half-open mouth on her pale face showing equal mixture of happiness and concern.

However, when Grandma told her I had spent time with Lola Dawson, Spring Valley's "single star" retreat for men and boys alike, I prepared myself for destruction. That's because all her letters from Toronto, for seven years, had ended the same way: Flinty, listen to your grandparents; wear clean underwear every day; give up cricket; and pick up your books. And remember my promise to you: if you get any girl pregnant, and if you ever get mixed up with either of the two Dawson sisters, I will be your mother no more. That whole family is trouble. I love you, and God bless you, son.

My dear Mother,

I have given up cricket. I am reading my books, even thick, heavy ones without pictures, and attending all my classes and writing long essays and compositions. The other day, Mrs. Black, my English teacher, sent all the boys in my class except me to the principal's office for flogging, for not doing their poetry homework. She told me that my creativity and imagination were the best in her class. Oh and every day I wear clean underwear to school.

How can I ever forget what you promised to do to me if I get any girl pregnant? I will never do it because I value my life. Plus, I am too busy studying to spend any time with girls—especially the Dawson sisters. Don't believe a word of Grandma's letters. I am your obedient little Flinty who loves you.

Love you, Ma.

Your son, Flint

P.S. Don't forget to send the cassette tape recorder you promised.

In fact, I only went to Lola Dawson because I had fallen on hard times; the other girls weren't biting my lines. So one evening, on a slow walk home from school, I tried out a new and improved string of pick-up babble on the one girl who I was sure would gobble it up: Lola. I wanted to nibble on the two ripe mangoes hanging from her chest—a one-time walk through her fruit market that no one had to know about—a little snack before going home to dinner.

Those two fruits bulging under Lola's blouse were ready and I was hungry. It had been many months since my hormone factory had gone into overdrive, engine steaming and burning but getting nowhere. That evening, Lola smiled at me, and her chalk-white teeth glistened between her full red lips. A large chunk of one of her front teeth was not there, chipped off diagonally to give it a perfect triangular shape, making her even more appealing. She looked like a warrior princess with a premium battle scar, the same way my many sprained and disjointed fingers from fast-flying cricket balls elevated my status on the cricket team as a tough batsman. She was a gifted fighter, delivering punches to boys and girls alike that equalled those of heavyweight boxer George Foreman, who had knocked out Smokin' Joe Frazier at the National Stadium in Kingston three years earlier. I did not ask, but I was certain Lola's front tooth had absorbed someone's big fist, maybe someone wearing an iron ring.

But on that warm, quiet evening, Lola Dawson switched her warrior soul from ice cold to sultry. I even saw a halo of grace glowing around her. Her big brown eyes brightened and, when she smiled, I was hers to be led by my school tie—stained with sugar cane juice—into the deep waters of seduction. I betrayed Mother's counsel and—in front of Lola's unkempt hillside home—lusted under the lush pear tree with little insects crawling on its scruffy trunk.

When Lola turned her head directly into the sun, rows of her dense patch of acne, which spread across her forehead and down both cheeks, lit up. My eyes escaped her gritty landscape by sliding quickly to her full red lips and over a dime-sized mangled healed-up area of flesh on her left cheek—another badge of honour from another fight—to trail along her thin smooth neckline and rest with great relief on her buffed-up bosom. But this time my exploring eyes were suddenly blocked by a tired but fully tensioned button in the centre of her chest, like a lonely, overworked security guard, on duty between her two fruits to stop them from bursting out of her yellow, skin-tight blouse and discouraging intruders like me. Her well-worn but clean white bra dotted with tiny holes—for ventilation—played peek-a-boo with me when she stretched her arms and twisted her body, her small waist and a butt that bubbled far away from the rest of her, bracing her short, skin-tight, white mini-skirt.

I quietly recited a prayer, asking Cupid to draw back her cute little bow, and shoot her arrow into that security guard pretending to be a button on Lola's chest and break it. I wanted my eyes to enjoy the images in my head: Lola's full-figured body rolling around with me on a carpet of dainty Spanish needles, smelling her musky perfume, her eyes soft, dried leaves stuck to her short, frizzy black hair.

My eyes closed as I inhaled her warm breath and kissed her lips, including a little bead of sweat just above her top lip.

But Cupid ignored my plea, so I took a deep breath, exhaled slowly, paced the black asphalt, rubbed my sweaty palms together and loosened my navy-blue school tie with the three slim white lines streaking across it. I dragged extra air into my lungs to sandbag the part of me swelling like a river. This made my chest rise and fall more slowly and deflate sinful thoughts of Lola, and I pulled myself back from falling into the bottomless pit of my imagination. I was brought back to reality by some small boys riding around us on skateboards and the bearded but respected Mr. Graphstine—a friend of my father's—riding his little grey donkey home, carrying a machete under his arm and balancing a bunch of green bananas on his head.

"Flinty, bowy, me never know you chatting up girls at your age already?" he shouted as the little grey donkey scurried passed us. "Me have to tell Oscar 'bout this."

"Only talking about school work, Mr. Graphstine."

"So why is your pant front bulging out like that?"

"I've a comic book in my pocket sir," I answered, with an embarrassed smirk, and removed my oversized Duke of Trelawny designer bag from my back to cover up my pant front.

As the tap dancing rhythm of Mr. Graphstine's donkey's feet faded, I gazed at Lola's eyes again. "I bet the West Indies is going to beat India, four of the five test matches," I said to Lola.

"I am in love with Lawrence Column. He is sexy," she said, laughing playfully while kicking her right foot at a Monarch butterfly fluttering in a neglected patch of grass on the edge of the road. Lawrence Column was the star cricketer of the West Indies team, who had scored the highest number of runs that year. The whole country was in love with him. Plus, he was the national television pitchman for the popular cologne.

"How can you be in love with someone you only see on television?" I felt cheated that Lola had chosen someone she'd never met over me, who was standing in front of her. But I took little comfort in Bob Marley's words that "Only the foolish dog barks after the flying bird."

I changed the subject fast to plug up the holes squirting out my pride into the street. I told her the country's state of emergency was necessary, but not in Spring Valley, where, like most small towns, people only wanted jobs instead of men with big guns dressed in uniforms. "Babylon searched Grandma on the bus on her way to Mandeville last week," I told Lola. "Almost gave her a heart attack."

The thought of police patting down my Grandma was terrifying to me. The only police officer Grandma knew was Fitzbright, her nephew, a detective and honourable crime fighter who wrestled bad boys in the streets of Kingston. Grandma worshipped the ground he walked on. Through Officer Fitzbright's eyes, lawmen were saints who risked their lives to protect women and children. So it was a shock for her, having men dressed in blue overalls brandishing M-16 rifles and ugly shotguns, ordering her around and patting her down. "I don't believe she will ever take the bus again," I told Lola.

"I bet Police Chambers was there when your Grandma was searched," Lola said with a sheepish giggle.

"Who?"

"Corporal Chambers."

"You know the policemen at the station?"

"I have been with all of them," she answered with a wink of her left eye. Then she burst into laughter.

Lola continued to laugh when I told her Principal Black used the school's public address system to demand that the student who stole six sets of underwear from a clothing store in Spring Valley Town bring them to his office without delay, before he called out the culprit's name at devotion the next morning. Still trying to wipe her adoration of Lawrence away, I told her the popular world cricketer was a bonehead who had no idea about history, while I was about to read Alex Haley's new book, *Roots*, which Mr. Binns—our history teacher—had recommended. But Lola, who stayed away from school for days at a time, just giggled and switched to talking about her love for motorbikers—the ones who rode aimlessly, dillydallying here and there, wearing gun-mouth pants and black sunglasses, bumping into adventures, from which many never returned.

"Those boys know how to live, Flinty," she said, almost scolding me. "You only play cricket and go to 4-H Club meetings. Sorry, Flinty. If you were Lawrence Column or had a red motorbike, so I could sit behind you and lean my chest into your back and cuddle your waist as we sped into the wind, away from here, to anywhere else—you would have a chance with me." Her bright eyes and white teeth were still lighting up her face as her cherry red lips moved, but I tuned out the rest of her rejection. It was time to go. I was neither Lawrence Column nor a Babylon, and my legs were my only transport, so all chances with the warrior princess had run out of gas.

I wobbled slowly home like a truck driving on deflated tires. All my pride leaked out of me and took my energy with it. I drifted slowly. I kicked at rusty tin cans along the side of road but missed. I kicked at a bullfrog hiding in the grass and missed it, too. It retaliated by squirting a yellowish goo at me; I had to jump fast from the streaming liquid. I grabbed at butterflies idling but missed them all, and when I tried to skip stones off the water of Garden River, they all sank. Suzy Danforth—supposedly a friend—saw me walking toward her and when I smiled, she flung herself to the other side, as if escaping from King Kong.

But when I got home, good old Grandma's dinner pumped me up again: cooked yam, cornmeal dumplings, codfish, ackee and avocado slices, all washed down with freshly squeezed sour-sop juice sweetened with condensed milk from America.

Grandma's story at dinner that evening was dreadful. She said she had been prevented from visiting her garden by a devil-possessed, two-headed, crocodile-sized croaking lizard, with fire dripping from its eyes, long razor-sharp teeth and a tail that lashed from side to side like a razor-sharp whip, cutting down shrubs and small trees in her garden. All of us had heard about this monster, but only Grandma ever saw it and only when she was home alone. That's when the giant mysterious reptile crawled from behind a crusty black rock on the edge of her garden and terrorized her. When this happened, she locked all doors and watched from her bedroom window as it wobbled around the yard. It would eat bugs and birds and slap its tail against the water apple tree and would catch and crunch the apples with its razor-sharp teeth. When Kende, the family cat, was found without its head, Grandma knew without a doubt that the evil crocodile-size lizard had done it.

But on that Wednesday, Grandma had planned to sit on her bench in her garden, under the lush June plum tree, and enjoy the afternoon. As usual, she would pray the lizards would be snoozing, so she could hum a few religious tunes and use her wood-handled pocket knife to peel and slice a ripe Julie mango and eat the juicy squares slowly, to savour the moment. I usually chowed down my dinner with great speed, grinning and nodding and pretending I was enjoying Grandma's boring stories, just like Hutch. That day, however, neither Grandma nor I had a chance to eat our mangoes, so I listened to the old lady's tale with a deep understanding. To me, that damned reptile that destroyed Grandma's day was Lawrence Column, motorbikers and Spring Valley Babylon policemen rolled up into one.

"You were not the only one who didn't eat your mangoes today, Grandma," I told her, touching her brown hand resting on the table.

"You wanted to eat Julie mangoes, too?" she inquired, wrinkling her face in confusion.

"Grandma. I will kill that giant after dinner," I offered, knowing there was no such monster.

A new pair of glasses would have shrunk the giant reptile into a scrawny piece of twig. But Grandma would never replace her glasses, which had been crafted in England by the great Sir Dennis Watson, dead long ago. But like everything made in England, the eye doctor's legacy was legendary to my grandparents' generation. Those wearing Watson's glasses needed nothing else, and it did not matter how old they were; in fact, the older the better. So Grandma would continue to scream and run from that brown, skinny piece of twig of a lizard she called "monster."

She always made sure the five of us ate the meal she had laboured all day long in the hot kitchen to prepare. And if by chance I left any food on my plate, she needed a thorough explanation as to why.

"You left the best of the meal on your plate," she would complain.

"Belly's full."

"A good man eats his own provide first, before eating other people's."

"It was only sugar cane juice."

"Whose sugar cane was it?"

I would give a name. There would be silence and then a new question. "Do you know that sugar cane farm is planted on an old burial ground?" Then she would laugh and toss a lump of sugar in her mouth.

Her revelation would cause my face to twist as I'd leave the table to change and hurry off to my Youth Club, 4-H Club meeting, or match practice or just to hang out on the Garden River Bridge with my friends, Sam, Ziggy, Mookie, and Stan-Chen, and eat bulla cake and cheese. But sometimes, Grandma hung out at the dinner table to fish for my daily wrongs, which would be promptly reported to Hutch as he listened to the news and sports on the radio. Not wanting to be disturbed, Hutch would clear his throat two or three times loudly, as a warning, and if Grandma continued talking, he would screw up his face and then turn up the volume.

"Hutchinson Griffin, you are just as rude as your grandsons!" she would scold before leaving the living room to sit in her verandah chair and hum one of her favourite hymns. Humming was her only pleasant singing voice, because whenever she sang out the song's words, the creatures around the yard would scurry for cover.

Hutch would remain quiet. All of his five senses, plus the extra one he used to figure out our tricks, would be tuned to the baritone voice booming out the day's sports news from his Telefunken radio. The radio was housed in a large, rectangular, wood veneer box, shaped like an old piece of Victorian furniture. It had six little ivory keys, like those found on a piano, with a large black and gold knob at each end. Its station display cluster lit up like Christmas lights.

After listening to sports news, Hutch would read the *Daily Gleaner* and loudly voice his disagreement with Prime Minister Michael Manley's policies; he named him "Manlie." "We have a communist ruining this country," he would repeat as he turned the newspaper pages. When he'd had enough, he would fold the newspaper neatly, put it away, and join Grandma on the verandah. He would sit in the chair on the left, closer to that grafted orange tree—one half grapefruit, the other navel orange. Grandma never sat in that chair. Lizards crawled around in it sometimes.

But the gleeful mosquito swarm—drunk from sniffing the burning mosquito destroyer coils Grandma had lit earlier—would welcome Hutch. The entire flesh-eating orchestra would buzz its annoying high-pitched soprano note and celebrate as greedy insects sucked his blood. He would slap the pests, missing often, but squishing some between his palms and against his clothes. Then he would cross his legs, right over left, dangling loosely, and smoke one cigarette after another. He inhaled and then blew the smoke into the pesky swarm of insects to scatter them. Then he sank deeper into his chair before trucking his mind to happy, faraway places. He would smile, mumble and grumble, and nod his head with every point he negotiated with himself.

On many occasions, I saw him moving his fingers as if he was pushing buttons on a calculator, maybe checking the amount of money he had to pay his workers or the amount of sugar cane he needed to sell to pay his bills. When there was a shortfall, he would hiss his teeth loudly and a quiet "rass" would slip from his lips before he'd move his hand through the air again, punching new numbers into his imaginary money machine until a smile came over his face.

Then the cigarette burning between his fingers would bring him back to the present. He would tap the ashes into the round, green bamboo ashtray beside him, and fill up his lungs with another great puff. Meanwhile, Grandma would be resurrecting all the bits and pieces of her day for her dear husband. And once in a while, her voice would break into Hutch's ear, and he would pretend as if he had been listening all along and nod in agreement with his dear wife. Sometimes loud laughter would burst out of Grandma, and Hutch, not hearing her jokes, would laugh just as loud. They would sit in this way until the sun sank behind the mountains. That was how my grandparents had spent their evenings ever since Mother was a child. Sometimes, though, when Hutch was at work, Gwendolyn Fluxby—Grandma's friend—would drop in with juicy gossip to keep her company. That's how the lie about me and Lola Dawson slipped into Grandma's ears.

CHAPTER 2:
Gwendolyn: The Lie Factory

Gwendolyn Fluxby topped the list in Spring Valley as gossip queen, one of those rambunctious women whom Satan had called to serve him at an early age.

Over the years, Gwen had mastered the skill of stirring up trouble in other people's lives. She was one of Spring Valley's restless, spirited women who would rock and roll their heavy bodies to Pocomania church, clutching their Bibles to their chests as if the Holy Book were their husbands. The short and stocky Reverend Ralston Morris would wipe streaming sweat from his face with his handkerchief, as his gravely, half-crying voice barked the saviour's precious words at them from the pulpit. He would command the sinners to repent for their iniquities. And guilt would trigger the women into a trumping chant until their bodies went limp.

Then they would throw their surrendered hands into the air and cry and shout, "Amen." "Hallelujah." "Praise the Lord." "Lord, have mercy." Many would drop and roll on the floor in shameless fits that seized and jerked their bodies. Some would fall into a trance, their eyes rolling backwards into their heads, as if making intense love with an unseen ghost, supposedly holy, to exorcise their demon. When it was over, they would stagger to their feet, their bodies bathed in sweat, their clothes and hair untidy. And stillness would come upon their faces as if they had reached their pinnacle of conversion—from storm to calm—that would light up their faces in an afterglow of divine ecstasy.

And heading home from the Lord's house, they would smile and wave, their heads held upright and saintly above the poison their tongues had injected into other people's homes only days before. But by the next day, Gwen's demon would return and elbow the Holy Ghost out of her, to make her normal again.

It was easy to believe Gwendolyn had her own news station feeding her lies 24 hours every day. For example, she told Grandma the exact date when Michael Manley's government would take away people's houses and lands, pigs, goats and cows, and give them to the island's lazy socialist people who had voted for him. And she was firm with Grandma that the cheaper condensed milk imported from Cuba was spiked with a potion to convert capitalist-minded individuals into communists. "Mrs. Griffin," said Gwendolyn, "it took only a few sips to do it. People all over the island are being converted every morning at breakfast. You notice how watery and yellow Castro's milk is? It's because of the mixture in it that converts hardworking people to lazy communists. The condensed milk from America is more expensive but not a threat."

Whenever I was home and Gwendolyn dropped by, I made sure to listen so that after she left, I could warn

Grandma not to believe her stories. But Grandma, who was home alone in the daytime, enjoyed Gwen's company and would not listen to me.

Still, I was shocked at the deceitful story Gwendolyn had concocted for Grandma about me and Lola Dawson. That scorching afternoon, I was inside my room being tortured by history notes about the 1865 Morant Bay Rebellion, in which two innocent heroes—Paul Bogle and George William Gordon—were hanged by Governor Eyre, because of their attempt to fight for the rights of the freed slaves. When I heard Gwendolyn arrive, I parted the curtains and cracked open the window to the verandah. She hobbled onto the verandah and dropped the heavy load of herself into a chair.

"The heat is murder, Mrs. Griffin," she complained as she fanned her face. Grandma brought her a glass of lemonade; she hastily gulped down half of it.

Gwen then bent her body forward and squeezed her puffed-out belly with her right palm and made loud ugly choruses of belches. It was as if her whole body was a deflating balloon: "Burp! Excuse me... burp! WOW! Pardon me, Mrs. Griffin... BURP! Goodness... BURP! Lord have mercy! I... I... BURP! Am getting dizzy! BURP! Excuse me... burp!" She apologized and burped for about two minutes and rubbed her belly until Grandma got frightened, jumped from her chair and started rubbing her back.

"Would you like a cup of peppermint tea, Mrs. Fluxby?" she asked.

"No, Mrs. Griffin, I will be fine soon. Give me a moment."

"You must drink some of the pot-soup when you cook dinner," Grandma advised her.

"Thank you, Mrs. Griffin. I will, but the gas has gotten worse since my Brownie's death. I don't eat well since." She took a sip from the glass.

"He was a good man," Grandma said.

Brownie was Gwendolyn's sweetheart and a logger who had died six months earlier from a falling cedar tree he was cutting down. He was a quiet gentleman, and many wondered how a nice man like that could live with Gwendolyn. People believed he was afraid of her.

Gwendolyn pulled a red kerchief from her bosom and mopped at her forehead, paying no attention to the loud creaks and cries from the little chair as she rocked her body from side to side to get comfortable. She bent down and removed her slippers, leaned back and stretched out her legs to full length.

"Hottest March month and Hutch forgot to wear his hat to work this morning," Grandma complained, fanning her face with her bamboo fan. Gwendolyn, still sitting, used her body to move the chair closer to Grandma's good ear.

"Flinty—your oldest grandson..." she began. She was whispering, but it was loud enough for me to hear every word.

"Lord, have mercy; what did he do now?"

"Last week Wednesday, him hide from school and spend the whole day inside Lola's bedroom. Through the wide-open window, I saw all the dirty acts he performed on her with my own two eyes." She continued. "That boy was so tired afterwards, he could barely stand up and could hardly carry his school bag, with only one skinny little comic book in it. For weeks, there was not one single condom in Miss Codner's shop, so whatever sexing him did, she bound to have a baby."

"Lola. You mean the Dawsons..." Grandma's troubled mind prevented her from finishing.

"Yes, Mrs. Griffin. Those wicked people your Flinty mixed up with," Gwendolyn injected quickly. Grandma sat speechless. She put down the fan and locked eyes with Gwen. Gwendolyn continued like a prosecuting lawyer, stating her case. "That boy has no ambition and isn't learning a single thing at school. Him the oldest; should set an example for his brothers and cousins. Make him apologize to the whole family for such a shameful act. Him think him is a man, spoiling up your good family name, mixing up with them bad-breed people. Look how the people them respect you and your husband 'round here. Make sure you write every word in your next letter to his mother up in Canada," she instructed.

Grandma continued to say nothing; she just sat there shaking her head.

"That boy out to commit first-class treason against him grandfather's good blood, blood that man spent all him life purifying through hard work, going to church every Sabbath and paying taxes and insurance to that crooked Mr. Blackstone Hammer, that damn big-belly thief." She paused for breath before adding, "You know say, that pickpocket insurance agent's car run over Miss Amy Jackson chicken last week, killed the woman one fowl and him didn't even stop."

She eased back in the chair and glanced at Grandma, who was still shaking her head slowly from side to side.

Gwendolyn smirked with satisfaction and gazed across the clearing at the Blue Mountain range.

"Are you sure it was Flinty you saw in Lola's room?" Grandma finally asked.

"What you mean if me sure, Mrs. Griffin? I know Flinty from he was a little boy; him can't hide from me."

Grandma explained to Gwendolyn, "That Wednesday was the day the crocodile lizard came out of hiding. He came home from school, ate his dinner like usual, but said he did not get to eat his mangoes and left for the 4-H Club meeting."

"Exactly, Mrs. Griffin, that boy had his belly full of Lola Dawson that day. That's why he had no more room left inside him for his mangoes," Gwendolyn snapped.

By then I'd had enough. I rushed from the living room and stood in front of Gwendolyn. I wanted to drive her from the verandah using some of the foulest words but could not because of respect for Grandma.

But Gwendolyn, who all this time thought I was at school, got up from the chair faster than a bullet. She rushed down the steps and then turned around and began reversing at great speed down the steps, her eyes snap-shooting pictures of my whole body like a Polaroid camera, to make sure I was not a ghost. She stumbled onto the concrete pavement but was saved from slamming her head on the concrete by grabbing onto the orange tree. Then she ran barefoot from the yard and down the street. I stood there, body frozen, shaking my head in disbelief. It was the first time I had seen and heard a person sow deceit against another person with such exactness.

TA-TA, GRANDMA

However, no matter what I said, it was obvious that Grandma believed Gwendolyn's version, because in her bedroom that evening complaining to my mother, she restrung every bead of Gwen's lies about me and Lola and hung it around my mother's neck.

"How many times must I tell you that Gwendolyn made up the whole thing, Grandma?" I shouted, appealing to Mother, whose lips were trembling, fearful her son was mixed up with Spring Valley's worse breed of people.

I expected her to explode like a volcano because the last of her four simple rules in her letters from Toronto was, Flinty, if you get a girl pregnant, I will kill you in seven different ways and bury each little piece in a different location, and don't think the police would arrest me because I have an arrangement with them to pay me instead.

I believed every one of her words because I put a reasonable price on my life, so I was careful not to violate that particular rule. As I began to tell Mother that I had only talked with Lola in front of her house on my way home from school that day, she cupped my chin with her soft hands, smiled, hugged my head, squeezed it against hers and whispered quietly, "I am so glad I came back, Flint. What would have happened to you if I didn't?" Her eyes softened with concern and drowned out Grandma's litany of complaints. Grandma was still on stage, but her voice faded away in the timeless grace and warmth of a mother's reunion with her child. It saved me from Grandma's overbearing love, one that sometimes hugged her family a little too tight. But Grandma had dropped a proverbial fly in my ointment—I felt it wiggling around, like a splinter in my shoe, and was sure Mother would be taking up every one

— 23 —

of Grandma's complaints about me at a time and place of her choosing.

CHAPTER 3:
Name's Bond: James Bond

I was relieved at Mother's cool after all that Grandma had told her and was about to leave the room when she asked, "So I hear you want to study in Canada?"

"Yes," I answered quickly.

"What do you want to study?"

"Audio engineering," I answered without hesitation.

"What is that exactly?"

"Build cool gadgets like those in James Bond movies," I answered, slipping her an untruth nugget to make her comfortable.

What I didn't add was that after graduating from engineering school, I planned to build the loudest sound system in the country—one with a bass that would wreck the place and traumatize Spring Valley's false Christians every time I played it. But I was brought up as a decent Seventh Day Adventist, who was not supposed to purposely lend my ears to swaggering reggae music. Aunt Buckingstone, our Seventh-Day schoolteacher, warned us that, if we were walking along Spring Valley Town's main street and heard reggae music blasting from jukeboxes, we were supposed to run away from the mind pollution. So I knew that just listening to Peter Tosh's song about wanting to smoke marijuana in Her Majesty's Buck-In-Hamm Palace, or pleading to the government to legalize the precious herb, would be enough to put me in front of a crackling fire, with Satan grinning. That's why I kept my subversive plan about blasting Spring Valley with thunderous reggae music to myself.

"Flinty—I mean, Mr. Bond, James Bond—I always said you could be a movie star," my mother said and then followed with sarcastic laughter.

"Oh, Ma, forget it," I said and left the room.

"Tell me at dinnertime how you intend to become Sean Connery," she shouted between bouts of giggles at my back. Then she turned her ears to hear seven years of the family's juicy chapter-by-chapter gossip that the five of us boys were not supposed to know. Like the one about the pretty, sexy, coolie girl Uncle Manstickle—Mother's younger brother, who we just called Uncle Manny—had met and fallen in love with all the way in St. Mary. He had packed his belongings and left Spring Valley to live with her, with Hutch's blessing, only to find out that she was a machete-wielding lunatic, recently released from Bellevue, the renowned mental hospital. He had to slip away from her one night while she was asleep, after a month of beatings. He came home with swellings, cuts and bruises all over his body.

As I was leaving the room, I noticed the bold imposing red maple leaf on Mother's Air Canada flight tag. It was strange to see a red leaf on an island where the trees are green all the time; except for sapodillas and cedars; they changed colours during autumn. When I went hunting with my father in the Cockpit Country, where mountains slanted down into valleys, nature's colours changed only from greenish to bluish, with shades of grey in between.

Canada using a single maple leaf to represent its people's dreams and aspirations seemed simple to me. Powerful countries used strong animals—lions, dragons and eagles—to sell their citizens' desires. The Soviet Union used a strong healthy bear. The United States boasted a fierce eagle—wings and claws poised to strike. Canada, on the other hand, although so close to the eagle's gaze, used a maple leaf—strange indeed. Even our island used a doctor bird—with a needle-pointed beak that can do some damage to those trying to badger it. And the black, green and gold flag boasted, "Hardships there are but the land is green and the sun shineth." Where were the strength and resilience in a flimsy maple leaf, representing a country I was going to migrate to, to build tools I would need to brave out the rest of my life? I was thinking about this as I joined my brothers and cousins in the yard, waiting for the noisy ice cream truck that came every Sunday evening.

Later that warm evening, the family sat down for dinner: my two younger brothers—Little Hutch and Brenton; two cousins—Reggae-Slim and Max; Uncle Terrence—Mother's older brother; Uncle Manny; Aunt Blanche—Mother's older sister; her two children—David and Marlene; and Grandpa Hutch and Grandma. Grandma laid out every piece of her fine cutlery, which had been locked away in two black boxes with soft red velvet cloth interiors until her prodigal daughter's return. Her silver knives with ivory handles, and forks that glistened like precious metals, imported from

Great Britain, were her prized possessions, which we saw with the same rarity as eclipses and comets passing close to Earth.

Hutch graced the meal before the clanking of knives and forks began. Dinner conversation was noisy. Marlene and David loudly described the fight scenes from *The Mark of Zorro*. They had watched the movie on their mother's television the previous night. Reggae-Slim bragged that the cassette recorder Mother gave him would help him become the best DJ in Spring Valley. Uncle Manny was quiet. Ever since he escaped from his machete-wielding girlfriend in St. Mary, he wore a blank stare.

"Thanks for the pair of shoes, Aunt Blossom," Max said.

"Try them on and make sure they fit," Mother said.

"The car needs a good radiator," Uncle Terrence complained.

"What's wrong with it?" Mother asked.

"It's leaking like a sieve. I used brown soap to stop the leak."

"I shoulda asked you to buy a new radiator for it."

Hutch complained about banana prices, saying Britain wanted to buy the banana for little and nothing. He joked that a hurricane blowing down the banana fields in St. Thomas would improve the price in Trelawny, because of inflation.

"Who's coming with me to harvest?" Uncle Terrence asked. As soon as the words escaped his lips, my cousins and brothers wolfed down their meal with turbo speed and left for the annual Spring Valley Seventh-Day church harvest. There were usually ice cream, fruits, cakes and puddings, and girls with ribbons in their hair, wearing black shoes with buckles and white socks and yellow dresses with frilly lace on them. If I had not promised to tell Mother more about studying in Canada, I would have gone with my uncle.

Aunt Blanche and Uncle Manny went to sit on the verandah, where he began to update her on the painting job he was doing on her shop.

Mother talked about Canada with beaming eyes, about subway trains that travelled underground. "The winters are cold," she said, squeezing her shoulders together and shaking her body as if shivering. But as I glanced at the sun about to sink behind the green mountains, heard a nightingale sing, and felt the warm evening breeze that ruffled the window curtains and tickled my face, I could only pretend to understand her stories about bulky winter coats and freezing fingers and toes.

"Canada is a good place to go to school," she said, turning to me. "And you will like the prime minister. His name is Pierre Trudeau. If I could, I would have voted for him. He is out for justice, for all the people, and has high expectations for the country; so you will have nothing to worry about, Flinty. Where in Canada is the school where you want to study?" she asked.

"Toronto. The Northern Institute of Technology," I answered proudly, for I had done my research.

"I know that school; it's across from the University of Toronto." Then she started her lecture. "The people are nice. As long as you go about your own business, your time there will be uneventful. A student's life bent on studying should be uneventful. No clubs and bars, and no need to demonstrate and mash up buildings while going to school.

"Make sure you don't wear those extra wide, bell-bottom jeans pants—those white boys would look much nicer in school uniforms and with decent haircuts. Make sure you do not idle on Yonge Street; you have no business on that sinful street. Lots of bad things happen there. Did you know it's the longest street in the world?" She smiled and looked directly at me. Then, changing the subject abruptly, she asked, "Have you told Oscar?"

"Yes, and he likes the idea."

When my parents divorced seven years earlier, Mother left for Canada and I went to live with my grandparents. I saw my father only on my way to school or at cricket matches.

"He should pay for it all; he has done nothing for you since your mother left," Grandma interrupted. At one time, Grandma liked my father, but after he remarried, she said he was selfish.

"You have only one year left at Spring Valley High; you need to get the ball rolling," Mother said, sipping her carrot juice.

"I cannot understand why Flinty wants to study engineering or anything to do with electricity; the same thing almost killed him at school," Grandma said. Turning to me, she added, "You would be much better off behind a desk using a pen to write about the good in this world. What do you have to say about it?" Grandma addressed this last part to Hutch, who had finished eating and was reading his newspaper.

"Catherine, leave Flinty alone. Let him do what him want," he answered, gazing over his glasses at the dinner table, where Grandma sat with Mother and me.

TA-TA, GRANDMA

"Grandma, I am not a writer. You have been talking about this writing for too long, only because of those stories I used to make up when I was little."

"But you haven't tried."

"Grandma, writers are creatures that crawl on their bellies and look up under the nation's skirt and write bad and ugly things. Is that what you want me to do?"

"Flinty, have you ever listened to the ridiculous things that come out of your mouth? But yes, that's how they expose the sins of people and nations," Grandma said, raising her voice.

"And that's exactly why writers are special."

"And where will all that money come from to learn how to fix up electric toasters?" Grandma asked loudly.

"Don't worry about that right now," Mother interjected. "I am just glad he wants to do something with his life."

Hutch, whose face was still buried deep into the pages of the *Daily Gleaner*, grumbled, "What a wicked rass."

"What is it?" Mother asked.

"A gunman killed three policemen in Spanish Town last night. One of the police is Miss Blackwell boy."

"Who is Miss Blackwell again?" Mother inquired.

"You know her," Grandma said. "She lives across from the Pentecostal church up the road. Nice boy—not much older than Flinty. Him only joined the force about two years ago."

"How comes the first time me hearing such terrible news?" Grandma asked her husband.

"I did not hear the news this morning; was too busy readying for the airport," Hutch replied.

"What a pile of wickedness," Mother said, shaking her head.

"Flinty, walk with me 'round to Miss Blackwell's house tomorrow evening," Grandma said.

"A can't."

"Why not?"

"I'll go with you," Mother injected, and quickly changed the subject, rescuing me from feeding grandma a string of lies. I had a cricket match I didn't want Mother to know about, because according to my letters to her, I was supposed to have stopped playing cricket.

"People don't wave when they say hello in Canada. I waved at people on the streets when I first went there and they stared back, confused. They don't use *ta-ta* for *goodbye*, either."

"Ma, that's an old way of saying goodbye," I couldn't help saying. "That colonial way of saying goodbye after drinking afternoon tea is out of style," I continued, under a stern look from Grandma.

"Flinty, I knew you would say something stupid like that," she said. "All you young fools' manners gone to hell since Michael Manley took over this country. *Ta-ta* is an affectionate way to see your loved ones off. It means you miss them and can't wait to see them again." Grandma was wagging her finger at me and Mother.

"The young people them want to get rid of everything British in this country since Michael Manley," she continued. "No one wears regular jacket and tie anymore but this damn ugly Fidel Castro-looking bush jacket."

As she spoke, I glanced at the old, framed, black-and-white pictures on the walls of Queen Elizabeth's coronation, of the Rt. Hon. Marcus Garvey, of Martin Luther King delivering his famous "I Have a Dream" speech in Washington, a headshot of Patrice Lumumba (while on a hunting trip, my father told me that Lumumba—who was the first black prime minister of Congolese Republic if only for two months—had refused to kiss his former colonial master's ass, and in his short but eloquent inauguration speech on independence day, exposed the cruelty of what colonialism had done to his country and released the bottled-up aspiration of the whole continent of Africa. He was quickly branded *Lenin of Africa*, and was assassinated, hacked into pieces and then burned), the state funerals for the Rt. Excellent Hon. Donald Sangster and the Hon. Norman Manley, and a new coloured portrait of Governor General Florizel Glasspole. They reminded me that Grandma had lived in a different time.

Grandma wouldn't let the subject go.

"Flinty, when I was a little girl, *ta-ta* was the last word before leaving loved ones. When you were a little boy in short khaki trousers, leaving to go home at evening time, I used to hug your little round head, squeeze it tight under my arm, laugh and rub your little forehead with my fist till it shine. Then I'd kiss it a few times, give you icy mints, sometimes paradise plum candies, a penny, sometimes a shilling, before you'd grab it and speed down those steps, giggling like a canary, to meet your father."

She paused and then started again. "Then Hutch and I would wave and shout loud ta-tas at you, and you would turn around many times with a big grin, wave and shout ta-ta back at us. Don't you forget those days, Flinty. I used to enjoy mornings when you ran and grabbed my frock tail, and I missed you when you left at evening time."

I wrinkled my face in embarrassment. "I did not pull your frock tail, Grandma."

"You did."

"These days, people say goodbyes 'cause they want the other person to disappear, perhaps never to return. Some slip the other person away quickly, with a speedy 'bye!' like flashing a whip to hasten them on, instead of saying the full 'goodbye'."

Grandma was so convincing, even Hutch put away his newspaper and listened as she talked. She sipped her unsweetened carrot juice—sugarless, because of her diabetes.

"Why are we talking about ta-tas and goodbyes when this dinner was about my return?" Mother asked, looking puzzled.

"Blossom," Grandma answered, "I am glad you are back, but I am getting old, and will hear more ta-tas than hellos. One day, all five grandchildren will be gone, leaving only Hutch and me alone in this house. I don't want to hear any damn goodbyes from them when they leave. I want to hear ta-tas."

"But, Grandma, you always complained that you and Hutch would have so much peace if it was not for us," I reminded her.

"Flinty, that's true. You boys give me and your grandfather troubles no end, and the sooner you all leave the better." Grandma said this giggling as she tossed a lump of brown sugar into her mouth as if she had scored the winning goal in a soccer match. Grandma sneaked a few lumps of sugar, sometimes, despite the no-sugar and no-salt diet Dr. Hector Goodwin had put her on for her high blood pressure and diabetes.

"Why do you think Canada used a little maple leaf to represent the country?" I asked, looking at Mother.

"What do you mean?"

"Like the Air Canada tag on your luggage," I said.

"Oh, yeah, that. Well, there's a beaver as well, but that little maple leaf is deceptive you know. You will never understand it until you see them Canadiens on Saturday nights, inside hockey rinks, skating around on ice. Those players wearing maple leafs on their chests are tough; they fight the same way George Foreman did when he punched out Joe Frazier.

I leaned back, bright eyes gazing at Mother, waiting to hear more.

She continued. "That little maple leaf is really about hockey, like the coconut tree on the West Indies uniform is about cricket. Cricket defines our pride, slapping India, Australia, New Zealand, England and all the other teams around, the same way the Toronto Maple Leafs slap other hockey teams around, even though they probably will never win the Stanley Cup. I watched all their games on television; in fact, there's a Toronto Maple Leafs jersey in my luggage."

I really didn't believe my mother knew anything about cricket or hockey for that matter. I had only read about hockey and American football at school, and I watched highlights from the 1972 game against the Soviet Union on Aunt Blanche's television once, apparently a big win for Canada. But to me, hockey was the exact opposite of cricket. The first skill in hockey is to learn how to fight, slap, kick and punch; second, how to unnecessarily crash into other players, knocking them senseless. All this mayhem on ice around shooting a little puck at a goalie in the net and scoring a goal is barbaric. I said as much to my mother.

"Cricket, you see, Ma, is a gentleman's game," I boasted. "Players respect each other. They don't slap each other around like warring men. No fighting among immaculately dressed men; even boots polished snow white."

"And to think you have given it all up for your books," said Mother.

"Blossom, don't believe a word about Flinty giving up cricket," Grandma snapped. And looking at me, she added, "If cricket was such a gentleman's game, why you come home limping and with swellings so often?"

I felt uncomfortable because I had no intention of giving up cricket for books, even though my letters to Mother had said so. In fact I had been playing in more games than ever.

"Ma, there are even breaks during a cricket match so team members can sit and enjoy time with each other like civilized men."

What I didn't say aloud was that I had played in matches where pace bowlers bowled so fast, the ball put fear in the batsmen, pinning them down at their batting crease, the same way a sniper firing his rifle from a rooftop makes a target still. I had sprains, bumps and healed-up flesh in places where, if she knew, she would cry out in pain.

"What are you saying, Ma? Is the maple leaf, representing hockey, as tough as our coconut tree, which represents cricket?"

She nodded with a burst of laughter that squeezed her eyes almost shut, and wrinkled her face. "I never thought of it that way," she said. "But, yes, that little maple leaf is a tough deception, and so is Canada. Don't judge the country by one leaf."

Grandma and Mother cleared the table as I ran and long-jumped over those steps into the street to join my friends already waiting on the Garden River Bridge. As I walked, I swung my hand like a pretend hockey stick, slapping hockey pucks into nets—just as I'd seen it done on television—instead of using them, as I usually did, as a pretend cricket bat to flick full-toss and leg-break off my toes into mid-on-four boundary.

CHAPTER 4:
Hurricane Flash

Next morning, I awoke at dawn. The bright moon still hung low over the silhouette of the mountain range across the valley. Warm wind tickled the trees into whispering in soothing laughter, punctuated by crowing roosters readying for their day. Grandfather Hutch, a large white towel hanging around his neck, stood before the mirror, shaving, already dressed in razor-seamed khaki pants and a spotless white shirt. He flashed a smile at me, pleased I was up so early. The old man and I were more like father and son; his words were few but all quality.

"Did your mother chase you out of bed?" he asked.

"Just going for a walk before my cricket match," I answered. In fact I had much more to think about.

I walked along a narrow track behind the house, through Grandpa Hutch's lush banana plantation and into a clearing, to get a panoramic view of the valley. As the sun rose and burned away the grey fog stubbornly hanging over the valley, I stood on a flat stone and marvelled at how Hutch had cultivated the uneven surface of the land into a quilted carpet. I could see the complete authority of my grandfather's handiwork: thick patches of green agricultural produce sowed meticulously into the soil that curved around and over massive hillsides, then dipped deep into the valley, stretching all the way to the edge of a dense bluish-green forest. My respect for his confidence in the land was immense. I do not have the faith of a farmer—a lifetime of planting seeds without any assurance of them growing or forces of nature acting against labour invested beneath the earth.

Yet as my eyes tracked the spread of Hutch's fruitful labour, I thought about my future. Studying in Canada would be costly and was only one year away. At dinner the night before, we avoided the discussion of price tag. *Maybe the same faith Hutch used to plant his seeds could help.* But I was not a believer in "the substance of things hoped for, and evidence of things not seen," which was how Aunt Buckingstone described faith to us in health and temperance class at school.

I sat and cupped my chin with both hands, elbows digging into my thighs, and watched as a noisy flock of black-billed parrots glided off from a distant mountain. It was as if they'd been choreographed—directed by an invisible maestro. They landed in a cluster of pimento trees to feast on their spicy berries only few metres away. I observed and listened to the birds celebrate their breakfast in a loud, quarrelsome tone, their short, curved, razor-sharp beaks slicing into fat bunches of green berries and removing the purplish spicy marrow from inside. Their flapping wings ruffled and battered against the branches, fighting amongst themselves as they invaded each other's space. It was as if they each believed that the berries their feathered mates were eating tasted better than their own. The quarrelsome birds reminded me of some of the people in Spring Valley, who fought for more of what they already had—like more land—causing rifts that lasted many generations, until they became old, sick and dead, leaving the land behind for strangers.

The thick flock of birds weighed down the branches, some of which snapped during their feeding frenzy. I estimated 200 in one tree. But something frightened them, and they suddenly exploded from the branches in a burst of panic. Their escaping bodies fluttered against each other and battered leaves and branches, their wings whistling loudly amidst the confused and erratic hollering. It was as if the birds were cursing the unseen intruder who had interrupted their breakfast. I locked my eyes on the green flock of escaping birds as they fled into the bluish-green mountain of camouflage, taking their noise with them.

Suddenly, there was, everywhere, a loud sound of silence. It was like switching off screaming soccer fans immediately after the home team scored the winning goal in a packed stadium during a World Cup final. In the calmness, my mind switched back to the reason I had awakened so early—thoughts returned of the cost of studying in Canada and where the money would come from. Suddenly, my eyes lit up with the most exciting idea. A thought so perfect, it kept the smile on my face. I had it! I would sell a small piece of Grandfather's land and just take off. By the time he found out I would have built enough audio amplifiers to sell and then I could pay him back. Wait—it was a bad idea, my better angel countered. You would be blacklisted by your uncles and aunts.

I sat on the stone, alone like a castaway once again, my chin in my hands, ignoring the buzzing swarm of mosquitoes already sucking my blood. Suddenly, I felt fingers about my body, lifting me slowly off the ground into the air. I looked down to see my super-white running shoes hovering about three feet above the stone I'd been sitting on only moments before. I could see the blue sky and green fields, the swaying of sugar cane leaves in the wind; I could hear the birds singing, and feel the hot sun on my forehead. I was not dreaming.

"Flinty Augustus Magnum, your grandfather's father is here to tell you that you have special, but difficult, work ahead of you. But you have my support," whispered a strong, raspy voice.

My heart thumped as loud as a drum. I tried to wrestle my body free, but the hands firmly holding my waist would not let go. I listened for more, but no more words came as I was lowered to solid ground. My feet touched the flat stone. It was over in an instant, even though it felt longer. I was not afraid, even though I had no idea what it all meant, but I was excited, as if standing on the edge of a steep precipice, being tossed around during an earthquake. I felt an urgent need to run home and tell my grandfather what had happened, about his father's words to me.

As I jogged home, my mind flipped between believing I'd been dreaming and being sure I had gone through something real. I wanted to question Hutch about his father—my great-grandfather—of whom he'd said with pride that he had worked himself to death, ignoring the many flasks of white rum that had helped him into the ground.

TA-TA, GRANDMA

The round-faced silver plated clock on the living room wall pointed to 8:10 when I got home; the kitchen was scented with fresh-cut thyme, June plum, scallion and ripe papayas. I grabbed one of the ripe, yellow June plums, gobbling it down before attacking my breakfast: three slices of fried ripe plantain; stiff, warm, black-pepper-drenched fried eggs that jiggled when I put them between the two slices of white bread; and a warm cup of mint tea. I thanked Grandma and planted a soft kiss on both of her cheeks, catching her off guard.

"That boy is up to something, and the quicker we know what, the better," she warned my mother, who briefly stopped washing the dishes to gaze at me.

Her face held a curious smile. "What are you doing today?" she asked.

It was the hot summer holidays, when boys played marbles and cricket in the streets. Others followed their fathers and grandfathers to the fields, but most had nothing to do. "I have a big cricket match in Falmouth today. I play for the Sport Development Division under-19 team," I answered proudly. Suddenly I realized I was admitting to a lie.

"You said in your letters that you had stopped playing cricket."

I said nothing.

"You mean Grandma was right, that you traded your books for cricket?"

I refused to answer any further questions and stuffed a big slice of papaya into my mouth. I quickly reversed from the kitchen to escape further cricket questions. But I really wanted to talk to Grandpa Hutchinson.

— 43 —

Hutch was about six feet and lanky, with a dignified air—some of which he had passed on to my mother. He wore brown-rimmed glasses on his slim, slightly wrinkled face. Lines etched into his forehead bore witness to all the triumphs and troubles that had concerned him at one time or another. He would easily burst into loud, warm laughter as he chatted with friends but could switch back to serious just as fast.

As the only boy among five sisters, as soon as he was a teenager his father threw him the burden of taking over the land and working all of it, as had happened with his father's father before him. He did this with diligence and grace, always rising early and working every minute of the day. Everyone liked his company, and when I was a little boy and travelled with him to one of his three farms, the journey took hours because of his many stops to greet friends with whom he never refused to have a drink. He would sit in Berti's Bar and laugh loudly with his buddies as their thundering, alcohol-spiked voices tumbled into, and solved, the world's problems. Every subject in their spirited debates, fueled by extra-strength white rum, would be trampled under their staggering feet.

But Grandpa never argued politics in public—only at home and mostly with Uncle Terrence and me, but sometimes with editors and columnists as he read the *Daily Gleaner*—the country's national newspaper. And, when he was in disagreement with them, he would give them a splash of his acidic tongue. "Those damn idiots don't know what the hell they are talking 'bout," he would grumble. "How can they agree with a government with only big talk? It's the IMF that owned the island. Them already kill off the sugar cane industry. Banana next, then aluminum, and then what? We borrow, spend, and give away the country to foreign banks, piece by piece."

Then he would fold and drop the newspaper on the table and swear not to waste his money buying it again. His resolve would last only until the next day. Because his political opinions were personal, when political debates got red hot in Berti's Bar, he would disarm his noisy comrades. He would laugh loudly, calling the prime minister by the nickname he gave him: "Hail to da great Michael Manlie!" he would shout. Then he'd burst into another cackle of laughter before throwing a shot of the scorching hot white rum directly into the back of his throat. The rum would miss his teeth and tongue altogether and burn its way into his belly. This would force a loud grunt as he screwed up his face, eyes squinted almost closed, as he compelled his stomach to accept the spicy rum. "That should kill those damn worms and clear up the voice box," he'd shout as he slammed down the empty glass on the wooden counter.

Before leaving, he would adjust his grey, Ivy-style hat, making sure it fit snugly on his balding head, and shout cheerful goodbyes to everyone, slapping their shoulders and backs before grabbing his machete and 12-gauge Winchester shotgun, usually kept out of sight, leaning against a wall in a far corner of the bar. He would then step outside, shove the gun inside Guidy's saddle and mount his obedient brown horse, its bridled mouth-suds a greenish froth from nibbling half-dead blades of grass, orange and sugar cane peels, or anything it found palatable by the roadside outside the bar. Meanwhile, I would gulp down the last of my pint of B&G pineapple drink before Hutch reached down and grabbed my hand, pulling me onto the saddle behind him. Slowly, we would ride as he waved and shouted until we reached his next batch of friends.

Many people worked for him, but only his wife—Catherine Griffin—knew which of his three farms he would be at. Some years before, someone had stolen and sold a ton of his prized yam while he was away on a three-day hunting trip. From this he learned his lesson and would never disclose where he would be from one day to the next.

"Where's Hutch?" I asked, pushing my head into the kitchen.

"You missed him by about half an hour," Grandma said.

I would have to wait until the evening, after the match, to tell him about his dead father's message. Disappointed, I quickly ironed and packed my white pants and shirt and whitened my cricket boots, leaving them in the sun to dry. I then wrapped it all in plastic and stuffed the package into my cricket bag.

At 10:55, the red-and-yellow Volkswagen van pulled up in front of the gate, its tooting horn sounding happier than a Brandenburg Concerto's trumpet. I shouted a loud goodbye, waving to Grandma and Mother on the verandah. I entered the crammed van and hi-fived my teammates, the 15 members of the cricket team. The normal time from Spring Valley to Falmouth is one hour. Scrammy took thirty-nine minutes, with the help of a giant spliff between his lips—zigzagging whenever he spoke, or suddenly swerving to avoid colliding into oncoming trucks and cars, appearing like magic around blind corners on the narrow, curvy road. Falmouth, Spring Valley's political capital, was founded in 1769, before the United States got its independence, and was famous for having plumbing before New York. It was one of the first planned towns in the western hemisphere. Its streets crisscrossed, creating rectangular and square blocks like modern cities. Our trusted driver, removed his hat, grinned and flashed his young sprout of dreadlocks a few times, as he weaved the van in and out of traffic, along the busy main street and into the town's square. Checking his watch, Scrammy shouted above the deep grumbling reggae bass and thick bluish-grey cloud of ganja smoke, "Dreads, give thanks and praises. We make good time!"

"Irie, Scram. You wire de van like a telegram from Spring Valley. Wicked piece of driving, wicked!" shouted our coach, his English-mixed-with-Spanish accent and the island's patois circulating a familiar unvarnished melody inside the vehicle.

"Irie, Ginger," said Scrammy, nodding in agreement, as a chimney load of smoke bellowed from his nose and mouth.

Coach Chris Sinclair—Ginger, as we affectionately called him—was wearing extra-dark glasses and a red, green and gold hat covering his curly, red dreadlocks. Like the great cricketer George Headley, who came to Jamaica as a boy, Ginger was also born in Panama City. His Jamaican grandfather helped build the Panama Canal, but his parents encouraged him to study at the University of the West Indies in Kingston, so he would learn about his ancestors. He studied social sciences, but enjoyed hanging out at the Rastafarians' herb farm, in the hills of the Cockpit Country. After graduation, he took a job with the government in community development and never went back to Panama.

When asked if he missed Panama, he would say, "This Island is my roots." His right palm would slap his chest as if he was pledging his allegiance to the land of his grandfather as he spoke. But sometimes I would wonder if it was the island or the stout ganja cigars to which he was being patriotic.

Every time I looked at him, or heard his voice or his name, I'd remember a hot day when I was 13. During match practice, I was hit in the head by a fast-flying ball. As I was leaving the field with blood streaming into my face and onto my clothes, Ginger ran after me, stopped me, and asked, "Are you a girl?" Shocked at his question, I wiped the sweat mixed with blood from my eyes. I wanted to punch him but quickly remembered the code of discipline against hitting coaches, captains and umpires. But many thoughts sprang up: *This idiot slave driver thinks he is George Headley because he is from Panama. If I see his little grey Hillman car at Berti's Bar tonight, me goin' to throw rocks on it.*

Our eyes remained locked. He stood firm, arms folded across his chest. I started off to the water fountain to clean up. Then I stopped and thought some more. If I turned around and continued to play cricket, I would be a toughie; if I continued toward the water fountain, I was a girl. I turned around, blood still dripping in my eyes, and played out the game, grunting, my hair strands caked together from dried blood and my shirt ruined.

After the match, while I was washing my bloody hair, the coach patted my back and said, "Flinty, a lesson in endurance—one day you will thank me for it."

My mouth flooded with contempt: *Fuck you and your endurance lesson.* But I swallowed the words and continued washing up and said nothing.

"Clean up and see you next week," he said, patting my shoulder twice before jogging off. Our relationship grew much better after that day. Coach could do no wrong, and we all enjoyed being around him. He was a father figure to some of the guys on the team, and would pull out the bus fares from his pocket for those without, after match practice.

That day of our match was market day in Falmouth. There were throngs of people in the streets, in all sorts of bright colours, some dancing to loud music blasting from jukeboxes, while others were hustling, bargaining, buying and selling their wares. A crowd of men argued aloud, their frisky hands moving around, helping their mouths to strengthen their point of view. A small clique of schoolboys on holiday from school smiled widely, waved and shouted at us as though they knew who we were. Scrammy honked the van's horn as we waved and shouted back as if we knew them. The van swung left around the tall central clock tower, then another left, and circled the roundabout, merging slowly into the dense traffic, past the courthouse and the historic St. Peter's Anglican Church. Finally, we made a sharp right turn into the newly built Falmouth Community Centre compound. The Community Centre had a tranquil atmosphere, with water sprinklers that kept the garden beautiful, and a panoramic sea view. It was my second time playing cricket there. One end of the cricket pitch faced the sea, where the strong wind ruffled the water, creating swift, rolling, white waves like the underbellies of twisting alligators wrestling to kill newly caught prey.

"The fast bowlers will be nasty. Expect bouncers in wholesale," Rankin' Whipper, our beefy but respected captain, cautioned as we alighted from the bus. Bouncers are used by pace bowlers to intimidate batsmen, unsettling them and forcing them to lose their nerve and make mistakes before the bowlers smashed their wickets into pieces.

"The pitch is quick; prepare to hook and glide your way to making runs," he further advised. He sounded like a concerned general advising his soldiers before leading them into battle. I was excited to be playing in my first semifinal match—Middlesex against Cornwall—for the coveted Sports Minister's Cup finals. It was a big deal, not just for me but for friends and community, too. We were three points ahead of all the teams in the division, and winning this match would put us in the finals. Many local sports analysts had picked our team to win. But I could hardly concentrate. My mind kept switching back to hearing that ghostly voice earlier that morning. I was still wondering if the whole thing was real, a dream, or—maybe worse— if I was losing my mind.

Lack of concentration on a quick-paced pitch like that one can cause serious injuries to a batsman—even death. So I forced myself to focus on the game. The hot sun hung directly over Shampoo Grill and me. We were the game's opening pair, but, most importantly, we were friends. Rankin' Whipper had won the toss against Hurricane Flash, captain for the Cornwall team, and decided to bat first. I held Shampoo Grill's shoulders and stared into his grey eyes.

"We have to beat the fire off the pace bowling," I told him.

"Yes, Flinty. At least a 50-run partnership between us," he agreed. "Watch out for that dirty Man Brown," he advised. "Almost killed off Ducky Warren last Saturday at Brown's Town. It's him and Hurricane Flash will be today's fast bowlers."

It had been big news that Man Brown slammed a fastball against Ducky's right jaw and knocked out six of his teeth—he kept spitting them out one by one in the ambulance on his way to St. Ann's General Hospital. Shampoo Grill bent his body in half, tying a blue handkerchief around his right pad for luck.

"Flinty, be careful. Five of Man Brown's six deliveries will be bouncers."

"You, too," I said, nodding.

But Percy Chang, Shampoo Grill's real name, who had played in all 10 games leading up to this match, had nothing to worry about because he handled his bat like an artist. I have seen his batting confuse and downgrade opposing teams, tiring them out before he slammed their careless bowling around the field like a loose piece of trash. Beyond Shampoo Grill's great batting skills, his manner was polished—he was quick to pluck the perfect word to fit and smooth out any situation. Above all, he was one of Spring Valley's top students. Most of the Amateur Sports Development Division's cricketers—not just those from Spring Valley—were of that caliber. But I struggled to keep my game in top tier, and, at the expense of my schoolwork, I chose green fields over classroom blackboards.

We walked on our shadows toward the wicket under the midday sun as it beat down on our heads. Our cricket uniforms were immaculate, except for that one stubborn drop of curry goat stain on my shirt sleeve. I'd fought it with detergent and bleach, but failed to get rid of it. I glanced at the blue sky and the deep green mountains rising from the sea to create a skyline against heaven, a postcard picture and perfect fit for any travel brochures calling tourists from cold countries to the beauty and warmth of the Caribbean. I felt privileged to be playing again in such a tranquil place.

The hometown crowd erupted into loud boos and jeers as Shampoo Grill and I took our position at the wicket and readied ourselves to play. I expected unfriendly treatment from the crowd; we were visitors and, worse, favoured to win the division in their backyard and bounce them out of the competition.

Shampoo Grill prepared to bat against Hurricane Flash's fast bowling. Hurricane Flash was way past six foot, with a wiry frame, long arms and skinny legs. He had a reputation for smashing batsmen's wickets and breaking bones. He stretched his hands to the sky and swiveled his head around like a gladiator preparing for his opponent in the coliseum. A coating of sweat caused his forehead to shine a menacing darkness as he ran, with the sea behind him, the wind boosting his strides. Long legs in white, laced-up cricket boots, ungracefully bounced up and down on the green grass as he picked up speed and delivered his 80-mile-an-hour missile at Shampoo Grill. He played the first ball nicely, shuffling forward gracefully to meet the fire with his bat and pad close together to kill the ball's pace, rolling it back to Hurricane Flash. He collected the ball and looked at Shampoo Grill with a grudging grin of respect as he walked back to prepare for his second delivery, which Shampoo Grill used his bat to guide to silly point position on the field.

Shampoo Grill tucked the third away from his right hip quickly, like using a sword to parry pointed steel thrust at his left side. The ball dropped to the ground and sped to the stretched arm of Doug Matheson, who was fielding in the forward short leg position. My batting partner was in fine form, a picture of confidence and control. He was playing exactly as he had been trained to do. He even cracked a wide smile at me before he lowered his head, tapped his bat on the ground a few times and settled down to meet the fourth ball the Hurricane was preparing to fling at him.

"Hey Grill! Lick this one into the sea," Morgan Campbell, one of our teammates, shouted.

His was the only friendly voice from the booing and hissing home crowd. They were on edge, wanting to see the quick ball slip past Shampoo Grill's bat and slam into his wicket, uprooting it to fly through the air like a broken helicopter propeller. The crowd was hungry to see the match's first wicket killed, like ancient Romans enjoying the feeding of Christians to the lions at the coliseum, when angry beasts ripped flesh from bone and spilt blood into sand.

Hurricane Flash wiped the sweat from his forehead, bathed the red ball with the salted water to make it slippery, and looked to the sun as if asking for help. Then he turned and ran toward Shampoo Grill. Picking up speed, his shoes bounced off the green grass faster and faster to reach his delivery speed, and he flung the fourth ball. It was the first bouncer of the match and a furious 90-mile-an-hour bullet that hit the ground short and slid chest-high at Shampoo Grill, who quickly leaned into his wicket, away from the oncoming missile, to create the room he needed to balance his body on his back foot and hook the ball into the deep square leg. If he had made the shot, it would have been a textbook play, one we would have talked about on the way home, a play Ginger would have had the whole team recreate at our next match practice. But Shampoo Grill missed the shot. His bat passed less than an inch above the ball, which hit him in the left side of his chest, over his heart. He thudded into the red dirt. I rushed toward my friend lying on his back and saw thick froth bubbling up from his mouth and flowing down his jaws, his eyes showing only the whites and his body in spasms.

The crowd sprang into a noisy triumph, growling like a pack of wolves after a feast. "Murder them one by one, Hurricane, and send them back to Spring Valley in body bags," a solo voice shouted above the buzzing crowd. "Don't worry 'bout body bags, Flash. Just lick them down; we'll send them to the morgue," I heard another voice shout from a leafy tamarind tree.

The first aid team sprinkled his face with cold water and slapped his cheeks; then they ripped open his shirt to see a bright red mark on the brown skin over his heart. They listened to his nose for breathing and checked his neck for his carotid pulse. They said it was weak and took him into the shade to wait for the ambulance to take him to Cornwall Regional Hospital, only three minutes away. The first aid team raced from the field to the screeching ambulance with my batting partner's body bouncing around on the stretcher like a ragdoll. As everyone digested the seriousness of Shampoo Grill's injury, the crowd that had been so hungry for blood calmed down and began to care about a human being who had almost died.

Hurricane Flash's face looked sad as he apologized to me. "Flinty, sorry about your brethren, but he will be all right," he whispered.

"You've started war against the Spring Valley," I said quietly but firmly. "Wait till I catch you on the Spring Valley cricket pitch."

The Hurricane stared at me and wrinkled his face as if I had annoyed him. He walked away from the ambulance getting ready to scream its way back to the hospital. I was not sure he was truly sorry, but, as Cornwall's captain, Hurricane Flash agreed with Rankin' Whipper to reschedule the match for another time, which was decent of him. He could have listened to the crowd and forced the game to continue. I was glad because I could not have continued batting while Shampoo Grill, my partner for two years, lay in a hospital bed coughing up blood. In cricket, good partnership is important. Like a pilot and co-pilot flying a jet, trust is built over a long period of training together and being able to predict each other's actions. As the van with 14 sad faces pulled out of Falmouth, headed back to Spring Valley that evening, I left one half of me at the hospital.

When I got home, I found out my two brothers had gone to Ocho Rios with Mother to buy their school uniforms. My two cousins were playing cricket on the street in front of the house. Grandma was sitting at the living room table, and Hutch was sitting on his old mahogany chair beside his radio, reading the day's newspaper. He hissed his teeth and twisted himself in the chair, convinced the country had gone over to the communists.

"Cubans building schools here now. To teach what, Marxism and Leninism?" he asked loudly and turned to the next page.

"Hutch, the country is finding its own way; education is its best roadmap," I said.

"Communism is a roadmap to nowhere," he shouted. "Flinty you have no talk until you start paying workers. So, how was the game today?"

I sighed and lowered my head on my folded arms on the table, looking at him sideways. "Ter-rib-le, Hutch."

"You lost the game you been bragging about for so long?"

He removed his spectacles from his face and gazed intensely at me, revealing some grey in his bushy eyebrows. I knew that whenever he removed his glasses, he wanted only the truth. I sat up straight and looked into his concerned eyes. He figured it out. "Was there an accident?"

"Well, yes. Shampoo Grill, my opening partner, got hit by a ball in his chest and is in hospital."

His face switched to astonishment. I had never used the word *hospital* when talking about a cricket game before. They just don't go together. Often we just throw cold water on victims of cricket accidents, sometimes give them syrup-sweet lemonade or let them sit and rest until the pain is gone, but never the hospital.

"Shampoo Grill. You mean Percy, Mr. Chang's son?" he asked, his voice softening.

"Yes. It happened at the start of the game, and Rankin' Whipper and Hurricane Flash, their captain, agreed to reschedule the match out of respect."

TA-TA, GRANDMA

Grandma touched my hand gently and stared at me, saying nothing, and left for the kitchen.

"Did you face the bowler?" Hutch inquired.

"No, only four balls bowled in the whole game; Shampoo Grill faced them all," I explained.

"Flinty, I told you many times, give up cricket," Grandma warned before placing a steaming cup of Ovaltine under my nose. Grandma reserved her kindest treatment for accidents. So much so that sometimes, my cousins, brothers and I would rub white dust on our knees, splash water on our faces and, pretending to be crying, limp home and tell her we had fallen out of trees or off bicycles. She would send us to bed and make all sorts of treats, which we would eat, and then we'd sneak off later to play.

"A game of cricket, as life, sometimes is cut short. A day-old baby dies without reason. You should know it was just an accident," Hutch reasoned, replacing his glasses on the tip of his nose. He held his newspaper up to his face to continue his reading but waited for me to speak.

"I guess you are right, Hutch," I replied.

He looked over his newspaper. "I told you many times: you own the smallest part of the big plans for your life. You know only a little piece. Try working closely with the man upstairs, who owns the bigger piece; see what I mean."

He paused and looked at me, and I nodded, maybe agreeing with him. He continued. "You left here to play cricket; that was your plan. But there was another, which you had no control over, and that plan got done. Always try to fit your small plan into that bigger one and you will be fine, as Shampoo Grill will be."

I nodded in agreement, and then said, "Hutch, I have something to tell you when we are alone."

"Tomorrow afternoon I am going to Kingston to buy shotgun shells and fertilizer; we can chat in two days' time when I get back. If it's urgent we can do it now."

"When you get back. I have to be early for 4-H Club this evening because of what happened to Shampoo Grill."

I could hardly wait to see Hutch's face and hear what he had to say when I told him about his dead father. Hutch sees his father—Hutchinson Nedikaya Griffin—in his dreams often, but his encounters are unpleasant. Hutch would shout and complain bitterly at his father, who was always giving him new and impossible tasks—same as when he was a boy. Most times, Grandma had to break up the loud quarrel by carefully waking Hutch. So I hoped my pleasant encounter with his father would not upset him and cause more tension between them in his next dream. But I had no choice; I had to tell him and listen to what wisdom he would impart.

CHAPTER 5:
From Cricket to Books

Exactly one week after Shampoo Grill's accident in Falmouth, Spring Valley Cricket Club, representing Middlesex Region, eliminated Cornwall from the under-19 Sport Development Division finals. The match took place in Spring Valley, and Shampoo Grill, who had lost weight, could only watch. His doctor, who feared his heart would not survive another bouncer, ordered him not to play cricket again. My new opening partner was Desmond James, an able player who batted well. But I was fearless at bat and slammed Hurricane Flash's fast-flying bouncers around the field as if I was swatting annoying mosquitoes.

One week later, Middlesex won the coveted Minister's Cup, defeating Alexandria in Falmouth. After the match, we grabbed our cricket gear and slipped away quickly from the disappointed crowd. Scrammy drove us home to a thunderous welcome celebration in Spring Valley Square. Rankin' Whipper stood on the back of a truck with the huge trophy above his head and shouted, "Thank you,

Spring Valley" over and over to the noisy crowd that sunny Saturday evening.

Summer was almost over; students who had gone to spend holidays with families around the country—mostly Kingston and Montego Bay—were coming home. A few spent the eight weeks in England with their parents and came back speaking with a bastardized British accent. But most came back wearing pretty clothes and telling fun stories about hanging out at beaches and dancing at fancy nightclubs. Once in a while, a girl came back pregnant without remembering the would-be father's name. But the usual foreboding farewell to the end of August hung like a dark cloud over many of the students, who wanted to turn back the frenzy of parents rushing to pay school fees and buy uniforms and books, to bring the summer holidays to a close.

One week before the September school opening, Mother and I went to buy textbooks at Sam Sharpe's Bookstore in Montego Bay. It was the first time I'd gone out with her since her return. It felt like when I was seven years old and had come home for lunch from Aunt Buckingstone's Seventh-Day Adventist Basic School. My father would be at work and my two younger brothers sleeping—one in a crib, the other in a bed. I would eat lunch, my feet sticking out of short pants, swinging under the table as I enjoyed the meal, and listen to some of the daily hurdles she had to jump. After lunch, she would rub lotion on my knees. Sometimes she would wet her thumb with her spit and wipe dry spots from my nose and cheeks, and I would try to push her hand away.

Then I'd run back to school with my cousin Reggae-Slim for the second half of the day in sun so hot, banana leaves quailed and refused to let the wind flutter them, and birds hid in shade, opening their mouths to cool down. I was sure those memories were far from Mother's mind as we walked amongst busy traffic and bustling people on Market Street, toward the bookstore on St. James St.

Mother wore a green sundress that went just below her knees, with skinny shoulder straps and black high-heeled shoes with sky-blue trimmings, which matched her blue handbag. Her afro style black hair extended over her round earrings. She gazed straight ahead and smiled at people, except when she glanced at me and commented about some of the men who whistled at her.

"Who is he calling to with that natty head?" she whispered.

Our agreement before entering the book store was that she would spend $500, which should cover the cost of all my textbooks.

"I will pay as long as you read them," she said. Mother watched my hands swiftly grab books about audio engineering and technology.

I carefully laid my prize books in the cart, totaling $480. The whole event took only 20 minutes. There was enough money for maybe only one other book. I was satisfied that finally I could calculate and select the electronic components I needed to tweak the transistor audio amplifier I had built months before, but which sounded terrible. Un-tweaked transistor audio amplifier inherently sounds harsh (electrons flowing through solid), but I wanted mine to sound as warm as any constructed using vacuum tubes (electrons flowing through a vacuum), and, with my new books to show me how, I should have no problem.

Apart from cricket, designing audio amplifiers was my passion. I would spend Sundays at Bill McIntosh's workshop. He was from Kingston and a whiz at building audio amplifiers. He was tall and slim with a bearded face. Bill was my undisciplined hero, who could build and fix anything that used electric current for blood. Many Sundays I waited in vain for him to arrive at his workshop. But while boys respected him, women enjoyed his company, so much so that he fled from Spring Valley because someone caught him in bed with his wife in broad daylight and threatened to kill him.

My plan was to tweak my amplifier so efficiently that my Treasure Isle and Studio One reggae albums would sound fresh and warm like two long-lost friends greeting each other with laughter and fond memories every time I played them. When that was done, I would celebrate by grabbing my cricket bat and heading to the cricket field to slam the ball around. Yes! I had all the books I needed and was ready to catch the next bus home. Mother was still browsing, so I sat on the edge of a stool, flipping through an audio magazine, while she gazed at books in the literature section. After all those letters I wrote, telling her I was a good English literature student, writing long essays and compositions, she expected me to join her. But I had no intention of getting too deep into reading literature—about people with characters that melded or built up tension only to tear people apart.

"Anything from over here?" she asked.

I had come to buy audio engineering and technology books, not books about literature. I usually scanned those books quickly and understood them but never read them deeply. Literature books were too thick and required too much work—books about Caesars, kings and princes plotting, dethroning, beheading, killing kings and queens and taking over kingdoms.

At school, I was expected to read and slice up the characters of these people into little pieces, sift and divide them into good, bad and ugly, and write about them. I was then expected to stand in front of the class and recite memorable moments from jealous schemes and fit their importance into greater human experience. Finally, I was to make moral and political judgments about whether those long-ago barbaric acts had faded in the face of our proud civilization, which was hard after my father gave me the inside story of one of Adolf Hitler's real missions had he won the war. "Flinty my boy, Hitler would have used black men's sweat instead of steam and water to run his machines—colonies of men, slaving 'round the clock, to generate a gushing river of sweat to spin turbines to produce electricity for factories of the Nazi's Third Reich." That bit of news depressed me for a whole month.

"No, Ma, I don't want any of those books. I have all the books I need. I am ready to go."

She was shocked, shaking her head in disappointment and walking toward me, but stopped and picked up V.S. Reid's *The Young Warriors* and began to scan its pages. This was my favourite book about five young Maroon boys striving to become warriors as they battled the British Redcoats in the Cockpit Country. One of the Maroon villages in the book is Trelawny Town, close to Spring Valley, which made me enjoy the tale of the five boys' odyssey into manhood even more. To me, there is value in literature when relevant and close to me, the same as being around family instead of strangers. From *The Young Warriors*, I learned how to walk on the soft portion of my feet behind my toes while hunting with my father and grandfather, the same way the five Maroon boys tiptoed to evade noisy marching British Redcoats in the Cockpit Country.

Except for Xaviera Hollander's *The Happy Hooker*, *The Young Warriors* was the only book I had ever read from cover to cover. Reading Shakespeare and Oliver Cromwell took too long. My rapid flow of kinetic energy all went into audio engineering and playing cricket, and my remaining potential energy, needed to concentrate on reading thick, heavy books with fancy words like *characters*, *protagonists*, *antagonists*, *villains* and *plots*, was a mud pit.

The exception was when I was really small and Grandma read *Beowulf* to me. My attention would bubble up to the surface. My eyes would brighten to track Grendel from the moment he left his cave to his feeding frenzy on drunken men inside King Hrothgar's meat hole. Grandma told me she'd had to study *Beowulf* for her English exams when she was a little girl and wore a sunny, bright yellow dress, black shoes, white socks and two red ribbons tied to her long plaits. She would jump hopscotch squares and play rounders with her friends on Mission Hill on Sunday afternoons, under the bell tower above Spring Valley's old Baptist church.

Grandma's eyes would snatch dread-soaked words from the pages, twisting and curling her lips until she emptied

Grendel's fury into the living room around me. I would cringe as she read about the greedy beast crunching and swallowing the drunken men. She would stop only after Beowulf ripped off one of the ugly beast's arms, which would leak the fright out of me onto the floor, leaving my mind standing ankle deep in a pool of terror. But Grandma would put away the book and give me ice cold lemonade and bulla cake with a little hole in the middle like a donut. I would eagerly eat the cake, gulp down the lemonade to scrub the terror off of me, and mop the floor so I could drive my red fire engine around the cold tile.

And all would be peaceful until another dark, cloudy afternoon, when heavy rain battered the zinc-roofed house, thunder exploded like clusters of bombshells, and flashes of lightning sliced the darkness, giving me terrified glimpses of trembling goats and chickens standing on white and grey tombstones under that old, fat-trunked cotton tree at the far end of Grandma's garden. That's when Grandma would begin reading that grey-covered *Beowulf* book again. That was all the literature that got stuck in me, a long time ago, when I wore short pants and spent days rolling around on Grandma's floor until my mother or father came for me at evening time.

Back in the bookstore, I stopped daydreaming, got up from the stool, stretched and went back to the technology section. However, Mother was still reading tales, fables, and conjectures from places where countless writers' minds had strayed over land and sea. Many, from their imagination, had fashioned words into chisels that shaped out meanings hiding behind the good, bad and ugliness of human character. Like the giant book with the stately portrait of a black man on its cover that Mother had pulled out and gazed at. Almost every continent has a story like his: an unlikely hero, brave in the face of every effort trying to cut him off from his rights as a human being. He refused to be unhitched from his senses that certified him as a man, above animals. So they jailed him and battered his body, but his character remained unbent against all odds. He forgave those who had treated him below the human base because of his colour, so they made him an ambassador of goodwill.

And because they could not break his will, in a mixture of befuddlement and grudging admiration, they pinned medals on the unconquered hero's chest, creating a stalwart citizen of him, naming schools and streets after him. But all the while, those who heaped praises upon the saintly champion of peace breathed sighs of relief. They knew in their hearts that vengeance would be their choruses instead of peaceful refrain, if they'd been trampled on the way he had been.

Those are the stories that Mrs. Black, my English teacher, wanted us to read and to measure ourselves against. Stories that lift the human spirit way up to triumph over evil. However, those books had too many pages and aimless wandering into politics and cultures before getting to the point of the story, and I had no time for them. Technology books—especially books on audio amplifier engineering, which I enjoyed—afforded me the precise description of the deed.

At school, I would complete my mathematics calculations and drop my assignments on Mr. Morris—my technology teacher's—desk with a high degree of confidence about my grade. Then I'd rush to the noisy playfield, where I calmed myself by slamming the cricket ball around the field. Essays and compositions are for girls, not boys, and it puzzled me how girls could write so much from the tiny amount of information Mrs. Black gave us. Once, she asked us to write our thoughts on William Wordsworth's poem, *The Daffodils*. As usual, everyone expected the girls to write four and five pages about the relaxation and enrichment nature brought to the human spirit. That all at once, nature is our theatre that entertains, like the maestro-breeze conducting daffodil blooms in a deliberate and spritely dance, and that we could use nature's sounds and rhythms to fill our vacant and empty moods with joy. That if we slowed down and paid attention, we would see nature as our beautiful loving parent, feeding us the oxygen and food we needed, but using typhoons and hurricanes to slap our busy fingers to keep them from messing up the beautiful home built for us.

I gazed at the paper with pen in hand, ready to write. All I could see was Grandma driving away lizards off daffodil blooms in her garden and praying for another shower of rain to water them. So I asked Mrs. Black if, since there were no daffodils in the schoolyard to inspire me, she would allow me to write something about the five Maroon boys in V.S. Reid's *The Young Warriors*, about hunting Coney in the dense woods of the Cockpit Country.

Mrs. Black snapped, "Flinty, *The Young Warriors* is for history, not literature." She sprung up from behind her well-used, dark, heavy, lignum vitae desk. She stuck out and wagged her dark stubby index finger with a red coated nail in my face. Her coarse, male-sounding voice was drenched in anger. "Flinty, it's you again! YOU AGAIN! Either you are crazy or just plain mad! I am not giving you any other assignment. You have yet to complete one of your poetry assignments this year."

Then she pointed out the window to a yellow blanket of dandelions covering a hillside and barked, "Flinty Magnum! Use the damn dandelions as inspiration for daffodils!" She paused to calm herself down. Her flaring nostrils aimed at me like a double-barrelled gun, and her spotless, white, blouse-covered torso rose and fell in anger from her vexed breathing.

She exploded again. "Flinty, you provoke me like this all the time. Leave my desk, go hunt down your lost, starving imagination, fatten it up and use it, for once in your life. And if you hand me any foolishness, you are getting a fat zero. I am splattering an egg—yolk and all—over your paper. And that goes for all the boys in here." I disappeared quietly from the carnage to my desk, leaving bits and pieces of my pride and ego scattered over the floor. It was a great relief to be on the cricket field later that afternoon.

Next morning, I dropped my half-page of hard labour on her desk. I stuffed the half page generously with *ands*, *howevers*, *therefores*, *nonethelesses* and *notwithstandings*, to bulk up the two paragraphs. I had stayed up late to complete the assignment, and felt proud. Ziggy, one of my friends, hastily copied it the next morning, saying mine was better than his, a sure sign my work was good quality. Nine of us wrote half a page as expected; only Cunchas—who betrayed his brethren—handed two full pages to Mrs. Black. Without missing a beat, she used Cunchas's work against the nine of us boys. She waved it in the air and looked at the girls, ignoring the column of boys in the corner, close to the window.

"This is what the boys in my class can do when they use the fluidity of work and lubricate their sluggish minds and flush away their sticky goo of laziness," she barked.

Then she smiled at Cunchas and handed him his paper. "Good work, Mr. Harold!" she said.

The nine of us stared at Cunchas as if he was a traitor whose assignment had lifted him into academic stardom while the rest of us frolicked around in our stagnant creative swamp. After Cunchas read his essay that day, Mrs. Black grinned and asked her new golden boy to stand. "The rest of you boys go to my husband's, I mean, Principal Black's office," she said. "You boys take my class for a joke. The joke stops today."

Cunchas stood in partnership with the girls. He grinned at us as we marched out of the classroom, turned right and walked along the corridor and down 15 flights of stairs like convicts; only rattling chains and handcuffs were missing from the procession. We entered Principal Black's office.

He growled at us. "You boys are here again because of your utter disrespect for Mrs. Black's poetry class?"

"Yes...sir," slipped from Stan-Chen's lips.

Principal Black's eyes scanned us from left to right. "The worst pauper house in any land is a mind with no creativity or imagination in it."

His eyes fixed on us nine in front of him and waited for us to say something. No one spoke. He continued. "Without imagination we are barren desert, create nothing, and destroy everything, like you boys in front of me."

He paused and waited again. Still no one spoke. "It's always you boys ignoring or failing Mrs. Black's English assignments and chatting the patois so loud I have to keep my office door shut to keep out the pollution," he said.

We stood in a line, stiff at attention, like scouts on parade being inspected by the governor general as he ranted. "For the whole term, she said you boys completed only one, maybe two of her five assignments. Mr. Magnum, Mrs. Black told me your lack of imagination is the worst in her class. Is this true?"

"No, sir. My imagination is mine— I mean *fine*, sir," I stuttered.

"Yes, Flinty, your imagination is yours. Keep it—no one wants it; worth nothing," he snapped.

He leaned back in his chair, took a deep breath, and then blew the air from his mouth as if he was exhausted. "The only thing you boys do well is show off your poverty, by walking and dipping your bodies like something's wrong with one of your legs, with your hands glued inside your pockets like you have money," he said. "Rich people's hands are never in their pockets because they are busy doing work!"

Then a derisive grin sneaked over his face, eyes glazed over by the sinister joy of a lion toying with a mouse. "One year ago, while idling with electrical gadgets, Flinty almost burned down the Industrial Arts Building. And just last month inside the science lab, Mookie poured sulfuric acid into Colin Rickard's schoolbag, destroying his pens and books. Teachers complain you boys act like a bunch of hooligans." He paused, gazed at us and waited. No one spoke.

"Do you boys have anything worthwhile to contribute to this world?

Silence. Only hard breathing. He leaned forward, put his right elbow on the table and rested his chin in his palm. Then, like an executioner speaking to a condemned prisoner already strapped into the electric chair, he said, "Starting with Mr. Samuel Jackson, explain why you are not completing Mrs. Black's English assignments."

Sam was nervous. "I always do Mrs. Black's assignments, sir. I ... I ... sir." Nothing else came out.

"Mr. Chen?" he barked. "Your father is well respected. Does he know you are not completing your work?" Stan-Chen cleared his throat and stiffened his shoulders. "Sir, the timeline Mrs. Black gave us for this assignment was short, sir. I just needed another day, sir."

"What about all the others you did not complete, Mr. Chen?" Mr. Black shouted.

Stan-Chen said nothing. Mookie told him he sprained his finger and could not write more than a few lines.

"Mrs. Black already told me about you, Flinty," he said. "But let me hear your story."

"One of my grandfather's cows had died and I had to attend the funeral. It was late when I got home, sir."

My lie slipped out of me while I was planning it—I swear. My premature untruth was the worst of the bunch. A laugh splinter burst from Stan-Chen, but died quickly when Principal Black shot his body up from the chair like a Saturn V Rocket shooting Apollo astronauts to the moon. He grabbed the cowskin leather strap from his desk. "I have had enough of you boys' slackness. You are wasting the government's money and, worse, my time!" He circled his desk and made two steps toward us, all traces of smirk disappearing, leaving his face in a grim state. His chest and shoulders rose and fell with greater speed than when he was sitting; his nostrils widened and narrowed as he breathed.

My eyes travelled up and down the black tie neatly clipped to his pressed white shirt, with little grey stripes curved over his potbelly. His black pants were pressed with creases running down his legs, his salt-and-pepper hair trimmed neatly and his moustache clipped with precision just above his nicotine-stained teeth.

A vengeful thought bubbled up inside me. *Smoke 10 packs of cigarette a day, you monster. Tar your lungs and die.*

"Mr. Magnum, do you really believe cricket alone can save you from your miserable future?" he asked.

Suddenly, I remembered our history teacher, Mr. Binns, telling us about the Roman General Julius Caesar advising his troops, "The die is cast," before he rallied them to cross the Rubicon—which he was forbidden to do—and thrust Rome into a civil war. According to Mr. Binns, nothing can defuse festered grievances gone too long, and the stockpile of grievances Principal Black heaped up in front of us had touched the roof of his office. Any answer I gave would not have saved me. So I kept quiet.

And with all the naked primordial instincts of an angry lion, his left paw flew above his shoulder and brought down the thick cowskin leather strap, to land three times, at great speed, upon our backs, to lash talents of imagination and creativity into our bodies. The loud blow, blow, blow of his strap slammed into each of our khaki shirts, raising up three welts. I screwed up my face, rushed to the cricket field and used up the freshly minted imagination he had raised up inside me. I imagined Principal Black as the little cricket ball, which I used my bat to slam around the field until the bright, shiny, red polished leather ball softened and turned into a dull bluish-black pulp.

My dreadful memories of Principal Black were interrupted by Mother calling out my name—almost shouting—and her brisk walking toward me. Her face had a sure and serious look. I put the magazine back on the shelf.

"Buy this book," she ordered.

"What kind of book is it?"

"*Federalism and the French Canadians*," she said. "It's written by Pierre Trudeau."

"Have you read it?"

"No, but I watched him on television. He is very smart. And did you know he and Michael Manley studied at the same school in England?"

"No, I did not know that."

It was way past midday when Mother paid for the books. The freshness had gone from her face as I carried the three white plastic bags to a waiting taxi. I was excited to have all the books I needed, and, to my happy surprise, Mother did not comment that I had bought only technology books. I could hardly wait to get home and start learning how to tweak the sound of my audio amplifier, but first, Mother and I must have lunch, our first time alone in over seven years. Even though I was hungry, because of Grandma's letters, I dreaded the topics Mother might bring up and the questions she might ask.

CHAPTER 6:
A Grilling at Lunch

The friendly taxi driver convinced us to have lunch at the new Island Green restaurant on a hillside overlooking Montego Bay. He said it was trendy and the food was really good. As the car travelled high into the green hills, the bay's natural beauty came into view—a carpet of calm, turquoise water. But I know the sea is a schizophrenic beast—a lamb in the morning and roaring monster by afternoon.

At the Island Green restaurant, I requested a window seat so I could continue to admire the beaches and hotels tucked in among the lush greenery—a city of aliens being nourished by the silent, ubiquitous bluish water. Looking northeast toward the International Airport, I could see airplanes taking off and landing. An impish smile snuck over my face as I climbed into the cockpit of an Air Canada jet, and took it over from the pilot. I sliced through the warm air above the sleeping Caribbean Sea, heading the massive iron-bird in a northerly direction. For many moments, the wide open, playful arms of freedom tickled my spirit, cheering it on, as the bird flew me above feathery clouds at cruising altitude above Cuba, until the waitress's voice breached my solitude and punctured my imagination. I hastily handed the aircraft back to the pilot, fell back to earth like a balloon loosing air, and ordered rice and peas and jerk chicken, and an ice cold Red Stripe beer in a tall, frosty glass.

My mother rolled her eyes and screwed up her face.

"Cancel the beer," I said. "Let me have an ice cold pineapple drink instead."

Mother ordered steamed callaloo and dumplings, and freshly squeezed mango juice. Maybe she was watching her figure. At 36, she was beautiful, and I told myself that I wanted my girlfriend to look exactly like her. Just like the sea, the moment with her was peaceful—like a date going well.

Sitting across the table, Mother looked at me and asked, "So, Flinty my son, how are you?"

I knew she was asking about more than my state of mind. It had been over seven years since we'd chatted up close, one-on-one, mother and son.

I nodded a few times. "Good," I answered, looking around apprehensively.

Just then the waitress carefully placed the meal on the white tablecloth. "Would you like some scotch bonnet hot sauce with your meal, sir?" she asked.

"Yes, thank you," I answered. "But stop the *sir*; call me Flinty."

"It's the restaurant's policy to call the customers sir or *miss*," she answered, smiling as she left for the sauce.

Mother placed the white napkin on her lap. "See, Flinty?" She leaned across the table and whispered, "You like her, but she is serving you and happy to do it like a professional."

"I didn't say I like her and was not trying to pick her up," I said. "I was just removing the master-servant business from the conversation."

"Your eyes always betrayed the lie from your mouth," she said.

She was right, because I did like the long-legged, brown-skinned, small-footed, wire-waisted, full bubble-lipped, sunny, smiling-face waitress. The bright red, green and gold colours, and two of Herbie Rose's paintings, gave the restaurant a festive, folksy air. But the alien saxophone notes of Ace Cannon's *Last Date*, hanging in the air, seem to have slowed down the tempo of the patrons inside the restaurant. I was surprised there was no dark-skinned waitress working there. "No different from banks and post offices," I whispered.

"Did you say something?" asked mother.

"No. Just mumbling."

I sipped my extra-sweet pineapple drink and soaked up the relaxed ambiance, while the air conditioner blasted cool air that ruffled my green, short-sleeved bush jacket and jiggled the white-starched tablecloth against my thighs.

Mother, enjoying her meal, glanced at me and smiled. "Flinty, congratulations. I heard you were voted this year's 4-H Club president."

"Thank you!"

"When?" she asked.

"Last week."

"Why did they vote for you?"

"It's hard to say. Maybe they liked the way I collected money and bought Shampoo Grill a present after his cricket accident in Falmouth, and the way I stood up to Hurricane Flash's bouncers in the final match against Cornwall. Or it could be because I won a noisy debate defending the Apollo 11 moon landing."

"Who were you debating?"

"Against Troy 4-H Club. I simply argued that God gives us knowledge to understand what's around us, which includes landing a man on the moon. Most agreed with me on everything except for the man on the moon, saying it was too close to heaven. God's home was off limits to sinful man, and pictures on television were lies. One lady cried shame on me to defend such blasphemy, and said my seed will be blighted and my life scarred for believing God would allow wicked men to put their dirty boots on his moon, so close to heaven."

"The woman you upset, what was her name?"

"Why?"

"Ignorance sometimes takes disagreement to extreme," she said. "Be careful."

"It did not matter," I said. "Two of the three judges said they liked my calmness in the face of the noisy objections. Maybe that's why they voted for me."

Mother gazed out the window briefly before turning with a glint of pride in her eyes. "No, Flinty, it does matter," she said. "They see the good in you." Then she suddenly changed the subject. "Flinty, not a day passed while in Canada that I did not think about you and your brothers. And despite Grandma's letters, full of complaints, and you misleading me about school, you did okay."

I knew the book thing was coming, but an uncomfortable spasm pricked inside my belly as she spoke.

"Your letters lied about giving up cricket and reading books. Now that I am back, you have to brush up on your lessons," she advised.

"Cricket provided me with some form of discipline, and I feel good when people sometimes asked my brothers if they were related to the Magnum who plays cricket for Spring Valley."

"Flinty, I was disappointed at the bookstore today," she continued. "You spent almost all the money on technology books. Not one other subject. I had to beg you to buy the book Pierre Trudeau wrote. And all those letters telling me you were writing long essays and compositions and that Mrs. Black said you were her most creative student were all lies."

I wrinkled up my face and kept on eating, hoping her spiel would soon be over. But she would not let it go. "How come you don't read? Look at the amount of books your father has and used to read to you when you were a boy. You need to get your act together."

"Okay, I will."

"Flinty, I am serious; that's why I came with you to buy books today, instead of renting them from school."

She gazed at the sea, her brown eyes lost on the wide, blue, endless road leading to so many dreams: people off to new lands, often to be washed away by raging storms. Water absorbs our excess; that's why the world's big cities are built on the water's edge. Maybe the sea would absorb Mother's concerns and spare me further grilling.

She put her right elbow on the table and spread her fingers over her sealed lips, eyes still gazing off into the distance. Suddenly she excused herself and went to the bathroom but returned shortly. Her face was grim, as though she had borrowed steel wool from the kitchen and used it to scrub the pleasantness from her face.

"What were you doing in Angie's bedroom?" she suddenly asked. Her words slammed into me like a missile. I almost choked.

"What?"

"You heard me!"

"Not here," I protested. "Do you have to bring that up in here—now?"

She pushed the slim, white plastic vase with a single red rose in it out of her way to see me clearly, and leaned forward. Her whole face and forehead creased and her lips trembled. "Yes, Flinty, right here and now. Grandma said the girl's father held up his machete, ready to chop your head off, and that you only escaped by jumping through the back door! Is it true?"

My defence mechanism clamped my teeth and sealed my lips together, making sure nothing escaped. But when I gazed over mother's left shoulder to the picture of three skimpily clad calendar girls on the wall behind her, advertising white rum, I realized that the one standing with long, smooth legs spread apart, bending over the domino table, wearing a pygmy-size green skirt and with two horizontal Mount Everest breasts bursting from her scanty yellow blouse, resembled Angie. Perhaps seeing the picture at the exact moment Mother asked the question was a sign I should tell the truth.

"When did it happen?" she demanded.

I leaned back, folded my arms across my chest erecting a defensive buffer between her and me, and told her what happened.

"It was sometime last year, on a Wednesday—about 7:00. The sun had gone to bed early; it was quite dark. It had rained long and hard. Angie and I sat on the couch in her living room, talking; she was home for a few days from school in St. Elizabeth. We sat having an innocent conversation when her father burst through the front door. The door lock flew like a fat rock through the air and left a gash in the wall on the other side of the room." I paused, sighed and sipped my pineapple drink. Mother screwed up her face, her unblinking eyes fused on mine, waiting for more.

"Angie's father flew into a fit, swearing and threatening to kill me. 'You piece of—.' I cannot say the word he called me. 'What are you doing in my house?' I jumped up from the couch. 'Stay right there; don't move an inch. I'll be right back,' he shouted, still pointing at me.

"He rushed to one of the bedrooms and burst out with a machete, held high above the torn black beret, with a picture of Che Guevara on his head. I grabbed my shoes, pants, shirt, and red-green-and-gold Duke of Trelawny designer cufflinks from the floor. The machete sliced the air, coming down to chop, but at the last minute, I jumped through the back door, in my underwear, and landed first in a banana plant and then on the ground. I got up and ran as fast as I could. He came after me, but he was too slow; I lost him in the dark. I heard him huffing and puffing behind me, cussing and tumbling around in the slippery wet grass."

"Let me get this straight!" She took a deep breath, eyes closed, and started again. "Let me get you straight. You and Angie were sitting on the couch having an innocent conversation, but before you jumped, you grabbed your clothes from the floor. Flinty, you think this is a joke?"

"No, Ma, it's not funny, but I want you to know the whole truth."

"You are reckless," she barked, and pointed her finger at me just as Mrs. Black had done so many times in her class. "Can you imagine, me hearing someone chopped you over a girl? Not even one I would…"

Her question was unfinished. But I already knew she wanted me to find a decent girl, one she would approve of.

"Your Grandma told me about Lola, and everyone knows about Angie. Her father told everyone about you in Berti's Bar while drinking. You cannot find any respectable girls to spend time with?"

"Look, Ma, this is all being blown way out of proportion."

Her bottom lip twitched. "Since we are on the subject of reckless behaviour, Grandma wrote that you came home drunk but she could not smell any alcohol on you. Are you on drugs?"

I leaned forward, looked in her eyes and then stood up. "What? How could you ask me such a question? First of all, I don't do drugs. If you think I am on drugs, then our conversation is over. Let's go!"

"Flinty, sit," she said. "This is my chance to find out who and what you have become. Grandma wrote that you were on something. I want the full story!"

"Is there anything that Grandma did not tell you? Alright then, I will give you the full story, but I cannot believe you would think I was on drugs."

I took a few deep breaths, and leaned back. "Since you want to know the whole story, I will tell you. I went to Dennis's farm in Kelton. He cooked a nice meal, but stuffed a branch of green ganja limb in the pot, which gave the yellow yam and white flour dumplings a dark green colour. I got worried and asked him if we wouldn't get high by eating the food. Dennis assured me that all was well, that that's how he cooked all his meals.

"The cooked ganja resembled steamed spinach or callaloo, which I thought was alright. I mean I like eating vegetables. So I tasted a little of it with the food, and it tasted really good, just like steamed callaloo, as Dennis had said. So I mixed it up with the codfish and ate ample amounts. But later I felt dizzy. Felt my head spinning, which started to worry me because the trees and mountains came up really close to where I sat. It was as if I could reach out and touch the mountaintops with my hand or climb up their steep vertical rock faces without any problem whatsoever."

"Then a headache came on, and I normally don't have headaches. I later fell asleep on the ground and dreamt I was fighting the Cyclops—you know, the Greek mythical one-eyed monster. It almost killed me. It grabbed and tossed me around until I shot its eye with Hutch's rifle, splattering blood all over me. I jumped up, shouting and wiping blood and gore off my clothes."

"'Flinty, Flinty! Wake up Flinty. You are dreamin'... It's time to go.' That was Dennis waking me up. I jumped up and saw his two red gums smiling at me—he had no front teeth; someone had knocked them out with a piece of wood in a fight. He gave me water to drink and we headed home. I remembered seeing our house from the hilltop, but I'm not sure how I got inside. Grandma said Dennis helped me inside, but he did not tell her what happened, so she just assumed I was smoking marijuana."

Mother's mouth opened in amazement. "So you and Dennis eat cooked green marijuana like vegetables?" she asked. "I never heard anything like this in my life. Flinty, my God, you blew in the wind to every bad corner while I was away. What happened to Dennis?"

"Nothing; he was sober as a judge, but I heard that some people who use marijuana often build up a tolerance. I never used it, so maybe I had none."

Mother, grim-faced, stared out the window, her fingers over her mouth. "The first thing they taught you at Aunt Buckingstone's School was to stay away from drugs. Not even caffeine you are supposed to drink. You learned that in Health and Temperance class."

"Ma, this happened about a year ago. Everyone forgot about it, except Grandma."

She took deep a breath. "Grandma wrote that the police broke up a riot at the Actor's Theatre last year and that you were part of the riot."

"Enough of Grandma's letters. I thought all the complaints were dealt with that Sunday evening in August when you came from Canada."

"Flinty, I have not asked you about half of Grandma's complaints."

I shook my head in disgust and took a few deep breaths. "Am I going to get a chance to eat my food in peace, Ma?"

TA-TA, GRANDMA

"What was the riot about?"

"What happened was not a riot. Spring Valley is a peaceful place. Only a few bottles were thrown at the theatre by some idiots. Gwendolyn just juiced up the story to excite Grandma. Okay, Ma? We watched karate movies on Thursday nights at the Actor's Theatre—all in Chinese with English poorly dubbed over the actors' moving lips. Often their lips moved widely, saying something different from the sound we heard. But that was never a problem as long as the kicking and punching were intense and exciting. We got used to expecting only Chinese and Japanese karate movie stars, until they advertised *Enter the Dragon*, starring Bruce Lee, John Saxon and Jim Kelly. They promoted it for many weeks. It was a big deal, the first black karate star, you know. For six weeks, before every movie began, we saw Jim Kelly punching and kicking, the crowd erupting into thunderous noise. Me and my friends saved our lunch money to see the film, which was the only talk in town. Jim Kelly, star of *Enter the Dragon*—only four weeks away, then three, two, one week away. It was a big deal."

I paused and sipped my drink and then continued. "On show night, the crowd swelled. Hundreds in the line made it long and noisy; security had to manage the crowd. When the show started, and the tall black karate star appeared on screen in his bell-bottom pants and extra-wide Afro, the crowd exploded. I could touch the anticipation; for the first time we were being entertained by a black man starring in a big karate movie."

Mother leaned forward and her eyes brightened.

"No one expected him to die, but Mr. Han killed him with his iron fists. That's when the whole theatre went

— 85 —

quiet. None of us believed he was dead. I thought he was just hurt, until the next scene when I saw his bloodied and battered body hanging from a chain tied around his neck like he was a slave, which was quite insulting.

"Some idiots threw peanut cans at the screen; others demanded their money back and blamed the theatre owners for false advertisement. 'It's because him black. Chinese karate movie star does not die like that.' 'Want my money back,' some shouted from the balcony. A crowd gathered outside, and some fools threw a few bottles at the building, but the police controlled the situation. That was it. Grandma just heard I was there and got scared."

Mother's mouth opened and she gazed at me in amazement. "Flinty, that's madness. Never heard such foolishness before. Any of them your friends?"

"Ma, I agree, the whole thing was stupid, but I did not throw anything and they were not my friends, just theatregoers. And second, there is a need for black male heroes, not only in karate, but in real life. I mean, except for Mohammad Ali, Pelé and Garfield Sobers, who else is there?"

Mother shook her sad face slowly from one side to the other, dismayed that she was involved in such a stupid conversation. "Flinty, you sound silly, defending those idiots. You have to do better with your life. 'Show me your friends and I'll tell you who you are'; those have always been your grandfather's words," she reminded me.

"Ma, that was almost three years ago. Let's drop it. You just congratulated me on being voted 4-H Club president. I am now 17 and not like that anymore."

TA-TA, GRANDMA

I smiled at one of the three pretty girls who walked in and sat at the table beside ours. One of the women, wearing a T-shirt with "Irie" written on it and a green towel wrapped around her waist, smiled widely and waved at me. I was enjoying the recess from Mother's interrogation, until she grabbed hold of my attention again.

"You don't have a girlfriend?"

"What?"

"A girlfriend. Do you have one?"

"I have a friend who is a girl—not a girlfriend."

"Where is she from?"

"Warville." I slid the napkin between my fingers.

"Is she pretty?"

"She is—she kind of reminds me of you."

She smiled. "Well then, if your friend who happens to be a girl reminds you of me, she is nice. A smart boy wants his mother's character in his girlfriend."

I chuckled. "Ma, like some fathers, not all mothers are good role models. If Gwen was my mother, I would not want my girlfriend to be like her."

"Flinty, I am sure Gwen has her good qualities."

"Name one."

Mother's eyes disappeared with her mind through the window into the sea again, and my mind travelled back to one of Gwendolyn's lies. It was the time when she told Spring Valley residents that someone at the Ministry of Health told her the reason why the drinking water tasted bitter was because it needed extra chlorine. She said the cemetery—which was uphill from the drinking water system—was leaking waste from dead bodies into the well. That lie caused a panic never before seen in Spring

Valley. It took the Public Health Inspector and the Water Commissioner dozens of meetings to quell the uproar she had caused.

Mother's eyes sparkled as she moved the slim white vase back to the centre of the table. To me, it symbolized a truce, a recess from my earlier grilling. "What is she like?"

"Who?"

"Who else? Your girlfriend."

"We are different—she is secretive; I am open. I am analytical; she is dogmatic. To her, what's written in the Bible means exactly what it says. I find that kind of thinking funny and refreshing, because my mind is from a place where nothing is above or below reason before being accepted as gospel. Having someone who just sees it as she reads it is strange but refreshing."

Mother gazed out the window for a moment and then turned her attention back to me. "But since she is only a friend, you don't have to worry about differences, right? Flinty, your whole family is an open book, and you in particular, do not like secrets or mystery."

"How do you know that?" I asked.

"Ever since you were a little boy, you've found ways to make complex things simple."

"So you think I am simple?"

"Absolutely not; it takes an intricate mind to break down a complex thing into simplicity. Your mind is complex, but not secretive. She must be really pretty for you to not care about the difference."

Then, smiling as she spoke, Mother advised me, "Remember, your spirit is free." Then she asked, "What's your girlfriend's name?"

"Peggy," I told her. "But she is not my girlfriend."

"Whatever you say, Flinty." Mother smiled. She stretched her right hand across the table and gently punched my chest. I could tell she was satisfied that I had something of a girlfriend. "When do I meet her?" she asked.

"You don't." I chuckled and ordered an ice-cold Red Stripe beer.

Mother rolled her eyes, so I settled for a Malt drink instead. Mother refocused my attention. "How often do you see your father?" she asked.

"Not much. We were close, but no more."

"There will be no divorce for me—you can bet on it." Then she added, "I will be happy if you and your brothers avoid getting divorced."

"You know Miss Warren from church; she told me one day after you left that a lot of people in Spring Valley, thinking you and Dad were doing well, got satisfaction that you two split."

"People get excitement when things break," she replied, "like an explosion in a movie."

"But Hutch and I go hunting often. He cannot see that well, and his hands shake when he points his rifle, so I shoot for him. He is good at packing the ways of the world into only a few words, for me to understand."

"I am glad you and your grandfather are getting along," she said. "He never said much in his letters about you, except that you can do things well but only if you choose to."

"Ma, I will brush up on my schoolwork next term."

"You only have a year left."

"I will cut out cricket and go back to the library."

"How many subjects are you taking?"

"Five."

"What are they?"

"Not sure."

"Five subjects and you buy only audio engineering books today? Whatever the subjects, pass them!"

I nodded, agreeing with her.

She glanced at her watch and summoned the waitress to bring the bill. It was my last chance to tell her about my ghostly experience.

"Ma, I was visited by Hutch's father behind the house, the same day the ball hit Shampoo Grill in Falmouth."

Her eyes opened wide and her face twisted up with an odd smile. "You mean your great-grandfather, a ghost?"

"Yes, and he spoke to me."

"You serious?"

"Yes."

She gazed at me, eyes sparkling, and then laughed. "Flinty, you had me for a moment. I almost believed you. It's stupid enough to tell me you see a ghost, but to say it talked. Well that's a riot."

"I am serious."

"Okay, then, what did it sound like. It talked through its nose?" she joked.

For a moment, I felt like Grandma telling one of her dull dinnertime stories. "That's it. Forget it," I said and sealed my lips.

She pushed her face toward me. "Flinty, ghosts don't talk; they just move things around and frighten people," she said. "Next time you have a ghost story, don't say them talk."

I gazed at her in disappointment as she paid and tipped the waitress.

As we headed home in the taxi cab, I gazed at the golden flickering light of the sun sinking into the sea, and listened to the booming reggae music inside the vehicle, and I wondered if Mother's years in Canada had closed her mind to listening to ghost stories. I remembered when she would tell me and my two brothers shockingly scary ghost stories just before bedtime.

"Flinty, don't forget to tell me and Grandma your ghost story at dinner this evening."

I nodded, but knew I would do no such thing. If Hutch hadn't been so busy, I would have told him already. I planned to tell him on our next hunting trip. In the meantime, enveloped in the intense, pulsating reggae music in the car, my heart pulsed with gladness that I'd got all the books I needed to recreate my audio amplifier to get the greatest sound when I got home. But I knew that with only technology books, and without improving my relationship with Mrs. Black during the upcoming school term, my dream of graduating from Spring Valley High and doing anything worthwhile with my life would be just that—a dream.

CHAPTER 7:
My Name's Mr. Malick Tabangi

On the morning of the first day of school, coach Downer called me into his office. He was smiling ear to ear. He grabbed both shoulders and shook them—hard. "Flinty, congratulations on helping to bring the Sports Minister's Cricket Cup to Spring Valley. It's a great achievement."

"Thank you, coach, but I had no idea you paid attention..." I could not finish.

"You must be joking!" he said. "I followed you, Percy Chang and all the others from this school that play for the Sports Development Division. I had a meeting with Coach Sinclair last week, and we both agreed you should be the captain of Spring Valley's cricket team this year."

I was shocked. "Are you serious about this, Mr. Downer?"

"Yes! And I wanted you to be the first to know."

I kept staring at him, nodding, but looking past his eyes instead, thinking it was my last chance to give up cricket and focus on my lessons.

"You are the best choice. Is there a problem?"

"No... sir."

"Good. Your first task is to help me select this year's school team. I will announce you as the new captain at next week's meeting."

I left coach Downer's office thinking about my promise to Mother to brush up on my school work. But being chosen cricket captain was a big deal. I knew I was not a good juggler—I could either play good cricket or do good school work, but not both. I would have to make a choice.

Later, the crowd at devotion overflowed. Many students stood outside the main assembly hall. The teachers were on the platform, being blessed by the Anglican parish priest, Sanguinity. It was one of the school's traditions. Priest Sanguinity thanked the Lord for returning everyone safe from their summer holidays. Then he reached out his hands and made the sign of the cross, as if he was blessing us with courage, and sang his standard prayer at us in Latin for the sake of edification: "Levo vestri pectus pectoris, exsisto non afraid, senior est vobis." This was followed quickly by a singing translation by Sister Smith: "Lift up your hearts, be not afraid, the Lord is with you."

To me, that part of the devotion always sounded like the priest was conducting a séance, because most of us had no idea what he had said until Sister Smith's translation from Latin to English. This made me wonder: if God blessed people by the language they used to talk with him, then Latin must be his favourite. People who prayed in Latin must be closer to him than those using any other language—until I remembered my father's book about Martin Luther, the German theologian, who was persecuted for translating the Bible from Latin to German, and King James of England, who also had the Lord's words translated to

English. I felt some comfort that both German and English people were doing well, enjoying their vacations by frying themselves in the hot sun on beaches in Montego Bay. So God must have answered prayers in their languages. But as the tall, grey-haired, black-frocked Anglican priest spoke and moved swiftly around the elevated wooden platform with his giant shiny cross ablaze on his chest, I thought about the struggling people of Africa and shantytowns in Kingston, and I wondered if God understood prayers in patois and Swahili.

The priest's stern voice grabbed my attention again. He looked where I stood and spoke as if he were talking to me: "Those of you in your final year, this is your last chance to make good on things neglected in the past." Then he instructed the teachers: "Let wisdom from above guide our teachers so the knowledge they impart will be tempered with patience but full of insights."

Finally, we sang the national school song to Mrs. Bartlett's piano playing, with our right hands over our hearts. The hymn was supposed to replace all remaining fragments of our summer vacation memories with honour, duty and country. Then we recited the school's motto: "Prayer and work conquer all."

After devotion, we marched in straight lines, but noisily, to our new classrooms. All my crewmates were back, and, like me, they were decked in gleaming Duke of Trelawny designer khaki uniforms. The uniforms were dark grey, the fabric soft, and the shirts had long sleeves instead of the standard short. The illegal red-green-and-gold cufflinks and matching epaulettes were always in our bags, ready to replace the school's dull white-and-powder-blue colours as soon as we left the compound. Principal Black only grudgingly tolerated our Duke of Trelawny uniforms, but banned the cufflinks and epaulettes. Once in a while, his green Volkswagen Beetle would burst around a corner and catch us off guard. He would stop and demand that we remove the Rastafarian colours from our school uniforms and would threaten us with detention the next time he caught us.

Later that morning, a new teacher walked quietly into our noisy classroom. He was almost seven feet tall, with a dark complexion. He was dressed in a colourful but loose-fitting African dashiki blouse, and carried a walking stick decorated with carvings. He hugged a pile of books under his right arm before dropping them onto his desk. His eyes were red and bulging from their sockets as if he had smoked something serious before class. My eyes followed the spectacle of him like they would a fresh suspect. He took his seat behind the old black lignum vitae desk and looked at the noisy and disorganized classroom. "Ladies and gentlemen, please be seated," he shouted.

My attention switched to my bloated right pant pocket—fat with a new cricket ball—and my polished black shoes under my desk resting on my bat, crafted from a specially selected virgin weeping willow tree from India. My bat and ball gave me comfort in times of uncertainty, times when threatened by the unknown; the new, tall teacher, wearing an Afro and dressed like a tribal chief ready to take over as ruler of a remote African village, made me uncomfortable.

He stood up and spoke, hands outstretched. "Quiet, ladies and gentlemen, please be quiet." Once we hushed, he said, "My name is Mr. Malick Tabangi." He paused and looked around the room. All eyes were on him. If a pin had dropped, we would have heard it. "I will be teaching you social studies, history and critical thinking, but most importantly, I am your homeroom teacher. I was born around the corner, just up the road from here, but left long ago for England. While in England, I studied history and social sciences at the University of Cambridge." He paused and smiled. "But like General Douglas McArthur, I have returned." He tapped his walking stick on the floor twice, between the size 16 brown sandals that strapped his slim feet with long skinny toes, nails clean and clipped short. Then a smirk came over his lips; his stalwart frame towered over us like a hero gladiator signing autographs outside the coliseum in Rome. We gazed at him. He seemed to be thinking about what next to say.

Mr. Tabangi's voice thundered and snapped my wandering mind back from ancient Rome. "I do not know any of you and none of you know me. That's entirely good. Together we are starting new, but I promise you this: that I will treat all of you with the same respect. In time, we will know each other."

He paused and laid his walking stick on the table. He rubbed his palms together, and then leaned his buttocks against the table's edge at an angle, using it to prevent him from falling. Then he folded his arms across his broad chest and looked at us. He spoke again. "I will teach reason always before passion. Reason removes prejudices and biases from discussions. Your duty will be to use reason in your dialogue, break down information into useful ideas, and build effective conclusions."

A half smile broke from him, making his face look younger and friendlier. The class remained quiet, all eyes on him. He glanced at the row of boys and said, "You are young adults—men and women getting ready for the world—and you must respect each other, not only in here, but on the streets. Soon, some of you boys will be marrying some of these girls." There was low moaning and grunts from the girls. Some rolled their eyes and screwed up their faces at us boys.

Mr. Tabangi gazed through the half-open window, where the late morning sun took vengeance upon the thirsty brown carpet of grass. Further toward the green rolling hill, closer to the newly built, white teacher's cottage, the grass was lush, with a garden of bright red, pink and yellow flowers. Visiting teachers and those from other countries lived there. He took his eyes from the window and beamed them on the row of 10 boys. "You cricketers are paying girls to do your assignments. As of today, that's over. Boys, do we have an agreement?" he asked, gazing at us.

I felt my body hunch down deeper into my chair as he spoke, because I had a score to settle with Paulette Chambers, who did not hand me a book report I had paid her for, way before the holidays. I had planned on getting my money back, but after hearing Mr. Tabangi's rant, I realized I might have to drop the whole thing.

"Yes, Sir," Cunchas and Stan-Chen answered.

The other boys, including me, just nodded. His arms folded across his chest and his face set like stone, he spoke again. "Mrs. Black also told me you boys are stealing food from the canteen for weekend bush cooking in the mountains around Spring Valley and, worse, some of you are selling the food and pocketing the proceeds. Is this true?" he asked. Not a word from the boys, but a few girls burst into laughter. He silenced them with a swift glance and then fixed his stare on us boys again. "Some of you are smoking ganja before class and falling asleep. Let me be very clear, if any of you smoke and come to my class, you will be barred at the door. Others use the terms *Irie* and *I-man* when addressing teachers. Use *Irie* and Rastaman's *I-man* among your friends and companions, not to your teachers."

He paused and the room remained silent. "Am I clear?" He unfolded his arms, glanced at his watch, and put his hands in his pant pockets, still leaning against his desk, and looked directly at us. "Indeed, it is most disgraceful that some of you young men—you know who—are paying the girls to steal white rum and wine from the home economics department. The school's alcohol is for cooking and baking, not for you to drink and get drunk. All of those things will stop as of TODAY! Am I clear?"

"Yes, Mr. Tabangi," some of the students mumbled. I glanced at the studious Paulette Chambers in her silver, wireframe glasses, looking as innocent as a Vatican nun. She was staring Mr. Tabangi dead in the face, shaking her head in disgust as if the despicable news was virgin to her ears, agreeing with the teacher's every word of rebuke. But I was estimating the downfall of Paulette's little enterprise. Two years earlier, when she had started to steal rum and wine from her home economics class to sell to us boys, she charged us 8¢ for one drink—one bottle cap full of white rum and Purple Label wine. We would give her 10 cents, but she would never have the 2 cents change. In no time, her price rose steadily, way beyond the country's high inflation rate.

Now she was charging 47¢, knowing full well she would collect 50¢, never having the 3¢ change. She would slip flasks of white rum and wine into her uniform pockets and meet us on Thursdays behind the industrial arts building, across from the agricultural farm and vegetable garden. She would measure every drop of the alcohol and pour it into a soiled yellow plastic cup from which we all drank. More than one cup would raise suspicion, she would argue, if we offered to bring our own.

The rules were simple: pay before you drink and no credit. This was ever since Martel Roberts tricked her and tossed five full bottle caps of Paulette's white rum down his throat and ran off without paying. That evening, while he waited for the bus, two Hercules-looking roughnecks punched his face to a pulp and took his bus fare. He had to walk the six miles from Spring Valley Town to Wait-a-Bit, and had to stay away from school until his busted lips healed and the swelling disappeared from his face. Since that day, no one messed with Paulette's little enterprise. Her business model was simple: we demand, drink and keep quiet; she supplied the product. As Mr. Tabangi heaped scorn upon this disgraceful behaviour, Paulette—dressed in a spotless white blouse and neatly pleated, powder-blue skirt, blue socks and polished black shoes—sat with a stern face that betrayed nothing.

Mr. Tabangi continued. "I expect serious regard for your lessons!" He looked at me. I returned the look and wondered if he knew that some of the senior boys were giving junior boys only 5¢ to buy $1 government-subsidized lunches, and demanding that they brought back change. But I was impressed with him; his expectations were fresh and clear, with no bullshit, which I had never encountered in a classroom before.

"I look forward to a successful term with you all," he said. "Are there any questions?"

The classroom stayed silent. He waited awhile, giving us time to speak, but there was only silence. "Good, alright then; tomorrow I will give you a list of the books you must read this term."

He opened a copy of Fitzroy Augier's grey cover book; *The Making of the West Indies*. I'd seen that book at Sam Sharpe's bookstore only a week earlier.

"The topic for today's lesson: Slavery—a demand for a large labour force. Read chapter 8 to 11, and write three pages of your thoughts for discussion tomorrow. You will find that slavery in the West Indies was the economic engine driving the British Empire. Yes, it ran on tears and sweat no different from a modern-day factory running on gears and oil to meet weekly demands." Then he paused. "I want you to focus on the quantitative side of slavery—raw data."

I had never heard a teacher use raw data and slavery together. All the other teachers, including Mr. Binns, whom Mr. Tabangi had replaced, talked about slavery using words like *cruelty*, *barbarians*, *wickedness*, and *genocide inflicted upon Black people*, and I liked it that way. Those words were my comfort zone. Words I could arrange into guaranteeing a pass mark every time. For I had watched every episode of *Roots* on TV, and saw Kunte Kinte's toe get chopped off for no reason. That episode made me want to fight the first white man I bumped into; luckily there weren't any livingin Spring Valley. So in history class, I would just put on a gloomy face and shake my head in disgust at the 300 years of atrocities, until the bell rang to end the period.

Then I would grab my cricket bat and slam the ball to a pulp around the field. And when exam time came, I would rant on for a paragraph or two about the wickedness of slavery for a pass mark. My scheme had worked well, but I could tell this new cat—Mr. Tabangi —was going to cramp my style, using words like *economic engine*, *gears* and *oil*. I had visions of me having to do some serious reading instead of glancing over the history book pages, getting the essence, and improvising my answer, as I usually did. The same with literature class.

I would have to do something about this quick, I thought. I would strike up a friendship with him. Get on his good side, so I could get away with light work—especially since I was the school's new cricket captain. I could not afford to let him trap me into heavy reading and writing anything, even though I had promised my mother. I wanted no stress. I leaned back in my chair—away from Mr. Tabangi's dashiki blouse and frog-bulging, red eyes, as he paced the classroom slowly with the book in his hand. I crossed my arms, placing a shield on my chest to block him out.

"Any questions?" he asked again.

The class remained silent. "Tomorrow I will take attendance; today was only an orientation. Class dismissed." He sat down and began to move papers around on his desk.

"We have to fren him up; else he's going to kill us with work," I whispered to Sam sitting behind me.

"I agree Flinty," Sam said. "He looks like a slave driver."
"Wait for me outside."

I waited until all the students had left before going up to him. Smile and chat nicely to him, I told myself. Be congenial; tell him how impressed I am with his good vibes, and how I look forward to learning all I can in his class. By the time he figures out my brainwashing scheme, he will have given me a pass and the term will be over.

Smiling, I reached out my hand to shake his. "Mr. Tabangi, sir, welcome to Spring Valley, sir."

He looked up from the papers with a smiling face. "Flinty Magnum, great cricket you played against Cornwall the other day."

I was shocked. "Sir... you watched... the game?"

"I like the way you handled Hurricane Flash's bouncers," he said. "After what he did with Percy Chang, someone had to cool him down, and you did."

"Thank you, sir."

"I am glad you are in my class. Despite Mrs. Black's warnings about you and your four friends, I believe you can set a good example for the others in here."

I screwed up my face and scratched my head, confused. I wanted to strike up a phony friendship with him, but there he was, using my passion—cricket, something true—to strike up his conversation with me.

"Example? Me, sir?"

"Yes! Yes! And I heard it through the grapevine you could be the school's next cricket captain. Another reason to set a good example."

I stood looking down at his narrow friendly face, not knowing what to say. "Well, sir, I wanted to... talk... about..."

"Flinty! That flick-shot off your left foot into deep fine leg against Cornwall had glory in it."

"Thank you, sir! Do you play cricket, Mr. Tabangi?"

"I did; long ago I played for Brixton Cricket Club, before going to Cambridge University." He leaned back in his chair. "Flinty, a cricket bat stroking a ball creates a moment's beauty, but graceful pen strokes create a better community. The pen is more powerful."

"Never heard that before, sir."

"You wanted to see me. What is it?"

I thought quickly; this man was a cricketer and a wacky educator. "Just to welcome you, sir."

"Thanks, Flinty. You know, you are the first student to welcome me. I want you to be my classroom assistant. I will explain what that means tomorrow."

"Sir... me... your assistant?"

"Yes. Yes. And I look forward to reading your assignment tomorrow." He pulled a pile of papers toward him as if he wanted me to leave.

"Yes... sir..."

As I walked along the corridor toward my friends—Mookie, Stan-Chen, Sam and Ziggy—I realized my chat with Mr. Tabangi was a swift and confusing conundrum. I wanted to trick him so I'd be able to do very little work in his class, and yet I left his desk as one of his assistants—more work.

"How did it go?" Sam asked.

"Man... The little half-pint tyrant told him everything 'bout us. He even watched the match with me against Hurricane Flash," I told my four pensive-faced pals. "And get this, he wants me to become his assistant."

"What was your answer?" asked Mookie.

"The whole thing was so quick; I am still confused about the answer I gave him," I said.

"That's dangerous, Flinty," said Ziggy. "He could be setting you against the four of us."

"I don't think so, man. He seems like a clever screwball; comparing cricket bat strokes with pen strokes... he used to play cricket in England..."

"Or he's about to use our love of sports to trap us into giving him what he wants," Stan-Chen chimed in.

That afternoon, in the school library the five of us spent two hours trying to understand the economics of why one set of human beings had squeezed out mass labour from another like wringing the contents of wet towels into buckets. I came to understand that slavery was not just a willful act of hatred as I had believed, but a warped business plan—a philosophy, twisted by unbridled greed. That slavery—that first clumsy automation technology—was based solely on a large number of burdened individuals tasked to meet daily production quotas, the same way modern car factories equip plants with robots to meet demands. And that if combine machines for planting and reaping sugar cane had existed, the business of slavery would have been obsolete on the island.

While reading, I kept thinking that Mr. Tabangi must have been good at balancing cricket and books if he could tell me about the flick-shot I made to deep fine leg in the match against Cornwall, and my respect for him grew.

During the months that followed, I assisted Mr. Tabangi by collecting and handing out assignments from students. He began to hand me books—fat ones like Tolstoy's *War and Peace*—to read. At first I took them, read a few pages and held them for a while before handing them back. But he began to ask about certain characters in the books. Not being able to explain, I would frolic around, giving silly answers. He would squeeze his lips together, look at the ground, then gaze at me and nod, and hand me the book. "Flinty, read it again," he would say and walk off. I would screw up my face, take the book home, read some more and hand it back. He would quiz me again and my answers would get a little better, with the hope that he would stop. But he did not; he just kept handing me more books, telling me, "Flinty, you're my class assistant same as your Paul Bernett is your vice-captain on the cricket field. He should be able to captain a match if you are sick, same as, if I am sick, you should be able to teach a history class."

After a while, I began to enjoy Mr. Tabangi's classes, and the stories my father and uncles had told me were in some of the books, which made me want to read more. But I never saw anything about Hitler wanting to use Black men's sweat to run machines—thank God. I was surprised my father had named his playful little dog Nero, after learning how wicked Emperor Nero was, but, like a mathematical equation, Mr. Tabangi told the class to read the stoic sensible reasoning of Emperor Marcus Aurelius to balance out Nero's atrocities.

Mr. Tabangi painted graphic pictures of historical scenes with words, speaking slowly and deliberately. When he talked about the American Civil War, it was as if he was at Gettysburg when Colonel Joshua Chamberlain charged the Confederate army at Little Round Top. His eyes sparkled as his words crafted images of the first Tzar Alexander's fighting men setting Moscow on fire for the Emperor of France to conquer the blazing city. And then took the whole class marching with the Corsicans' decimated grand army back to France, watching frozen solders eating their dead horses to survive.

In his Critical Thinking classes, Mr. Tabangi selected precise words from his thoughts to form ideas, and then shaped them like a stone cutter before inserting them into airtight slots to build a strong wall of reason. "You have no reason to bounce your fists off anyone's body when you have reason as your weapon," he would say.

I began to sit in the front row and ask questions. Let him see that I enjoyed his classes. I spent my spare time in the library and hung out with students whose future was stamped with insignias of assurance their parents had handed down to them—those who were going somewhere good in life no matter what. From them, I heard stories about summer holidays with mothers and fathers in Africa, Spain, England and America and adventures only my imagination could see. Marlon Anderson, for example, chatted with friends in the cafeteria about walking in snow—freezing while climbing halfway up Mount Kilimanjaro in Tanzania. I had no idea it snowed in Tanzania. Marlon and his crew used the library like an intellectual soup kitchen: books filled their brains with nourishment. Mrs. Puncy-Jay, the school's diligent and stoic librarian, was like their mother; she treated them the way Grandma treated me, feeding me snacks when I fell and scraped the skin off my knees—directing them to every reference book until they found exactly what they were looking for.

Boys who were born in England dominated the school soccer team, but those who were born in the United States and came back to the island with their parents didn't know about cricket and didn't care. I would tell them about my adventures in cricket matches played in Westmoreland or St. Thomas, far from Spring Valley, to balance out their exotic holiday trips. They told me they had no time for a barbarian sport that takes five days to finish. Some of them would sit in the library, close their eyes, lean back with bulky headphones over their afros and listen to classical music.

One afternoon, while listening to the prime minister's recorded speech on Education and National Youth Service, Marlon removed the headphones from my head and said, "Flinty, your mother lives in Canada; listen to Vivaldi's *Four Seasons*, and hear what winter sounds like." He handed me his headphones and I listened for a while.

"What do you think?"

"It sounds lively," I answered.

He took the headphones and listened. "Oh, my mistake, that was spring." He moved the turntable's arm to another track on the record and handed me the headphones. I listened again.

"What do you think?"

"Sounds sad."

"Not sad, Flinty, dark. There's no sun," he said and laughed. I handed back the headphones and he put them on his head, closed his eyes and let Vivaldi's winter music freeze his mind. I walked outside into hot sunshine and thanked God there was only one season on the island: summer.

TA-TA, GRANDMA

By the end of my first term as captain, I had won five games and lost two. I began to spend less time on the cricket field, using the extra time to read, and began to write full pages of assignments for Mr. Tabangi's classes, but still only a few paragraphs for Mrs. Black's. Mr. Tabangi told me that if I wanted to write with passion, I should write the same way Herbert Morrison reported the *Hindenburg* disaster in New Jersey on May 6, 1937. It took Mrs. Puncy-Jay a long time, but she worked a miracle and was able to borrow the rare recording from somewhere and let me listen to it. After that, I vowed that if I were to write a story, I would try to write with the honesty Morrison used when describing the disaster. The hydrogen airship was docking when it burst into flames; he instinctively described the scene with such colourful details it seemed as if the words were streamed to him so he could tell the sad story honestly without a glitch.

In February, Mr. Tabangi asked me to help coordinate the Rt. Hon. Marcus Garvey's history competition, which involved the whole school. Students were asked to travel into the past, pick an event, and reconstruct the ending to create a sensible but different outcome. I reconstructed the Maroon battles in the Cockpit Country against the British Redcoats and, instead of having them sign a peace treaty in 1740 with the British, I gave the Maroons a clear victory. And, encouraged by the Maroon victory, the slaves rebelled, joined and fought together with the Maroons and liberated the island. At first, the British thought the night-time attacks were only an irritant, but they realized too late that the wilderness-dwelling fighters were well organized and motivated; they fought at night and slept in deep caves in the daytime. After numerous coordinated sugar cane burning campaigns across the island, the British cut their losses and negotiated a new peace treaty, not only with the Maroons, but with the slaves, freeing them in 1780.

My simulated rewriting of history changed our ancestors from victims to victors, and many students—especially boys—attended my three presentations. They cheered loudly after each session. My presentation won for overall creative thinking and self-esteem building. From that experience, I learned that history is more about the present than the past. My interest in reading and writing improved, and I borrowed more books from Mr. Tabangi's home library and read them.

One day, I handed Mrs. Black a four-page essay entitled *The Matter of Truth*, in which I reasoned that "In a society where truth is swift flowing like *liquid* in the ways it is practised and distributed by governments and citizens alike, that society will prosper because truth builds *solid* foundations. But when leaders use politics as dividing lines between people, it brings mistrust and deception, and the people sizzle in violence; their dreams fizzle like *gas*." Mrs. Black called me to her office after class. She was waving my essay in her hand as if it was the primary evidence—exhibit "A"—to be used to convict me for fraud. "Where did you get this topic? Isn't this the three states of matter?" she bellowed as I entered the room.

"You said the class could choose any topic, Mrs. Black, so I picked that one."

"Your essay is a jumble of physics and bits of literature sprinkled on top. For that alone I should give you zero—my class is literature. But whoever wrote this has a gift for plucking and crafting information. Despite what Mr. Tabangi thinks, I don't believe this is your work, Flinty."

"Mrs. Black, I wrote the paper. It took me two days."

"You may fool Mr. Tabangi, but not me. I know you and your friends much too long," she said. "Which of the girls did you pay to write this? Paulette? Marilyn?"

"Mrs. Black, if one of the girls had written it, wouldn't there be fewer punctuation errors in it?"

She glanced at the paper again and said nothing;

"Mrs. Black, I wrote it myself."

She rolled her eyes up to the white-painted ceiling, where a flickering, amber-coloured fluorescent light bulb witnessed the interrogation. Ever since my history presentation won the Marcus Garvey Competition, she had begun to smile at me when we passed each other in the hallways. And once she jokingly told me that Mr. Tabangi told her I had potential, with which, from her aggressive questions, she did not agree. "OK, Mr. Magnum. Pick any topic and write an essay right here in my office. That's the only way I will give you a mark for this one in my hand," she said. She was as stern as a sentencing judge.

I picked my topic, "Politics of Self" and wrote without a hitch, flashing my pen along the page like I was jogging along happily in a lush scenic valley, listening to birds chirping. I was enjoying myself, which disappointed Mrs. Black. She really wanted to see me sit and stare into space, not being able to write anything, so she could hand me a harsh punishment—perhaps expelling me to set an example for the other boys in her class.

I felt her gaze over my shoulder. "Flinty, stop the writing and tell me when you learned to scratch more than a few lines of your usual nonsense," she demanded. She pulled the almost full page from the table. She read it quietly. Then she handed it back to me and told me to finish it later.

"Mr. Magnum, if you are not smoking ganja, I think you have finally tapped into something, and good things are flowing out. These assignments are Bs at least." She gazed at me in grudging delight; her round, gold-plated earrings with the peace sign jerked around, bounced into her neck and cooled her wrath. She smiled, nodded, gazed at me and wrote a B on the "Matter of Truth" assignment that had started it all.

"Thank you, Mrs. Black."

Since my science marks were good, in April, I applied to study audio engineering at the Northern Institute of Technology in Toronto, and I sat my final exams in May. I breezed through engineering sciences, mathematics, physics, history and religious education, but I scratched my head, took deep breaths, looked at the ceiling and used up almost the whole four hours to pass English literature.

In mid-June, I screamed, jumped and then ran two miles home from the post office with my letter of acceptance from the Northern Institute of Technology. I left the letter on the living room table for everyone to read.

Hutch burst into loud laughter and slapped my shoulder. "Congratulations, Flinty. You did it."

Grandma rolled her eyes at me and, tossing a lump of sugar into her mouth, said, "Flinty, congratulations. You get to do what you always wanted."

I felt as if I had climbed the tallest mountain in the Cockpit Country and was looking down and around the valley below. Mission accomplished. There was nothing left to do but secure my tuition, keep out of trouble and enjoy my final summer on the island until September. That would be easier said than done.

CHAPTER 8:
Under the Spell of Joshua's Rod

> "When I use my memory, I ask it to produce whatever it is that I wish to remember. Some things it produces immediately... some are forthcoming only after a delay, as though they were being brought out from some inner hiding place."
>
> —St. Augustine

Later that June, I sat on a wall overlooking Spring Valley Town, waiting for Stan-Chen, Sam, Mookie and Ziggy. Stan-Chen had gotten his learner's permit, which allowed him to practise for his driver's licence. He was taking us for a spin in his father's Volkswagen van. We intended to have a drink at Blue Vail's, our favourite hangout, and then go on to no particular place, as long as fun lived there. As I gazed at the rusty old weather-beaten clock towering over the roundabout, I smiled at some of my memories of Spring Valley Town.

The town was small and quiet but busy on weekends because of the market. The grey, brick community centre was located beside the Shell gas station, which was owned by the short and stocky but fast-walking Mr. Magnum, who always wore black pants, white shirt and a black tie, curved over his potbelly. Mr. Magnum told me all Magnums are from the same roots in St. Elizabeth, and he always encouraged me to use my time wisely. Whenever he saw me leaning against one of the town's buildings, or prancing around chatting noisily with friends before or after school, he would shout as he scurried about his business, "Young Magnum, time is your friend only when used well. Otherwise it's your worst enemy!"

I would nod as I shouted back, "Yes, sir, Mr. Magnum. Thanks for the good vibes, sir!" Then as soon as he turned his back, I would be back to my noisy self, chatting about cricket, girls, karate movies and my favourite serial cartoon strip, *Rude Boy Jammy*.

My friends and I would save our lunch money for movies at the Actor's Theatre located across from Mr. Bennett's bakery. There was always stomach-vibrating reggae bass from the record shop, next to the health centre, across from the Public Works Department and next to Blue Vail's Bar, where Jah Spike, our brethren to the bone, was the bartender. My friends and I hung out there. Jah Spike would put cold beer in the freezer just before school break for lunch and slip us the ice-cold Red Stripe and beef patties under the table—no charge. Next to Blue Vail's Bar was the Love 'n Light Bookstore. I hated that white-and-blue concrete bookstore, and I will tell you why. Its many shelves were stocked with romance novels only. Their covers boasted erotic pictures of pretty women and youthful, sexy, half-naked men with long hair blowing in the wind—none having any resemblance to the people of Spring Valley. Miss Cherry Michaels, a full-figured Englishwoman, owned the bookstore. Her business model was simple but precise: girls read books; boys didn't. And so, there was not a single comic book in her store.

At lunchtime, the Love 'n Light Bookstore would be jam-packed with Spring Valley High School girls, all of them with romance novels covering their faces, their minds vanished into fantasies. Gone with their tall, shirtless, broad-shouldered handsome lovers with shoulder-length blonde hair. In those books, their lovers kissed the backs of the girls' hands, fingers and toes, and whispered the language of love to them in exotic accents: "Pardon me, madam. I am Jacques French. If you don't mind, would you please accept this bouquet of fresh red roses I travelled five miles, barefoot, dodging flaming arrows fired by savages to cut just for you?" (Although I never read these books, I liked to imagine what happened in them.)

A few lines down—on the same page, after Jacques handed her the roses—he moved closer. He kissed her neck softly and promised to transport her to exotic places: Tuscany, Casablanca, Paris. But never Africa. By page 15, the heat of anticipation would grow sweat beads on the girl's forehead as Jacques spread a picnic basket on soft grass under blue sky. He surprised her by pulling a bottle of rare Chardonnay from his knapsack, whispering that it was her destiny, because he had saved the two bottles of wine for two years just for this moment. By this time, her heart was an erupting earthquake about to burst from her chest. She had to use the book to fan herself, and walk around inside the bookstore for a few minutes, before joining Jacques again.

Suddenly, Jacques whipped two glasses from his pockets; he wiped them with his kerchief and poured the wine. The girl would be surprised by the Chardonnay's dry, tangy taste—nothing like the fruity Purple Label wine she was used to—but she gazed at Jacques and sipped the wine slowly. Jacques then caught a butterfly and cupped his hand around it, giving the captive creature to the girl, asking her to close her eyes and make a wish before setting it free, telling her, "True love always returns when set free." After that, Jacques gazed at her dreamy eyes and, as she thanked him for the beautiful picnic, he leaned over and kissed her lips. She giggled, acted shy at first and pretended to elbow Jacques away, but a few lines down she was rolling around in the grass with him, breathing hard and making soft grunts... until the bell rang for afternoon class.

The schoolgirls would grin, straighten their uniforms, wipe their sweaty faces, place their hands over their heaving chests to calm down, and mark the pages to continue the next day's reading. Some would kiss the book many times and giggle before putting it back on the shelf. A few would ignore the bell, skip afternoon classes and continue reading. Others would give Miss Michaels their lunch money to put the book on layaway until they could afford the additional two dollars needed to take home their Prince Jacques, the romantic saviour created entirely of words. The cluster of girls would drift on cloud of dreams back to afternoon class and want nothing to do with us schoolboys, after comparing us with Jacques and reducing us to the status of immature and uncivilized brutes.

TA-TA, GRANDMA

Deloris Peckham was one of Mrs. Black's best students. She won the school's top poetry awards more than once. The whole community was proud of her when she dressed like a man in a pair of banana-stained khaki pants and shirt and gestured with a machete while she recited Evan Jones' *Song of the Banana Man* at a concert on a hot Independence Day holiday. Her performance was so good she became a local celebrity for many weeks. Deloris's white blouse was always spotless and her tailored skirt, hosting her long smooth legs, gave her the look of a supermodel. She was graceful and effortless when she moved. Spring Valley boys lusted after her dreamy grey eyes and cherry lips poised always to smile. Her shiny black hair wrapped around her face when the wind blew, and she lazily cleared the silky strands from her eyes with her long, slim, delicate fingers.

However, Deloris Peckham was so addicted to romantic novels she refused to take her textbooks to school—she took only romance novels. As a confused romance junkie, she was no different from any of Spring Valley's alcoholics—men who washed their faces with white rum, drank it for breakfast, lunch and dinner, and took late night shots to quell their demons.

She would smile and blow kisses to her book-dwelling romantic phantom lover—Carlton Sheldon—and walk around dreaming of being rescued by him. But after many warnings from Mrs. Black about reading novels in class instead of her textbooks, and failing her exams, Deloris Peckham was suspended on grounds that she was a romantic adrenaline junkie (RAJ, for short). And because there were no doctors trained to help RAJ disease in Spring Valley, Deloris was left to wander the streets.

One evening after a heavy downpour, Deloris was waiting for the bus outside the Love 'n Light Bookstore where she still hung out. As I walked toward her, she wobbled her long legs as if fainting and dropped herself suddenly in front of me, hoping I would impulsively swoop her up, just in time before she hit the wet pavement—the way one of her tall, handsome, romantic novel-dwelling heroes would. I stepped over her and continued walking. She screamed at me in a strong soprano voice, the same one she used to recite poems. "Flinty Augustus Magnum, you are no Carlton Sheldon! Shame on you! You are a pitiful wretch."

I turned around. She was getting up from the muddy ground, her blouse soiled and debris stuck to her hair. "Who the hell is Carlton Sheldon?" I shouted. "Why didn't you have him catch you rass?"

Picking off bits and pieces of grit and wiping mud from her clothes, she continued. "Let his name not come from your lips, Flinty, for they are unworthy to call my lover's name. Carlton Sheldon is a man's man, but you are a beast of darkness, walking in daylight in the frame of a man."

She paused and waited for me to speak, but I just gazed at her as she continued. "Leave me alone. Go. Surrender your heart to its beastly desire, for your puny heart is a chunk of coal that repelled my radiance."

I'd had enough and walked off. She continued to rant, waving her hands around as if she was reciting in Mrs. Black's poetry class. I put both hands in my pockets, grinned mischievously and left the romance-crashed site.

Jah Spike saw the whole thing. "Flinty, why you let Deloris fall on the wet pavement like that?" he asked.

I pointed at Deloris still brushing debris from her hair. "Jah Spike, the government should round up these romantic junkies from the streets, the same way they should rid them of alcoholics. The Love 'n Light Bookstore is the cause and should be closed. Look at what it turned that nice girl into!"

"Flinty, the government should do no such thing. These are harmless girls, starving for love, adventure and affection, which those books provide. They are not drunken, swearing alcoholics."

"Jah Spike, alcoholics and these romance junkies see the world through distorted lenses that match their unreal expectations."

"Flinty, if you read one of those novels, you would find the men heap attention on the girls, which they enjoy. You should try heaping attention on a girl sometime and see what happens."

"Jah Spike, since that bookstore opened, girls are bleaching their skin to fade out their blackness to make them look like the pictures on the covers of the novels. You heard Deloris; I am no Carlton Sheldon. I bet Carlton Sheldon looks like Robert Redford or maybe David Carradine from *Kung Fu*."

"Flinty, it's not the romance novels that cause skin bleaching, but lack of self-awareness. I thought you were smarter than that!"

I was not sure if Jah Spike was right, but the bakery's aroma swallowed me. I suddenly felt hungry for a chunk of crusty hot bread and a thick slice of cheese before catching the bus home. "Jah Spike, you want a piece of hot bread and cheese?"

"No, Flinty, I am heading to Christiana, to watch the movie, *Jaws*. I hear it's wicked."

While Spring Valley High School girls were hooked on romance novels, boys were hooked on *Rude Boy Jammy*, a roughhouse cartoon strip on the back page of the *Kingston Daily News*. My friends and I never missed an episode. Sometimes I woke up in a cold sweat from nightmares about how Jammy—my hero—would escape from the sticky jam in which he found himself.

One afternoon, after wolfing down two beef patties washed down with an ice-cold Trelium pineapple juice, I leaned against the Actor's Theatre, soaking up the day's episode. Jammy was about to park his red, bullet-ridden S-90 Honda in a Kingston plaza, unaware of three police officers inside, waiting to kill him. The lawmen wanted to avenge the bank robbery he had pulled off in broad daylight the day before, splitting the loot equally between the poor people of Troubli Gardens and those of Remaville. To us schoolboys, he was Robin Hood, but to the police who wanted to squash him, Jammy was a plain, low-down hoodlum.

From inside the plaza, three lawmen trained their guns at the tall, cocky, dark-skinned zebra-stripe-pants clad, big afro, self-anointed Robin Hood. He turned off the motorbike's engine and lightly patted his oversized afro with his palms, wet his fingers with his lips, and straightened his pencil thin Errol Flynn moustache. He adjusted his gold-plated cufflinks crafted like pistols. He pulled his black shirt over the two guns (Capone and Clyde) stuck in his waist to hide them. Finally, he whipped his super-dark sunglasses from his shirt pocket and covered his eyes and almost half his face. He skipped off his wiry six-foot frame from the motorcycle and made a quick, fancy-dance move to Dennis Brown's new hit tune *Here I Come* blasting from the jukebox across the street.

Four men playing dominos and shouting at each other in the bar, where music thundered, cheered Jammy's dance move. The stocky fellow in the green vest with a red headband and craggy moustache slammed a domino on the table. "Say you pass!" he shouted.

But the skinny one in the full black suit and long dreads took a swig from his pint of Guinness. He studied the four remaining dominos in his hand and shouted, "I am going to kill your hand now!" Then he gazed at Jammy, stepping toward the three guns inside the plaza with a suspicious grin, as if he knew about the ambush, and slammed his domino on the table so hard he almost turned it over.

A pretty, fat girl with supersize breasts, wearing a bright, skimpy, red-and-white blouse, came through the door Jammy was about to enter. He smiled at her, took her left hand and kissed the back of it, and then patted her horizontal protruding butt, wrapped tightly in yellow shorts. "Sexy daughta', you pretty like a bunch of ripe cherries."

She grinned at him from her round face.

"I'll be right back; just wait a minute, man," Jammy said.

She stopped, and the black of her sparkling eyes danced hastily around in her head, taking in every unruly inch of the urban outlaw's body. Then she laughed out loud, patted her jiggling chest and waved at him. He winked, reversed, took a few steps, and then turned around and stepped through the door, into the Babylon guns and his doom. That ended the day's episode.

I can't take any more of this, I thought. My hands shook and my palm sweated against the newspaper. My mouth was dry and eyes open wide—I couldn't blink, my breathing had stopped, and my heart thumped fast. I let out a long, loud sigh as I imagined what was going to happen to my hero. "Jammy, turn around. Go after the girl. The police are going kill you. There's no way he can get out of this. Can't wait to see what happens tomorrow," I whispered.

Still lost in my thoughts, I folded the newspaper and slipped it into my yellow-and-red oversize Duke of Trelawny designer bag. I was about to find my friends to talk about our hero's grave predicament when I heard someone call my name.

"FLINTY, FLINTY, didn't you hear me calling you? I was bawling out your name so loud!" It was Lavern Milton, a classmate and friend. She was eating a beef patty and coco bread sandwich and drinking a cherry-flavoured box juice.

"Hey, Lavern!"

"What's in the newspaper that deafens you to the world?"

"Sorry, Lavern," I answered. "I very upset right now. My Jammy's in a tough jam."

"Jammy? You mean that criminal who ride around terrorizing innocent people?"

"Lavern, what you talkin' 'bout? Rude Boy Jam's a Jamaica bowy, helpin' out oppressed people."

"Flinty, last week you complained to me and Jasmine Graham about girls reading too much romance novels," she said. "But it's alright for you to read about that crook, Jammy. Keep up your hypocrisy."

"Lavern, do you know how much poor people Jammy help out? A real Robin Hood, that." My mind still clung to the tension between my idol and the three policemen about to snuff out his life in a wicked shootout. "I won't be able to sleep tonight. Tomorrow will be dread."

"Flinty, I have something for you," Lavern said and hastily tossed the last of her patty crumbs into her mouth. She rubbed her hands together quickly to clean them off, reached into her bag, pulled out a pink-covered book, handed it to me, and burst out laughing. "It's a present from the Love 'n Light Bookstore," she whispered.

"A book?" I asked. "Lavern, you know I don't read books from Love 'n– *The Happy Hooker*? I shouted. "You got me *The Happy Hooker*!?"

"Quiet, Flinty."

"I read about it in a magazine," I said, grabbing it from her.

"Quiet, Flinty. I stole it," she confessed. "Put it in your bag, and don't show it to anyone."

I did exactly what she said. She left for afternoon class and I skipped off to get my friends' opinion on Jammy's doomed situation.

Later that evening, after dinner and Grandma's story, I closed the door to my room, lay on my back, and devoured the pink-cover book for dessert—digesting every word. While everyone slept, I travelled with the high-priced call girl around Manhattan to apartments and hotels and witnessed all her erotic acts and tricks. I enjoyed her so much, I flew through the book and started it a second time and read until I heard roosters crowing; it was near daylight. Except for *The Young Warriors*, this was the fastest I had ever read any book. I slipped the book under my pillow and caught about a half-hour of sleep before school, where I was my happiest, and smiled with the female teachers—even Mrs. Black.

That evening, my mission was simple: gobble down my dinner, lock my bedroom door and snack on the sinful book for dessert again. But at dinner, Grandma's face looked sad and for the first time, she had no story. I was about to cheer her up with the day's episode of Jammy's backward somersault, triple-twist in midair, evading the volley of police bullets. How he landed on his feet in a banana field and leaped over a barbwire fence, all the while bobbing and weaving his body like an American football player slipping the bullets whizzing by his head. One of the bullets went through his afro, leaving a narrow channel from back to front, just missing his skull by an inch. Capone and Clyde fell from his waist as he skipped over a retaining wall, into a yard where three dogs chased him, nipping his heels, attracting a woman with a broomstick, who joined the police and the dogs chasing him onto Delford St., where Jah Skillet, his Rastaman brethren, lived and where he would spend the night. I wanted to let Grandma know how I can't wait to see what death-defying act Jammy is going to pull off to get back his guns from the Babylon them, in the next episode.

But before I could speak, Grandma held her right hand above her head like a preacher and shouted, "Flinty, as Almighty God is my witness, every scrap of you is going to burn in hell. Just like the filthy book I found under your pillow. No wonder you were so tired this morning. You cannot be learning anything good, reading such filth! As soon as your grandfather comes home I will tell him, and that will be my first complaint to your mother in my next letter!"

My face twisted up and my stomach felt hollow. "Where's the book, Grandma?"

She pointed at me and shouted, "Flinty, I burned every sinful word of that book and spent the whole afternoon praying for Jesus Christ to cleanse your soul. You are turning into a vagabond and need to go back to church."

There went my after-dinner dessert, I thought. I wanted to escape from the table, but the dinner was really good, so I chowed down the final fried dumpling, stuffed a man-sized avocado slice in my mouth, scooped up a generous spoonful of codfish and ackee, guzzled down the carrot juice and then fled Grandma's tongue lashing.

But there was more to Spring Valley Town than reading Jammy's episodes and the Love 'n Light Bookstore. Further up the main street were the Workers' Credit Union and Scotia Bank, beside the police station, across from the hardware and agricultural shops. The post office and the public library, where I borrowed many books—were under the same roof, across from the roundabout, which had a wrought-iron fence around swaying willow and pine trees that whistled when the wind blew.

The three concrete benches inside the roundabout were always empty, except when Prime Minister Michael Manley held a political rally there. When that happened, Spring Valley Town was scrubbed clean; buildings, tree trunks, and stones were whitewashed; and buildings were decorated with streamers in orange—the political party colour. Smiling pictures of the prime minister plastered the town. Thousands jammed the town and made hurricane-loud noises.

There were hundreds of Rastafarians, with long, waxed locks caked together like tree-root prongs sprouting from their heads, some down to their waist, some that swept the ground. Others wrapped their locks in bright red, gold and green wraps. All of them clutched homemade rods and walking sticks with carvings like chief elders of African villages. They came out of the deep jungles of the Cockpit Country to see and hear the prime minister—Joshua, their leader—speak.

Rasta Binzy, a friend with long, thick dreadlocks sprouting from under his oversized hat, walked up to me. "CIA is helping to mash up the country. Marcus Garvey would be proud of how Joshua is taking the island from the greedy baldheaded, capitalist," he shouted before joining his other Rasta brethren.

Spring Valley's tall but fat member of Parliament introduced the prime minister. Dressed in a sky-blue, short-sleeve bush jacket suit, he grabbed the microphone and mounted the stage. He moved his slim, but fit body around, dancing to the loud music, singing along to a popular tune, listing his first-term accomplishments. Everyone sang as if the whole thing was a sing-along. The prime minister boasted about leasing lands to those without and giving free education to those who could not otherwise afford it. He stirred up the crowd with a heavy dose of his charismatic brand of politics, never heard in Spring Valley before. The crowd roared, danced, swayed and cheered him like he was a reggae superstar. Spring Valley High School girls fell instantly in love with him; their dreamy eyes latched onto him the same as they would with the sexy heroes they read about in romance novels from the Love 'n Light Bookstore. In fact, the prime minister's tall, athletic frame; white, wavy hair; square jaw; straight nose; and tanned boyish face were the same as the features of those heartthrobs from the covers of the romance books.

The girls from the high school drama class danced to deep and heavy African drumming for him. We whistled and shouted when he said there would be no increase in book-rental fees for textbooks. One of his aides handed him his "rod of correction," and the crowd exploded into a deafening roar. Many believed the rod had magical powers, which they had all come to see. The thick pine tree inside the roundabout, where I sat with Sam, Jah Spike, Mookie, Stan-Chen and Ziggy, swayed from being overloaded with men and boys—even girls. I climbed higher to get a good glimpse of Joshua's rod. His right hand pushed the rod above his head and shook it firmly, and the massive throngs of people broke into a chorus: "Whip them with the rod of correction, Joshua... Whip them..."

The noise quieted down as the people waited for the prime minister to speak, but he just smiled, gazed at the crowd and pumped the rod like a mischievous schoolboy. The crowd roared some more. Then he brought the microphone really close to touching his lips, like he had a secret to break, but only at the right moment. The tension swelled.

He cleared his throat. "Eh-hem." The crowd roared. And with his ivory and black rod of correction—given to him by Ethiopian Emperor Haile Selassie—in his right hand, pumping the air above his head, the retiring evening sun glistening from the rod and his silver watch on his left, his voice thundered, "We have them under heavy manners! Heavy manners! Under heavy manners as we have them! We have them!"

This meant the opposition party was trapped in Joshua's suffocating charisma, which was pure oxygen to the people. The crowd erupted into pandemonium, jumping up and down with hands in the air and shouting, "Hail the man! Joshua! Joshua! We love you, Joshua!"

The prime minister held out his rod over the crowd, the same way Joshua, leader of the Israelites, did when he commanded the sun to stay still in Bible days, so he could be victorious over the Amorites. The mesmerized crowd gazed upon the rod, outstretched like it was delivering a miracle blessing upon his flock. Then, like a maestro conducting an orchestra, Joshua moved his rod from left to right, choreographing the mourning crowd. Then, with his right fist with the rod in it pumping the air, he thundered into the microphone, "Forward ever! Backward never! Democratic socialism forever! Forever! Forever!"

The crowd buzzed like a disturbed beehive. Women and girls jumped onstage and jiggled their hips and flung their feet in fancy style in all directions with Joshua, who giggled and danced like he was schooled in his moves.

The people sang and danced, hoisted the prime minister above their heads, and carried him around on stage with his rod hoisted in the air. All of the homemade rods, walking sticks and canes in the crowd—many with lions carved on them, some that looked exactly like Joshua's rod of correction—were held high and waved around to deafening festive medley. "Power to the people! We love you, Joshua! Heavy manners!" The crowd threw hats and hibiscus blooms, some women threw their brassieres, kerchiefs—anything they could find—at the prime minister, adoring him. Joshua waved his rod and blew kisses at his people like the triumphant return of a local hero, basking in his people's adoration.

Later that night, I walked along the main street toward Blue Vail's Bar for an ice-cold pineapple juice—maybe a free Red Stripe beer, if Jah Spike was working. The whole town was still buzzing with excitement. Even the wind blowing through the pine, eucalyptus and willow trees sounded joyful. All people and creatures in Spring Valley, including goats, chickens, donkeys and cows, were ready to vote for Joshua and give him a second term in office.

The crisp trumpet-sounding horn of Stan-Chen's father's Volkswagen van interrupted my flashback and alerted me to Stan-Chen's smiling face gazing out of the van window with his jet-black sunglasses. We greeted each other as I entered the vehicle.

"Irie, Flinty!"

Stan-Chen sped off with screeching tires. "Let us test this baby!" he shouted.

"Where are we going?" I asked.

"Mandeville!" Mookie shouted.

"What about a drink at Blue Vail's?"

"Mandeville!" Ziggy screamed.

"Stan-Chen, what if you run into your father?" I asked.

"He's in Kingston," answered Stan-Chen.

"OK, Mandeville, here we come!" we all shouted.

Mandeville was almost two hours away, and Stan-Chen had had his learner's permit for only a few days and should not have been driving that far. Besides that, a licensed driver should have been with him. But we were in a festive and noisy mood, Sam stretching over Stan-Chen's shoulder and banging the horn, Mookie switching on and off the air conditioning. My head hung out the window, wind battering my face as I waved and shouted at drivers as we overtook them.

Stan-Chen was driving so fast and erratically that drivers pulled over to the side and waved us along. We called them idiots and chickens as Stan-Chen circled and zipped past them. We slapped Stan-Chen's shoulder and heaped buckets of praise on our rookie driver. The van flew around blind corners on the wrong side of the road, Stan-Chen all the while gazing over the rim of his super-dark sunglasses. He could not see through them, but they made him look cool.

Suddenly, Stan-Chen flashed the van around a corner and headed into an oncoming truck. He swung a sudden right to avoid slamming into the truck, and the van, airborne, flew over a gully, but landed on its wheels. It skated into a banana field, slamming into tree branches, shrubs, rocks and red dirt. It bounced up and down and flipped to one side and back. Debris scattered as we slid into the steep gully, bouncing inside the vehicle. Stan-Chen wrestled the steering like a demon-possessed bumper car driver. Mookie, Sam, Ziggy and I screamed like 10-year-olds on a roller coaster ride, but this was no joy ride. Mookie cried out for his mother as we tumbled over one another, head over shoes in an untidy bundle. The van stank of gasoline, and thick smoke rose as it continued on a fast track down the gully.

TA-TA, GRANDMA

The van dipped to one side, careened off a Mahogany tree and then straightened up and continued down the hill. Broken glass blanketed our faces and clothes. I heard explosions—tires bursting open. Stan-Chen let go of the steering wheel and put his hands over his eyes to guard them from the splintered windshield. The van zigzagged between two houses, hitting goats, pigs and chickens. A woman waved her machete and cursed at us but ran for safety as the vehicle careened toward her.

The van stopped suddenly in a river, and water began streaming into the vehicle. We screamed as smoke rushed in from the fire that had broken out in the engine. We panicked. My heart pounded, wanting to escape from my chest to safety somewhere else. The van started to sink. We punched the doors without success, trying to escape from our communal coffin.

Stan-Chen escaped through the windshield and I kicked out the back window and jumped into the water, with Ziggy, Sam and Mookie following. We swam briefly and then ran from the smoking van and stopped at a safe distance to look back at the half-submerged vehicle. A stout woman ran toward us with her machete raised, shouting, "Not one of you leave until you pay for the chickens and goats you killed!"

We galloped through a stinking pigpen—shit stuck to our shoes—escaping the angry woman. Again, we stood at a safe distance, watching the smoke rise from the van. Stan-Chen put both palms on his head and dropped to his knees. "My father is going to kill me!" he shouted.

But we had a more pressing problem. We had to get away from the gathering crowd closing in on us with machetes, pick-axes and sticks, demanding payment for the damage we had caused. We ran across the gully through tall bushes and followed the river, not knowing where we were going until a farmer directed us toward the main road. We hitched a ride to Spring Valley on the back of a dump truck.

News of the accident travelled faster than a telegram, and like all Spring Valley's news bulletins, was dead wrong: we were all dead, burnt to a crisp. So my ghost walked through the gate to Mother and Grandma's loud bawling inside the house as they got themselves ready to visit the accident site to see my ashes because, according to Gwendolyn, the van had caught fire and burnt us all, and she saw the five smoldering piles of black ashes inside.

All crying stopped when Grandma and my mother saw my ghost enter the house that night. Mother fainted, falling on her bed, and Grandma bolted into her bedroom and slammed the door. Shortly after, she cracked the door open, peeked out, and screamed at me, "Everyone said you was dead!" Grandma was trying to erase that fogginess between readying herself to see my ashes and accepting me standing in the flesh before her. Mother lay on her bed, her chest heaving, like a runner with a sick heart who had just completed a marathon. Her eyes rolled back into her head.

Grandma's trembling hands scattered vials of pills and tonic bottles inside her medicine cabinet, some falling to the floor, as she searched for Bay Rum, camphor, and asafetida to sprinkle on my mother's head and face to revive her. The whole time she didn't stop staring over her shoulder at me, still frightened, not sure if I was a ghost or her grandson. I stared back at her, trying to understand her frantic behaviour, not realizing they really thought I was dead.

"Jesus Christ! You are giving everyone in the house heart attacks. Look what you are doing to your mother!" she hollered as she sopped Bay Rum on Mother's face, head and neck.

Mother sat up in the bed looking dazed and confused, her stringy black hair she had washed earlier scattered all over her eyes. She swept the hair from her face and shouted, "Flinty, you are all alive—thank God! Everyone said you and your friends dem dead."

I stared at her. She jumped from the bed and squished me with her strong hug; her wet hair splashed my face and spread the strong smell of Bay Rum. Grandma's troubled eyes still searched mine, her face changing back from white to her normal brown. Her nervous right hand covered her mouth—still lost, not sure what to believe.

Having digested so many of Gwendolyn's lies for so long, her mind veered between the glare of deception and reality, still not sure if she was staring at my ghost or me. "Flinty! I am happy to see you alive, but I swear to God in heaven, you are trying to kill your mother and me at once. Thank God your grandfather gone a Kingston and not here to see this!" she shouted.

"Grandma, Ma, I only sprained a big toe," I assured them, patting Mother's back. "Who told you I was dead?"

"Gwendolyn said all five of you died in the van!" Grandma shouted.

"That snake!" I snapped. "I told you not to believe her stories." I was torn between feeling sorry for Grandma and wanting her to learn a lesson.

"Let me sit down," Grandma whispered. She took two shaky steps toward the bed, her trembling right hand holding on to one of the tall, dark, wooden Victorian bedposts. She sat down gently, her wide eyes locked onto mine without blinking. "Pass me two of my Dodd's pressure pills and some water, Flinty," she asked quietly. I gave them to her and she took them and lay on her back, closing her eyes. "Let me rest a little until my blood pressure come down."

Half an hour later, my father arrived and knocked hard at the front door. When I let him in, he put both palms around my shoulders; his arms were trembling like banana leaves in a hurricane. He looked into my face, squinted, and then closed his eyes for many seconds and took deep breaths, leaving me to notice two sunken crevasses above his eyes sockets.

He opened his eyes and stared at me, still standing in the doorway. Then he shouted, "Do you have a death wish, boy? What the hell were you doing in Mr. Chen's van? Stan-Chen was driving his father's van without license!" Mr. Chen was one of Dad's good friends. "Stan-Chen took his father's brand new van without permission and mash-it-up, and you were part of the whole damn wreck!"

"It was just an accident," I said.

"First I heard you were dead, then minutes later that you were alive. Do you know what that can do to a father's heart, boy?" he demanded.

He dropped his arms to his sides and slapped his khaki pants—same standard outfit as Grandfather's. I noticed that the green-lit face of his wrist watch showed 8:30—long past Grandma's bedtime.

Dad finally walked into the house and greeted everyone, including Mother. This was the first time I had seen him and Mother together in years, and it made me feel awkward. My parents together because of me—worried, thinking I was dead. It was sobering to see my father looking uncertain. He was always in control, and even though he read all sorts of books, his mind had two colours—he painted things he liked red, and his dislikes, black. Which made it difficult to reason with him.

Grandma made a pot of strong mint tea. My father and I sat quietly on the verandah, sipping steaming tea while being entertained by a symphony of cheerful chirping insects. Mother and Grandma went inside to pray with hands in the air, thanking God for sparing my life. I sat in a quiet but anxious state, waiting for my father to begin one of his lectures, which he was good at. And even though I still revered him, I mentally drew a line in the sand as to how much of his grand theories about life I was about to let him pummel me with. He'd been a good father at one time, but I hardly saw him anymore. As my mind kept replaying the full-length movie of the accident, I felt lucky that my friends and I had survived without major injuries. But I worried about what Stan-Chen's father was doing to him for wrecking his van.

CHAPTER 9:
Father and Son in a Storm

A warm wind bathed our faces as I waited for Oscar Magnum to speak, but many moments ticked by without him saying anything. He kept staring at the outline of the Cockpit Country Mountains and sipping his tea. In that quiet, peaceful moment, a mischievous thought sprung up inside me, that I should get involved in more accidents so we could spend more time together.

As I sipped my tea and smirked at the ridiculous thought, my father finally spoke. "Flinty," he said, "you are pushing all the buttons to end your beginning." I said nothing, just sipped my tea and listened for more. "Alfred almost chopped your head off when he found you in his daughter's bedroom and now this crash," he said. "What next?"

"What happened today was an accident," I answered, thinking about all the many good things about me he knew nothing about.

"Flinty, you are skylarking in hurricane-bound winds and thinking it's a cool breeze," he continued, almost shouting. Suddenly I remembered how good he was at customizing his thoughts, so I kept quiet and let him enjoy being on stage for a while. He continued to lecture. "Flinty you are... Flinty"

I had enough and tuned him out, slipping away from his piercing voice of instruction, and drifted back to one of our hunting trips when I was ten. One afternoon, we were deep beneath a mysterious part of the Cockpit Country—where grown men knelt and prayed for guidance before entering, and gave thanks to God for allowing them to leave safely.

It began to rain, which was not unusual, but the forest suddenly switched to night-time darkness, even though it was only 3:00. We could not see the narrow track and had no flashlight. It was no use continuing, unless to our deaths—falling off cliffs onto razor-sharp rocks, or slipping into narrow crevasses. We sat for a while, waiting for the darkness to clear up, but the blackness was punctuated by lightning and the heavy rain only intensified, wrapping us in a blanket of dread. After lingering for several minutes, our survival instincts kicked in.

We nervously manoeuvred our bodies slowly along a steep reef, spreading our fingers apart and moving hand over hand along the vertical wall of rocks to stabilize ourselves, like mountain climbers. We inched forward until our fingers wrapped around life-saving vines—we could tell by their crusty texture and sticky stains. They hung from stout trees above the rock, trees competing with each other for hundreds of years to touch the sky. We swung to the far side of the ridge, where the rocks were fewer and not as sharp, but the rain continued to batter, and frequent lightning flashes lit up the wilderness, followed by growling thunder.

The shiny metal rifle slung over Dad's back attracted deadly lightning flashes that enveloped us. For the first time, I felt terror. Sometimes the bursts of lightning lingered along the ground to provide extended daylight around us, so I could see how fat the raindrops were. At one point I glimpsed a huge Jamaican Boa coiled up beside my feet, its head buried under its thick fleshy trunk. The unflinching serpent had the same cold equanimity of the towering rocks and mountains around us, waiting for the storm to end. I jumped from the snake and hastened to close the gap between me and my father, who was ahead. I told him about the snake, but he said my eyes had played a trick on me, because cold-blooded reptiles would have expected the storm and crawled to one of the sunny hillsides earlier that day.

I was sure I'd seen a snake as large as those I had seen at the National Zoo in Kingston on school trips. (Weeks later, Dad told me he actually saw the snake but did not want to put any more fear in me.) My body shook with dread when my senses assured me the reptile was closing in to coil itself around me and quietly strangle me to death. No matter how many times I was told that the yellow boa was harmless, like most, I was afraid of them and never trusted them. Once, at a 4-H Club, a Spring Valley resident asked one of the two scientists from the University of the West Indies who were conducting a seminar on how to survive in the Cockpit Country, "How can a snake be so big—some six feet and more—and not be dangerous?" One of the young scientists smiled and said, almost pleading; "Ladies and gentlemen, it's a fact; the yellow boas are unique to Jamaica and are harmless to humans. Please, do not kill them. If you encounter any, just call the forestry department."

We laughed, and someone shouted, "I will report snakes, but only if I forget my machete." The soft-spoken scientist had been quiet until then, but her eyes popped wide as she pleaded with both hands outstretched toward the crowd. "Everyone, please, please, the yellow boa in the Cockpit Country and across the island is not poisonous. They are constrictors, and are found nowhere else in the world. They suffocate their prey—mostly rats and birds, but never human beings." Despite her efforts to reassure us, I was sure many, myself included, did not believe her.

So now I kept glancing behind me, expecting to hear the serpent's body slithering on the wet leaves toward me, but all I heard was thunder as I watched the flashing lightning illuminate the trees and rocks. At one point, an explosive burst of lightning swallowed us up, causing Dad to toss the shotgun from his back over a cluster of rocks. The frisky lightning danced around the gun's outline as if electrocuting it, leaving a sizzling glow around the weapon's profile, like chalk outlining a murder victim.

Trees tumbled around us like a thousand men were felling them without stopping. But despite the terror of the storm, I heard the sounds of animals in the distance. It cheered me up, and I told Dad. I led the way, guided by the animals' bleating, to a dry, cozy, but dusty cave. Wild goats stamped their feet to keep the pesky swarm of mosquitoes from eating them alive as they sheltered from the storm. Like Maroon warriors of old, a good hunter in the

Cockpit Country knows wild goats do not like water, and seek shelter as soon as the rain starts.

As quickly as hungry scouts returning from a dangerous patrol, we started a fire that cleared out thousands of annoying mosquitoes. We sat on stones around the crackling fire and huddled our bodies to dry our clothes. We enjoyed hot cups of cocoa from our dented red Thermos, and watched bright flashes light up the jungle. We listened for the great thunder that followed, as buckets of fat, sideways-falling raindrops battered the forest. It was as if the lightning and rainstorm were punishing the wilderness for wrongs it had done before we got there. Further along the cave's ridge, it was dark where frightened owls hooted, reminiscent of a scary movie.

"Have you ever seen anything like this?" I asked Dad, my voice drenched with excitement and dread.

"Never," he said. "This is not normal." Then he blew a mouthful of air into his cup to cool his cocoa, sipped and continued to gaze at the storm with sparkles shining from his eyes. Then he interrupted our quiet and said, "Flinty, I've been hunting in these forests since I was a boy, hunting with my father, and have seen it peaceful and angry, but never like this."

He paused, sipped his cocoa and spoke again. "One thing I know: you have good ears. They saved us today. For through all that noise, you heard the animals, which led us to shelter. Thank you, because if it was me alone, I would be still fumbling around in the darkness."

As he spoke, I remembered something Aunt Buckingstone had told us: "The leopard will lie down with the goat, the calf, and the lion and the yearling together; and a little child will lead them."

After an hour or so, our clothes had dried, and we felt warm and comfortable, but the storm still raged. "Flinty, you know that story about Androcles and the lion?" Dad asked, gazing at the trees being whipped by the rain and wind.

"Yes, I read it at school," I answered, nodding and turning to face him.

"If that escaped slave, Androcles, had had a rifle when the lion entered the cave in which he was hiding from the Romans, what would he have done?"

I hesitated, thinking that the question needed inspection. I had learned not to answer any of his questions before examining them properly, because some were hazardous pitfalls. However, he quickly fired his answer at me: "Flinty, Androcles would have shot that damn lion, roasted it, and eaten some of it, and would have found the thorn in its paw only while eating the animal's foot. And the famous story about friendship would have been about survival—man against beast—instead of friendship and kindness to an animal."

He poured a new steaming cup of cocoa and glanced at me, my palms cupping my chin, elbows digging into my thighs, staring at nature's rage. I was thinking I had just used the animals' kindness to find shelter, but was sure if the weather continued until the next day, Dad would have no problem shooting one of the goats for food. My father was no Androcles; he was a hunter.

He threw dried leaves on the shiny rifle lying beside him, making sure all its metal was hidden, to prevent it from drawing any lightning into the cave. "Not all kindness is deliberate. Unarmed people, like weak nations, are kinder and gentler than those who are armed. An ugly woman is friendlier than one armed with beauty," he said confidently.

"A beautiful woman is not a weapon, Dad," I said, thinking about Angie, who was in my class.

"Flinty, I know since leaving Aunt Buckingstone for that other idiot school you stop learning anything good," he said. "Beautiful women can elevate men to greatness, but can be a deadly political weapon, same as any nuclear warheads," he continued. "The flashpoint for many wars (wholesale and retail), have been triggered by tag-o-war over women armed with beauty."

"This is getting out of hand," I grumbled. "How did I stumble into this trap?"

"Did you say something?"

"No, just, mumbling."

"Bowy, speak up when you have something to say."

I nodded at Dad to shut down his lecture, and then turned my head to the seven animals stomping their feet and chewing their cud at the far end of the cave and raised my cup of cocoa in a toast to them, thanking them for rescuing us from the storm and hoping for the weather to improve. Which it did, so my dad did not have to shoot one of them for food. And, like Androcles, I hoped they would remember me the next time we crossed paths in the forest.

That's how I used to bond with my father while hunting and developed an instinct—knowing when to debate, when to listen and when to tune him out. That night on my grandparents' verandah, I listened for a while, but tuned him out once his lecture began to sting. But then his voice found me again.

"Flinty, remember our hunting trips?"

"I was just thinking about one of them."

"I miss them," he said, "but we will hunt again one day."

He sipped his mint tea and put his left leg over his right, adjusting his buttocks on the chair, which shifted and screeched loudly against the tiled floor. "Do you remember that book, John Bunyan's *Pilgrim's Progress*, I used to read to you?"

"Yes," I answered, dragging my memory back to when I was seven or eight years old, before he and Mother divorced. *Pilgrim's Progress* was one of his favourite books. He used to read it aloud to me many times.

"Tell me what you remember," he said.

"Well, that in life, we may face the world's good, bad and ugly forces. Sometimes the bad is cleverly disguised as good—intended to throw us onto life's wrong path. But we must always be determined to turn around and start on the right road, no matter how far we may have gone down the wrong. That we should never accept wrong, no matter what."

There was no sound from him for a while. He just sat there staring ahead, perhaps trying to find holes in my answer, maybe agreeing. I was not sure. He glanced at his watch, took a deep breath, leaned back and blew a big volume of air into the night. Then he turned, looked directly at me and said, "Flinty, make this night the start of your journey on the right, drop everything and turn yourself into the right direction. Soon you will be going to a foreign country with many deceptive roads, to study. Stop the skylarking. You know better."

Instantly, I felt like challenging his authority. Who gave him the right to instruct me like that? But just as suddenly I realized I was leaving for Canada in about two months and this was his last opportunity to be a father, so I cut him some slack.

"I agree, Dad. I have some changes to make, and I will."

"Good," he said. "Flinty, you have great potential. Go and use it."

I shrugged my shoulders, maybe indifferently. I had nothing more to say, for I had given up cricket in time to graduate from school, but he knew nothing about that. There was a gap in our conversation, which the night creatures filled with their chirping and whistling, until I chimed in. "Dad, thank you for that cricket bat and ball you bought me and the coaching behind the house when I was small. I was the only one on the school team with such early training."

"That's OK," he said. "I heard about a match you opened and walked away 'not out' with your bat on your shoulder. That's amazing, Flinty. Something I always wanted to do when I used to play. I wish I was there to see you do it."

"That was a big day for me. I still don't understand how I did it; at times while batting, I felt like my confidence was a rock—unmovable," I told him as I replayed in my head the cheers and festive noises from four years earlier when I was 14.

"I should have been there," he said, nodding and gazing across at the mountains.

I suddenly closed the guilty trap door, and said, "You were there—many of those shots I played you taught me in the backyard when I was small."

"Thank you, Flinty, but you are being generous to me."

I closed the guilty trap door again. "I don't play much cricket anymore. I use some of the time to read."

"Good—reading's good," he answered, nodding and looking over his shoulder toward me. He glanced at his watch and announced, "It's midnight."

"Our longest conversation in almost eight years," I said.

"No, Flinty, the start of our new conversation going forward."

I grinned at his midnight dream as he got up and stretched both hands into the wind that had turned cool. The bones in his arms and legs cracked and creaked like an old bed. It was time for his sleep. We stepped toward each other in the middle of the verandah and hugged briefly—a hug born from my accident more than anything else. The razor-sharp aroma of his aftershave stung my nose. I whispered goodbye to him. He reversed slightly and touched his lips with his finger, as if he was trying to remember something. Then he walked down the steps, glanced behind and waved as he strolled between the silhouettes of Grandmother's garden, columned gates onto the street. He waved one last time and kept walking until all fragments of my father that were lit by heaven's stars disappeared into the darkness.

CHAPTER 10:
The Tonic Wine

Hutch came home from Kingston about midday the next day. He looked tired and unshaven and went straight to bed and stayed there for three days. He complained about a pulsing pain in his left side. During one of our hunting trips, he had complained about the same pain, grabbed his side and grimaced often. When I asked if he was all right, he had answered, "It's nothing a strong hot cup of mint tea won't cure." Mint tea was the emergency fix for all of Hutch's ills, but I believed that pain was serious.

Grandma's mouth swiftly spilled out my accident to Hutch as soon as he entered the house. He called me into his bedroom, looked up at me from his bed, grunted a few times and said, "Be careful, Flinty." That was all—a sure sign he was a sick man. If Hutch had not been ill he would have given me a sound lesson in few words, like when the ball hit Shampoo Grill in Falmouth almost a year earlier. And if I had blamed Stan-Chen, who was driving, by saying that I was only a passenger, he would have said, "Flinty, show me your friends and I will tell you who you are." There was none of that from him. I left the room thinking the old man must have been sick in Kingston and had a terrible time.

Grandma called us—her five grandsons into the kitchen for the official announcement. She simply said, "Your grandfather is lying down." Those five simple words actually meant that her husband and friend was in poor condition. It meant friends had to visit us instead of us visiting them, no late night coming home from anywhere—doors would not be opened for anyone after 9:00—and no carousing around the yard. All vulgarity, including laughter, was suspended. No barking dogs were allowed, not even those passing on the street. Owners were at risk of being reprimanded by Grandma, who would shout at them, "My husband is sick, you know! His head cannot take the barking. Walk up fast with your dog!" The owners would apologize for their dog's bad behaviour and speed along to their business.

She also doubled the price for us to shoot down the loud chirping birds in her garden with our slingshots, and loud clucking fowls risked being served for dinner. Only mourning doves got a free pass—their sad cry cheered Grandma's spirit while her husband drifted closer to heaven's door. The house had to be quiet, except for religious songs playing at low volume on the little RCA record player in the living room: Pat Boone, Chuck Wagon Gang, Mahalia Jackson and Jim Reeves. Sometimes, Uncle Manny sneaked in one of Skeeter Davis's sad pieces like *Don't they know it's the end of the world*. Grandma didn't mind that mournful number. That was it. But absolutely no reggae music while she used all sorts of remedies to pull her husband from greeting his maker. And for the three days while Hutch was in bed, after dinner, Grandma would sit alone on the verandah, on bright sunny afternoons with her face overcast by a grim shadow like a woman searching for her lost love. Longing for her Hutch, her quicksand husband who she would sink her large daily volume of talk into, the one who listened, heard nothing and said very little, but agreed with her every word. Her darling husband who sometimes would take deep drags from his cigarettes, blow the smoke into the ceiling and mumble a few "rasses" under his breath when Grandma's nonstop chattering got too much for his right ear.

But I don't want anyone to think my grandfather was St. Hutch of Spring Valley. No, sir. There were times when his voice thundered and shook us to his attention. Like that Easter holiday when the five of us drank off his three bottles of Wincarnis wine. An act of high treason for, to Hutch and his friends, that wine was tonic to kill any destructive microbes inside his aging body, so no one except him should pour any liquid from those extra-black bottles. He would ignore us stealing his white rum, Appleton rum, or rum punch. He would even overlook his rum-fortified sorrel disappearing from its bottles at Christmastime, but never his precious Wincarnis wine. The only exception was the very rare occasion when he invited us to have a sip, because one of his favourite cricketers had scored his first test century at Sabina Park. He called all five of us boys, one by one, to have a drink of the great tonic—pouring just enough to cover the glass bottom—and he watched in satisfaction as if he was enjoying draining the glass with us, saying, "Good for you, boys! It's medicine, you know. Not supposed to drink too much." Then he'd close his prized bottle of healing remedy and put it away.

But to the five of us, Hutch's hallowed wine tasted like cola spiked with alcohol. So that Easter holiday, while Hutch was away, some of our friends came over, and we drank the carrot and sour-sop juice and all the rum punch in the house, leaving the three unopened bottles of Wincarnis wine inside the cabinet. Those bottles of wine stood like religious shrines, tempting us to crack them open. We resisted and went about our mischief—for a while. But like that colourful beguiling serpent in the Garden of Eden that whispered sweet pick-up lines into Eve's ears, those bottles of wine were long smooth legs and succulent breasts for us to be fed from. After our friends left, I cracked open the first bottle and, along with my two brothers and two cousins, gulped down the liquid as if it was ice cold lemonade on a hot day in a desert. We belched loudly, grinned at each other, and, because the first bottle tasted so good, like Eve, who enjoyed Satan's fondling and ran to her husband for more, we drank the second and third bottles, and pleasured ourselves with Grandfather's tonic of meat extract and grape juice.

I gulped down two full mugs and wanted to wring the bottles for more of the tasty thirst-quenching wine. At one point, Reggae-Slim and Max each had a bottle to his head, guzzling as if they were thirsty cars being filled with gasoline. But suddenly, as if we had flipped a switch from happy to sad, we gazed at each other with deep concern over what we had done. Then we put our heads together, literally huddling like American football players, to flush out a believable lie.

We almost agreed to tell Hutch that Detective Fitzbright, Grandma's well-respected nephew from Kingston, had made a hasty holiday visit with his friends and drank the three bottles of wine, but quickly we agreed we could not fib on him. He carried a gun and had graduated from the police academy with a yellow "X" stitched into the right shoulder of his uniform, letting everyone know he was a marksman. One time, he told the five of us that he had shot the yellow part of a thief's foot bottom from one hundred yards away as he stole a woman's purse and was running away. Then he sipped his carrot juice, grinned and looked at Brenton and said, "To make sure that thief began washing his feet before bed." There was no way we could take any chances with someone like that. So we filled the Wincarnis bottles with water and put them back as if nothing had happened.

Hutch came home in a great mood that Easter holiday evening. He was mangling every note of one of his favourite songs, and when his voice smashed the notes into bits and pieces, he used his whistling to recover them and then mangled them all over again.

For whatever Hutch's business was that day, it had gone well. He greeted his five grandsons with a big grin, his gold teeth glistening at us. He gave me a friendly slap on the back before handing me a heavy brown paper bag with lots of goodies for the family. He then gave the five of us one dollar each. He bathed and changed into his standard evening uniform: white shirt, brown cardigan with two black lines running down the front from both shoulders to his waist, ivy style hat and stiff, starched and ironed khaki pants. He slipped his sock-covered feet (to protect them from mosquitoes) into his brown sandals and sat in his chair with a copy of the *Daily Gleaner*. He cleared his throat and set free his mind upon the pages for the news to take him on a rough ride around the world. He smiled sometimes, hissed his teeth, bit his lip and sometimes popped his eyes. A piece of good news hoisted his mind up to make him smile, but then tumbled it down with the bad as he turned the pages.

After much grumbling and teeth hissing, Hutch's mind returned from his bumpy roller coaster ride. He put away the newspaper and sat at the table for dinner, which Grandma had readied with care: white tablecloth, knife and stainless steel fork and Royal Albert china, crafted in honour of one of Queen Elizabeth II's visits to the island or a jubilee for one thing or the other.

Finally, came his bottle of Wincarnis wine to complete her husband's holiday dinner decoration. Grandma then sat at the table and began to update her husband about her day while he ate. But on that evening—Easter Monday evening—Hutch's Wincarnis wine was clear water when he poured it, instead of red. He held up the glass and examined the water in it. Then he shook his head quickly to clear it. He must have thought, maybe my mind is playing a trick on me; maybe I need a new pair of eyeglasses. He was not sure, so he shouted at Grandma to bring the second bottle, which also proved to be water. Hutch's three bottles of precious wine had turned into water—a full reversal of his saviour's first miracle. Turning wine into water was Satan's miracle, not his Christ's, to whom he prayed every night before bed.

Every single line in the constitution that governed his kingdom had being violated, warranting swift and decisive action. He barked loud, like a rusty old broken tuba, "All you five fools come here—now! Who the hell drink my Wincarnis wine?" None of us answered.

"You know I don't drink wine, because of my high blood pressure," answered Grandma, quickly removing herself from Hutch's inquisition. Then she barked, "It's a disgrace that you boys would drink the three bottles of your grandfather's wine!"

Their husband and wife alliance was now fully cemented, leaving their five grandsons hanging off a proverbial dry half-broken grapevine, waiting for Hutch to chop it clean off, which he did. His tuba voice growled again, "Until you idiots put back every drop of my wine, all of you will be sleeping tonight, but not in *this* house!" The broken tuba voice fell silent. Suddenly, I felt like a fish fluttering around on hot sand. In situations like that, Grandma would jump in and pick us up from the hot sand. She would say something like, "You boys are the worst. How could you do something like that? Flinty! Catch the bus and buy back the bottles of wine with money your mother send last week." But it was a holiday, and everywhere was closed early, leaving no room for her to help. So she kept quiet and accepted Hutch's decree.

We boys spent many minutes gazing at each other, deciding where we would sleep.

CHAPTER 11:
Rasta Binzy

That night, I slept at Rasta Binzy's. Binzy, a Rastafarian, was only three years older than me and had won a five-year scholarship to the prestigious Cornelius College in Ocho Rios but was expelled after many warnings about his passion for smoking ganja. During his hearing to be removed from the school—his weeping mother beside him, begging the school's stone-faced board of governors to give her son a second chance—instead of defending himself, Rasta Binzy stood up and pleaded eloquently not only to be allowed to stay, but also to keep on smoking. He told them, "I have attended this school for two years now, and if it was not for the blessed herb, I would have failed my exams. But as you all can attest, my academic record will show that I am one of the school's top students. Instead of expelling me, you should legalize the weed, so it can help other students improve their grades."

The five grim-faced custodians of high education, expecting Rasta Binzy to beg and plead, was so shocked, the chairman shot up from his chair, and, pointing at the

Rastaman, shouted, "Mr. Anthony Emanuel McIntosh, otherwise known as Binzy, it is with extreme prejudice but deep sadness that the board of governors of Cornelius College forthwith expel you from this institution, effective this minute, of this hour, on this date, January 28th, 1974."

Binzy came back to Spring Valley with his suitcase and crying mother and his head full of academic babble, but nothing to do. He just sat around and increased his daily herb intake. Many in Spring Valley were shocked that he had blown such a great opportunity and thought the weed had maddened him, but my friends and I enjoyed listening to him talk about the rise and fall of kingdoms. He told us that Cleopatra betrayed the great Pharaohs before her, losing Egypt to Rome by falling in love with Julius Caesar and Mark Antony, the same way Adam and Eve lost the Garden of Eden because Eve fell in love with Satan. "School youth," he told us, "love, romance and business are unstable mixtures that caused many kingdoms to fall into ruins."

He would lecture us on our way home from school, waving his hand with a stubby half-smoked ganja cigar unlit between his fingers, wearing a red, green and gold headband, green shorts, red T-shirt and sandals, with a big towel slung over his shoulder against his long dreads and his walking stick leaning against his thigh. Rasta Binzy took pride in his long dreads and washed them regularly, making his hair black and shiny, with a healthy glow. He had a youthful spirit that shone bright from his eyes, and he always volunteered to help young people at youth and 4-H Clubs, where he advised them to read their books but think for themselves. "Think before using your brains to swallow words, the same way you chew your food before sinking it into your belly," he told them.

That warm Easter holiday evening, as I skipped over boulders along the narrow track leading up to Rasta Binzy's two-room house nestled among a cluster of pimento trees, he shouted, "Flinty! What are you doing up in my hills?"

"Binzy, can I rest at your gates tonight?" I asked.

"Irie. Anytime!"

He did not ask why I wanted to sleep at his house, but that night he cooked ital chow as he called it—cabbage, okra steamed in coconut milk, young green banana, yam and corn meal dumplings—everything fresh. I meant the food was fresh—absolutely not one grain of salt in it. At first it tasted blah, like the food Grandma ate for her high blood pressure.

"Flinty, all Rastaman a vegetarian—anyone looking like I eating meat is not true Rasta," he said.

I nodded, maybe agreeing with him, looking around confused as my taste buds adjusted to the tasteless food. "You have any salt?"

"Flinty, salt rots bone. There's none here, so don't search."

But as I ate, my taste buds adjusted, and after a while, the meal tasted so good that I had extra. "Thanks. You right—the food's nice, Binzy."

"It's Jah food, Flinty. Not mine. I am just glad to share it with you."

He lit his first of many tree-branch-stout cigars for the evening and sucked the smoke into his chunky body, where most of it stayed because when he blew, only a thin fume came out of him. He sat on a stone and lectured me on the ways of Jah, as he called God. "Flinty—my brethren—never use Babylon System to fortify your life," he said. "You see those lights over them tree-tops, and the damn loud music? You and I have no business in that noise with dem type of people." His voice had the sureness of a seasoned philosopher, and his eyes were as red as fire. But as I watched frisky sparks burst from the lively fire and dance briefly in the air before dying, a comfortable feeling engulfed me—same as bonding with Hutch and during my father's hunting trips. That's when I thought about Hutch and Grandma alone at home, but pleased that Reggae-Slim and Max were safe with Aunt Curry, while Brenton and Little Hutch were with Gwendolyn for the night.

My thoughts went away as the tall, scrawny Jah Starki dropped by with his well-used guitar slung over his back. He bounced his bony fists against mine and then Rasta Binzy's and we shouted loud, warm "Iries!" before he planted himself on a stone next to me. Rasta Binzy handed him a fat cigar—freshly lit—and he dragged the smoke from it with passion, as though he was making love to it. Then he gazed at the virgin ciggy as if he was admiring it. Then he positioned the guitar across his thighs and began to strum it as he chanted.

The melody of our untrained voices rebelled against the calm, starry night. Then Jah Starki gazed at me and said, "School youth, you are a fool to not smoke the good herb—Babylon misled you. But I respect you still. I know you father and grandfather; a good people them, but until you understand the wisdom the herb gives, you will be twisted in the wind by Babylon shitstym, thinking it is a good system."

I nodded, not sure if I was agreeing with what he said or just with the night's vibe.

Rasta Binzy put a piece of dry wood on the fire and dusted off his hands on his green gabardine pants. Then he grabbed up his half-finished cigar from the stone beside me, dragged a big mouthful of smoke, blew it triumphantly into the air, slapped my shoulder, locked his red eyes with mine and shouted, "Yes-I, Jah is with us. You feel him, Flinty!?"

I gazed into the darkness, nodding, though I didn't see Jah. I thought, maybe if I was smoking I would see and feel him.

Jah Starki pulled a huge volume of smoke, but it choked him. He had to let go of the smoke from his mouth prematurely and coughed deeply many times to prevent suffocation.

"A de real collie weed dis, Binzy. A weh you get it?" Jah Starki asked, almost choking.

"From Virgin Mountain. Me fertilized it with pure rat-bat shit."

"Me will tell me brethren them 'bout it."

Then gazing at the two of us, Jah Starki wrapped his lips around the cigar, grabbed his guitar and started playing again. Our corrosive voices struggled to harmonize with the sounds of the guitar's tuned melody, crackling fire, chirping crickets and croaking bullfrogs. Moments when we were not singing were replaced by bursting ganja seeds as the two dreads made love to their spliff in the warm night.

"Rasta Binzy, I will see you in the morrow," Jah Starki suddenly said as he got up.

"Flinty—school youth—respect, take care a you-self," he said.

"Irie, Jah Starki."

Rasta Binzy and I bounced our fists against Jah Starki's and shouted Irie, peace and love to each other. Jah Starki slung his old Gibson guitar over his shoulder, and his legs carried him away from us until all of him disappeared into the darkness. Moments after that, Rasta Binzy and I went inside.

"Flinty, you know King David was a Rastaman—a man who loved God's creation, a man of nature, right?" he asked.

"Who told you he was a Rastaman?" I asked.

"Flinty, there was nothing artificial about King David. That's why he was a Rastaman." Grabbing his Bible, he tied a red, green and gold headband around his head and reclined in his wicker chair to get some comfort. He started to read Psalms 121: "I will lift up mine eyes unto the hills from whence cometh my help..." Then he put the holy book down and sucked his ganja cigar until I could no longer see him through the smoky cloud but heard his counsel coming out of the fog from the other side of the room. "Flinty, hear I now!"

"Yeah," I answered.

"All King David psalms are about green hills, fertile valleys and rivers—nothing about noisy big cities, because Jah is about peace and quiet. You a hear I, Flinty?" I nodded yes, but he could not see me. He asked again, "Flinty, school youth, me right?"

"Yeah, I don't know, Binzy," I answered. It was late and I wanted to sleep.

"Take Psalm 23rd for example: 'He maketh I to lie down' where?... In green pastures." he said, answering his own question. "You see what I mean, Flinty? Man should live in green and fertile valleys, hills, not congested cities. God destroys cities—Sodom and Gomorrah, Jericho, for example. Except for the great flood in Noah time, when the whole Earth was under water, God never destroyed any hills and valleys—he just used volcanoes and earthquakes to make them prettier. You agree?"

I coughed a few times to clear the smoke from my throat and wondered what my clothes would smell like the next day.

"God leave hills and valleys fertile for peaceful people like you and I to live, Flinty, not the war-minded."

I heard his wicker chair squeak on the floor. I could not see him, but maybe he just leaned back in it. He began to preach again. "From afar, Jah shall lick them with his rod, left and right. And they, all of them shall be left naked in their priceless garments and big mansions. Flinty!—school youth—make sure you are not one of them. Leave Babylon business alone and come to the hills—where there is peace. Only among green hills and valleys, moon, stars, and Jah Rastafari, Lord of Lords, conquering lion of the tribe of Judah, will you find the peace you seek."

I nodded.

"Flinty! School youth, you a hear I?" he shouted.

"You may be right," I answered, hoping he would leave me to fall asleep, but without any luck.

"Tell I, school youth. Have you ever see a Rastaman not peaceful?"

I said nothing.

"Flinty, answer the question," he demanded.

"No," I answered in a hoarse voice.

He was right. I had never seen or heard of any Rastaman committing any crime in Spring Valley. They mostly chanted the herb gospel, mostly about its healing powers, that it should be legalized.

He walked over with a brand new cigar to the bed where I lay. "Flinty, I like how you reason with the youth them at 4-H Club meetings. Remember the night after you stood between two youths and broke up the fighting and told them that their first and second man inside them—ego and pride—were on stage performing too loud, taking all the attention. You tell them to give the third man, truth, a chance."

"Yeah, I remember that night," I said.

"That was a wicked piece of reasoning, Flinty, but you just said it and left. I like that about you, the way you tie up your ideas into neat and simple bundles."

"Thanks man," I replied. I yawned a few times and stretched my hands to the roof, trying to stay awake.

"I cannot say the same thing 'bout the pork-eating bald heads them who runs the shitstym," he continued. "Dem chow down the pork, eat, sleep, drink and wallow in the corruption 'till them look like the hogs."

He sucked in and released another cloud of smoke.

"Binzy, open up the window and let in fresh air?" I asked.

"Flinty, leave the window close to keep the pestilence out," he answered.

Those were the last words I heard. I coughed many times after that and drifted off to sleep. I woke up several times that night because of grunting and wailing sounds I heard coming from outside, which I thought were duppies or bad spirits roaming around. I pulled the sheet over my head and tried to sleep. I woke up early, tired and with a pounding headache. My struggling Afro stank from stale marijuana smoke. But Rasta Binzy was in a deep sleep in his wicker chair, snoring loudly. I squeezed his hand, left the dollar Hutch had given me the evening before on the table and staggered off to catch the bus for school. That day, I slept through my classes.

All day long I felt bad about drinking all of Hutch's Wincarnis wine and wanted to buy them back, but was short on cash. But when I got home he had cooled off because Aunt Blanche had brought over a new bottle for her father. This calmed him down and got us off the hook. That was three years ago, the last time I saw Hutch's fury. I was only weeks from graduating and hoped to never see it again.

CHAPTER 12:
Waltz of the Unbloomed Hibiscus

It was Friday, June 30th: Spring Valley High School's official graduation day. But the sun refused to rise that morning, leaving the district in darkness. It was as if the previous night had stretched itself far into where daylight should have begun. Except for the usual 90 degree temperature, darkness had blanked out the morning's light like a December winter's day in Finland. But according to the weather forecast, the sun was supposed to rise at 6:30 a.m. So no one could explain the cause of the stubborn gloom that had lingered and stolen many hours of daylight from such a special day.

"Your graduation day is Ipernot's day," Grandma announced as she tossed a lump of sugar into her mouth.

Everyone in Spring Valley had heard the story of Brother Barber Ipernot, who lived long before Grandma was born, a notorious Obeah-man, who could stop people's hearts from beating in their chests by chanting their names a certain way when the moon was shining full. The people were afraid of him, and when he fell into a deep narrow sinkhole, the Spring Valley citizens left him in the blackness to die. He cursed and threatened the villagers for two days for not pulling him out, and on the bright sunny morning of the third day, his voice fell silent. Darkness blanketed Spring Valley District only minutes after, and a howling windstorm battered the village.

"Grandma, Ipernot's day is a legend," I said. "Just like Anancy stories. People made them up."

"Flinty, you think you know everything," Grandma retorted, and began humming a hymn, as she walked slowly to the kitchen, using a candle to see her way.

But at exactly 10 a.m., the sun suddenly burst through the clouds. There were shouts of jubilation around Spring Valley. Someone even sounded Daniel Butterfield's double-quick bugle call from a hilltop with an Abeng. Maroon scouts long ago used the Abeng horn to warn their village of approaching British Redcoats. The elders still sounded Abengs on special occasions. Spring Valley was alive again and readying itself for graduation. Except for Cricket Matches, Christmas and New Year, graduation was the town's biggest event.

At 3 p.m., Hutch, Grandma and Mother were all dressed in their best. They inspected my powder-blue Kariba suit and gleaming black shoes as I entered the living room.

"Flinty, boy, you looking like a real man," Hutch shouted. I high-fived my cousins and brothers, who were also dressed in their Sunday best for the occasion. I posed with the family for pictures as Ma's camera clicked away. Uncle Terrence gave the car horn a long toot.

We arrived at Kingsway's Anglican Church, with its tall, white steeple gazing down on Spring Valley High

School from a green hill, like a big brother guarding his younger, unruly sibling. During his weekly devotion, Priest Sanguinity would drive our heavy load of sins committed at the school up that steep gravel-road hill, and use prayer to scrub those wrongs until they were as white as the collar he wore around his neck. Gravestones were scattered about the grassy hillside around the church, some from the early 17th century. Important tombs were painted white and black, with wrought iron fences around them, like the Johnson and McIntosh families, Spring Valley's first business leaders. The first general hardware store was theirs, going way back to when the original McIntoshes first arrived from Scotland and settled in Spring Valley.

But I had not liked that church since the funeral of my first year music teacher, Miss Palmer, four years earlier. She was so beautiful that I fought every week to sit on the front bench to get a good look at her. All I learned for the whole year in music class was "doh re mi fa sol la ti doh." I could sing it backwards, upside-down and sideways, but that was all that had stuck to me from her class. I was happy just to sit and gaze at her white blouse and smooth legs that extended from her black skirt under the table toward me every week. Once she caught me gazing intensely at her under the table. The next day she demanded to know what I'd been looking at. My lie was snappy and convincing; I told her that she had dropped a piece of red chalk under the table and her feet had been moving on it and drawing something that looked like a monkey's face. She wrinkled her face and scratched her forehead with her index finger, trying to recall, but nothing came to her mind, so she reset her face back to pleasant, nodded and dismissed me from her office.

It was as if she was playing with me when she squinted and bobbed her head when she strung musical notes together to make them sound sweet. She would snap her fingers and jiggle her narrow hips when she played the piano to encourage the rhythm—all were glue for my eyes to never leave her. That is, until she became sick and her dark smooth skin stripped away from her face day after day, leaving patches of awful pink. Then she died suddenly. I attended her funeral and had hated Kingsway Anglican Church ever since. It was as if the church had taken her, leaving me in quiet sorrow.

However, on this, our graduation day, my friends and I were jubilant. We planned to watch the sermon slip out of the way so we could enjoy the graduation ball. It was planned for students only, down the hill at the school. Mookie, Ziggy, Stan-Chen and Sam were sharply dressed the same as me. I glanced often at the red digits on my new digital watch Mother had given me for the occasion. She snapped pictures of the five of us boys posing together and giggling like young roosters circling around hens. We gazed at the girls as they arrived in their flowing mauve gowns with white trimming.

Marilyn Fisher, my dance partner for the ball, was stunning, her eyes bright and her cheeks and eyebrows plucked and painted, perhaps for the first time. Every strand of her shiny black hair was steamed with a hot comb and drilled into place like an obedient soldier on parade. A category five hurricane could not move a single strand of her hair, and her make-up made her face fresh and smooth. Like magic, Marilyn Fisher, who often put her hand over her mouth and giggled mischievously in class, had transformed into a full-grown woman from the shy dancing partner with whom I had practised the official graduation waltz just days earlier.

We sat in the mauve-and-white decorated church and listened to Priest Sanguinity's words of commencement, his six-foot frame in full priestly black frock with white collar, his white wrinkled face and blue eyes gazing at us through silver, thin-rimmed glasses, the warm evening wind ruffling a few strands of his unruly greying hair. He had the air of a caring father, not only for students, but for the whole community. When Saddle-Head, a popular Spring Valley High student, had urinated on a piece of live electrical wire some years earlier and was electrocuted, the priest's calming words soothed the people's sudden shock and replaced students' fears with courage. But on our graduation day, the priest spoke to us like the adults we had become under his pastoral stare. He first thanked our parents and guardians for supporting us. Then he commissioned us, "Graduates, your duty is to go boldly from here, into the world; take nothing from it, but give..."

The leftover echo of his English accent that lingered in the hot, quiet, old church transported my wandering mind to President John Kennedy's inaugural address on January 20, 1961: "...And so, my fellow Americans, ask not what your country can do for you, but what you can do for your country."

However, when I glanced at my fellow graduates, I saw many taking much and giving back nothing. What did we have to give? I wondered. We were poised to give the world happiness and pain, but the priest expected only comfort from us. Head boy Marlon Anderson, with his perfect afro and self-assurance bolstered by good grades, would have no problem giving good to the world, I thought. His valedictorian speech was inspiring. He spoke with poise and confidence: "...In time, perhaps in this decade, through diligence and hard work, graduates here today shall work proudly, shoulder to shoulder with the world's best, finding solutions to global problems. This unassuming island, in its defiance and against all odds, has already struck a proud pose on the world stage, as we saw at the Olympic Games in Montreal, Canada, two years ago. Graduates, let us be proud of ourselves and our country and carry it in our hearts wherever we may roam."

His words were eloquent—perhaps with a few too many spoonfuls of sugar—but he was leaving for the United States within days after graduation to attend Howard University and climb the ladder of success. Probably the only time he would come back was on vacation with his wife and children, taking pictures like a tourist.

I glanced over at the gruff Mike Dules, who sat in the corner grinning and nodding at the charitable priest. He had given many freshmen only 5¢ to buy $1 lunches and threatened them with harsh punishment if they returned without the meal and change. The thought crossed my mind that he was geared up to use a scheming shovel to scrape away much from this world, giving back only fumes of stinking gas from his loud belches. And what would I give? Grandma kept telling me I could write, but I didn't believe it, and I once played a good game of cricket but had given that up so I could pass my exams.

Maybe giving up cricket had been a mistake. At least I was good at it, and, with practice, maybe I could play for the West Indies and become popular like Lawrence Column, buy a big bike and come back for Lola Dawson. Shit, I forgot Lola was pregnant for one of the policemen. Wonder which one.... But my dream about playing for the West Indies was too ambitious. I had never heard of any test cricketers from places like Spring Valley. They were from Kingston and Montego Bay—places with big playfields and clubs with lots of cricket gear.

"The world is yours but for a short time, so use your moments to full..." Priest Sanguinity's voice alerted me, before I drifted away again.

Okay, Flinty, I told myself. I will stick to my secret plan to build the loudest sound system in the country, one that rumbles like earthquakes and pollutes God-fearing false Christians. But that would unleash Priest Sanguinity's wrath. Perhaps he would drive his blue Vauxhall to my parties and whip the dancers and beer drinkers like Christ had done in Jerusalem. That wouldn't work; maybe my promise to build Grandma a dream machine after graduating from engineering school was my best plan. She wasted her mornings trying to remember her dreams.

Hutch did not need a dream machine. His dreams were loud adventures, especially when he met up with dead friends and relatives. Whenever that happened, he called them by their names first, and then told them 'bout their "rass"—demanding that they go back to hell, where they came from. And if they ignored him, he punched and kicked them back to their misery. He would roll around in the bed, fighting under the sheet, kicking and punching like Mohammad Ali, sometimes worse—like Smokin' Joe Frazier.

I had seen him get up from his bed, bobbing and weaving, sparring like a middleweight boxing champion—straight punching, hooking, jabbing and throwing uppercuts at the unseen dead. But the most dangerous thing anyone could do while he punched out ghosts in his dreams was wake him because the person who disturbed him became the ghost and ran the risk of being knocked out cold.

I glanced at Hutch and smiled as I recalled only one month earlier. I was in my room reading Henry David Thoreau's *Walden Pond*—the chapter on sound. Trying to escape Hutch's boring see-saw snore, I began to read. "All sound heard at the greatest possible distance produces one and the same effect, a vibration of the universal lyre... There came to me in this case a melody which the air had strained...." Hutch's snoring, strained by his nostrils, had an ugly melody about it, and was quite louder than a buzz-saw, so I put away the book and gazed at the ceiling. Suddenly, I heard him shouting. No big deal; just another dream, I told myself. But then I heard him call out, "Uncle Bark, but you no dead long time, man. What the rass you doing in here?"

For a moment there was silence, until the peace exploded into intense loud cussing. "Get your dead ugly rass out of this house now!"

I heard his bed jerk as if it was breaking apart. He was punching and thumping. I heard his fists landing in quick succession on Uncle Bark. "Take that. How about this one in your head! You want some more?" he asked the ghost. "How the hell did you get in here? Through the front door?

TA-TA, GRANDMA

You telling me you just walk right in? But look how far from here them bury you, and you find your way 'round here. You lucky I left my machete inside the kitchen, else I would chop you up into pieces!" A new wave of fists landed on the ghost: Grandma sleeping beside him.

She woke up screaming. "Hutch, it's me! Hutch, HUTCH, wake up! Wake up! You are dreaming! It's a dream. It's not your Uncle Bark; it's me!" I ran into the room. Hutch was half-awake and sitting on the edge of the bed. He was in a foggy twilight between his dream and Grandma restraining both his hands from throwing any more punches.

"It's alright. It's just a dream," I told him firmly. Grandma released his hands and held her forehead with a confused look on her face, staring at her husband, by now fully awake. His head hung low and his face sank into a gloom. He kept apologizing.

"I am sorry, but that damn idiot dead so long, still walking around."

Next day, Grandma walked around the house with a plastic bag of cold water on her head to shrink her swollen face, complaining about being Hutch's punching bag. Hutch stayed home and apologized to her non-stop throughout the day.

While Hutch's dreams were adventures of fighting dead people, Grandma could not remember any of hers, and so my dream machine would suit her well. The machine would have a hat made of soft cloth with electrodes clipped to it, which she would wear to bed every night. The hat would scan her brain for intelligent activities and sniff her dreams while she slept. The hat would be linked by wires

— 175 —

to an intelligent amplifier/analyzer that would collect, amplify, and store the complex, low-amplitude signals from Grandma's brain. It would then feed them to an interpreter/translator/recorder that would finally be fed into a video processor/enhancer for pictures, which would be stored on a magnetic tape, the same as a video cassette recorder. My dear old grandma would only have to push the playback button each morning and enjoy her dreams, like watching television. I could see her gathering the family to enjoy her dreams with popcorn each morning.

Other than Grandma's dream machine floating around in my head, I had no idea how to live up to the priest's call. "...But I can ask no more from you than to do your best. Spring Valley graduating class, congratulations and God's grace goes with all of you."

The sermon ended and we sang the national anthem and shook hands with the priest. Principal Black smiled and handed out diplomas. I gave my parchment paper with my full name printed on it and the Holy Bible—a gift to all graduates—to Grandma. Then I pecked her and Mother's cheeks, and exchanged smiles with Hutch as he patted my shoulders, before walking off down the hill toward the evening's main event: music, dancing, girls and gossip, but regrettably, no alcohol.

I met with Sam, Ziggy, Mookie and Stan-Chen in the foyer of the school's main building, where we stood and watched cars pull up and beautiful girls get out. Some were careful to hold up their gowns so they would not sweep the dusty ground as they strolled along the corridor toward the elegantly decorated assembly hall. Doxie Chambers, sexy and classy, slithered out of the back seat of her uncle's white car like a cat ready to prowl long into the night. Earlier, at the church, her graduation gown, cut much too low in front and back, was so revealing a lady had to drape a sweater over her to prevent Priest Sanguinity from having a heart attack. She arrived stripped of the sweater and exposing her bare slinky frame, all her curves uncovered for our eyes to drive over, under and around as she floated by us. She smiled at Sam.

"How do you and Doxie get away with that secret between you two?" I asked Sam.

"Flinty, I told you before; we are just friends. You and I already talked about that at 4-H Club." He laughed to mask his lie. They had fallen over the edge of love, all the way down into its deep bottom, but Sam's and Doxie's families hated each other because of a land feud going back many generations, so they kept their relationship secret.

The graduation ball commenced with a long line of graduates paired off outside the assembly hall. My beautiful, perfume-drenched Marilyn Fisher stood beside me, holding my hand with her sweaty palm, her buffed chest nervously rising and falling. Every breath she took into her body and released had gaps in it. At the quick wave of Mrs. Simpson's hand, the music started and we waltzed down the corridor into the long rectangular hall, decorated in mauve and white. Couples coordinated in fashion and spirit, future leaders and idlers, danced down the centre of the hall to the *Waltz of the Unbloomed Hibiscus*. The music was composed by Nadia Smelt, Spring Valley's most creative student. We practised the spirited piano waltz for many weeks until we got our steps right. The way Mrs. Simpson—our music teacher—explained the waltz was that, one day long into the future, some of us would bloom by doing good deeds that benefit others. She also said, it was our duty to reach out for the sunshine we need in order to blossom in this world. But at the moment of graduation, we were just buds and sprouts, and many of us were still seeds struggling to get out from under the soil.

But on graduation night, the ladies held their heads erect, chins and chests lifted up, their slim necklines stretched to expose every inch. Their bright eyes were firmly fixed over their partners' right shoulders, gowns floating like swans gracefully rising from a lake of glass. My cheek lightly touched Lady Fisher's as my right hand rested on her lower back, and my outstretched left hand clasped her right palm, our feet barely touching the floor as we harmonized our steps and let the music melt us with the other dancers into a graceful dancing stream. Beads of sweat sprinkled her forehead. I stole a quick smile that put a dimple on her cheek. I felt her bouncing heart against my body and smiled at her some more.

Many awards were handed out afterwards. Mine was for history, given to me by Mr. Tabangi. He had the biggest grin he'd ever allowed his face to show as he handed me the heavy wooden plaque, shook my hand firmly and posed with me for a photographer. "Well done, Flinty," he whispered. Mookie received the award for outstanding athlete. He had set regional records for the 100 metres all the way to the mile. He was so fast we sometimes lifted up his shirt and jokingly searching for a hidden engine. Ziggy got the school's highest award for mathematics. He would passionately argue algebra and calculus with mathematics teachers, sometimes embarrassing them in front of the class, but that was all he was good at. He had a gift for arranging and seeing numbers performing all sorts of useful things for the world.

After the prizes had been handed out and the formalities were over, DJ Superman cranked up the music. I was pleased with the rich acoustics inside the dimly lit hall as the sound bounced off protruding objects hung from walls to create a pleasant resonance. Big empty halls sometimes destroy harmony, creating a thin and hollow sound, forcing the DJ to turn the volume up much too loud and send party people home with pounding headaches, but not this time.

DJ Superman fed us with hits like The Four Seasons' *Oh What a Night*, and Hot Chocolate's *You Sexy Thing*, which pulled everyone onto the dance floor, especially the girls, their slim bodies rocking, holding their brand new toe-burning high-heel shoes over their heads as they flung their bodies and feet in all directions. But the joint vibrated and rumbled when DJ Superman exploded sweet reggae nectar into the speakers. He blasted us with Little Roy's *Tribal War*, the Maytones' *Money Worries*, Althea and Donna's *Uptown Top Ranking* and all the '70s greatest hits. The thundering music blew the lid off our compressed ire that had simmered for five years: detentions, lashings, demerit points, lock-ups, lock-downs, fights, floggings, bad report cards, too much bad and too little good, lack of this and lack of that. As if fallen into a trance, our whole bodies zigzagged and twisted to the proverbial sound of the rusty chains of academic binding that had tied us to exams. Principal Black's strangulation of rules and regulations snapped from our wrists and ankles as the rhythms pulled our minds and bodies from the five-building penal institution to new freedoms. We danced and sweated until the bad vibes lifted off us and drifted away to set us free.

We waved, shouted, clapped our hands, hugged and stomped our feet in cadence with the rhythm, like marching soldiers coming home victorious from a well-fought battle. We skanked forward four or five steps loosely, allowing our bodies to move at the whim of the rhythm. Then we let the rhythm bend our slinky, surrendered bodies in half at our waists. We dropped our heavy heads to let them dangle forward, and waited for the next jolt of rhythm to pull us up straight, and, reversing our steps inside the rhythms' familiar shell, back to where we had started. We repeated our dance steps over and over again, chanting deep into the night, until our clothes were drenched with sweat as we celebrated and shouted toward a crescendo of musical fireworks. Medicine to start our new lives.

Later that night, I went outside into the cool night to take a break from the heat on the dance floor. I saw the silhouette of a woman's elegant frame leaning against a railing on the second floor of the science building. She was gazing at the moonlight with contentment, a statue of peace, as if she had surrendered all of herself to the mystery of the night, undisturbed by the loud music.

Ah, it's Deloris Peckham, I thought; I mounted the steps and walked toward her.

Deloris had sorted out her addiction to romance novels the way I had cut out my addiction to cricket in time for graduation. We had much in common. I folded my arms across my chest, leaned on the rail beside her, and said nothing. I gazed at the night just as she was doing. She turned to me and smiled. She was more beautiful than ever.

Her new-found strength she had used to break her addiction from romance books had put radiance on her face that glowed even in the dark. After her suspension, her parents had cried buckets of tears in Principal Black's office, asking him to take her back.

Principal Black readmitted her after she promised to keep away from the Love 'n Light Bookstore. I had reached out to her and offered my help with mathematics and history whenever I could. Perhaps it was out of guilt for stepping over her when she deliberately fell in front of me, expecting me to save her when she was hopelessly lost in love with the sexy characters from romance novels. We later became friends.

Deloris put her left hand on my shoulder and looked at my eyes. "Flinty, thanks again for helping me with my math assignments," she said.

"No problem, Deloris. I am just glad to see you leaving this place."

The gentle wind ruffled her hair. She smiled, and her sparkling eyes added an extra sheen of warmth to the moment. "I was wrong to call you a brute with a dark puny heart," she said.

"But I am a brute, on a night like this, just before the moon comes out."

"You mean like a werewolf."

"GRRRRR!!!"

"Flinty, stop! That's not how a werewolf sounds," she said, chuckling.

"Deloris... I was wrong for letting you fall that evening. But I was stubborn in those days."

"I am glad we both left what we were behind."

I nodded and glanced at the sky, my mind leaving the music's thumping bass behind. "Congratulations," I said.

"For what?"

"I heard you and Nadia will be attending the Kingston School of Drama."

Deloris smiled and nodded, but said nothing.

"Bet you will be on TV one day."

"Flinty, do you think the future is already planned, and we are just wasting time trying to make it our own?" she said, changing the subject.

She'd caught me off guard. I screwed up my face and squinted, trying to reason out an answer. "Deloris, that's deep. Come on," I said. "Tonight is graduation, not one of Mr. Tabangi's critical thinking classes."

"Flinty, I am serious! What do you think?"

I felt my mind begin a lazy churning—as if climbing a steep hill, not wanting to answer her question. But I felt her hungry eyes on my lips, begging my mouth to feed her something.

"Well, maybe there is a plan bigger than ours. Hutch, my grandfather, always said so. But even if that's true, we still have to make choices that give us a say in the way the plan turns out. You coming back and graduating was your good choice."

"Only because I tried to implant Carlton Sheldon into Splinter—who used to live next door to me—but it didn't work. And when we broke up, I came back to school."

"Splinter! His name's Splinter!"

"Yes. And he was nice. Why?"

"I just can't see someone name Splinter looking the way you described Carlton Sheldon."

"You think I was crazy wanting Carlton Sheldon from romance novels."

"No more than my dreams of making the West Indies Cricket Team. Okay, back to your question about the future. Why are you concerned?" I said.

"I am too dramatic," she answered. "Often I create mountains out of anthills."

"That's because you have strong survival instincts."

"Really?"

"Yes. Take my grandmother, for example. If she saw me getting ready to ride my bicycle without brakes, she would describe the accident scene to me in detail, her hands slicing the air like a knife, to make sure every word from her dark recital stuck. 'Flinty, you are about to ride that bicycle without brakes again? The big six-wheel bus is going to slam into your little two-wheel bicycle, around Miss Codner's blind corner. Run over and pulp your scrawny body. The ambulance will find you on the asphalt, twitching, with your tripe hanging out of your belly—in the dirt. They will have to pick up your stringy gut off the ground and brush off the dirt and push it back into your belly, before taking you to Spring Valley Hospital. And me not coming 'round there to visit, because me tell you over and over: you not supposed to be riding anything that cannot stand up by itself, much less without brake. That's the first complaint in the next letter to your mother this month.'"

Deloris wrinkled up her face uncomfortably as I spoke, but then a grin came over her puzzled face. "What would you do after hearing that?"

"Sometimes I'd screw up my face and swallow, trying to block her out. Then I'd put on my bravest face and ride carefully to wherever I was going, but I'd stay away from Miss Codner's blind corner and make sure to get back before the bus. Other times, I'd leave the bicycle and walk to where I was going, and fix the brake as soon as I got back."

"She'd scare you away from having any accidents."

"Yes, and she was good at it, Deloris. Except for the police bus search during the state of emergency, which almost gave her a heart attack, I have never seen her involved in a single mishap; she never broke a dish or a drinking glass. Her graphic horror pictures inside her head steered her clear of accidents."

I continued to think about Grandma. "It's easy to think she is gloomy, but she is not, because she spends her mornings in her garden, searching for new blooms and sprouts. She is an optimistic woman but with a dramatic flair for survival. Don't complain about your dramatic flair," I advised Deloris. "Use it like my grandma, to survive."

"Thanks, Flinty. Amazing the way you have changed. I remember Principal Black calling out your name over the microphone at devotion, saying you and your friends were a bunch of hooligans."

I chuckled. "Deloris, I have changed, but not too much," I said. "Many times I ignored Grandma's warnings and squeezed out fun juice from whatever I enjoyed."

"But you survived."

"So far so good. My fingers are still crossed."

We listened quietly to the music for a while; then I asked her to dance.

I took her left hand in my right, kissed her hair, and we walked slowly down the steps and moved onto the dance floor. We leaned, almost collapsing into each other. I embraced her gentle beauty the same way Grandma cupped a delicate forget-me-not bloom in her garden. I wanted Deloris to know my heart was not a puny chunk of coal that repelled her radiance as she had screamed at me one year earlier.

She dropped her head on my shoulder, her right hand slid around my waist, and our bodies lingered lazily in the moment, wrapped in each other's arms. The two of us were survivors of our addictions. Our bodies melted into one, resisting all efforts to move, not wanting to hasten the end of the tune we were supposed to be dancing to, Manhattan's *Let's Just Kiss and Say Goodbye*.

After the dance, I kissed her hand the way Carlton Sheldon—her book-dwelling romantic hero—probably would have done. She smiled and I thanked her, wished her good luck and walked outside for a final look around the compound before meeting my friends.

CHAPTER 13:
A Matador at the Wicket

Many students were scattered along the building's corridors and around the compound, some dancing, embracing—maybe kissing—others just standing around, recalling favourite moments. A cluster of boys in darkness, behind the library, chatted quietly as they spewed strong ganja smoke into the air. I was surprised Shampoo Grill was among them. I heard his foggy, baritone voice, though it was down many decibels. I waved to them and walked past the broken water fountain that forever squirted water that kept the grass around it lush and green. I sat quietly on the wall that divided the cricket field from the pavilion, my arms folded across my chest. Reggae bass grumbled in the background, but after a while my thoughts grew loud and blocked out the music, leaving me and my memories in the dark.

As clear as television, my memory rebroadcast a cricket match from a sunny Tuesday, when I opened for Spring Valley against Christiana High School and retired from the field unconquered, carrying my bat on my shoulder off the field after watching my 10 teammates' wickets fall. It was a record that remained unbroken. On that incredible day, I used my bat like a sword, to protect my body and wicket from dangerous bouncers, but slammed bowlers' mistakes into the boundaries. There were times when I felt invincible, as if I were protected by forces outside myself.

But after batting for so long, to the astonishment of my teammates and the grudging admiration of my opponents, I shuffled forward and stepped into a deceptively slow, spinning ball in flight and hit it into the hands of my opponent, fielding at mid-wicket. I was lucky; he dropped the fast-flying ball, giving me a second chance, but I was ungrateful. I was tired and had had enough. The sun was too hot, my hands were sweaty and they trembled, for I had not prepared for batting for such a long time. I expected to bat for the usual 30 minutes, so I was not prepared to manage my new success and was about to throw it away. My concentration drifted, like straddling a fence between failure and success, but all the while the intense alertness of my opponents to remove me from the game remained high.

Suddenly, I was reminded of my father's favourite book—John Bunyan's *Pilgrim's Progress*—when travelling Christian, on his journey, was lured off course by deception and tricky guides, whom he had befriended and trusted. He meandered into walls of discouragement until he was baked soft from exhaustion, tired and confused, ready to be destroyed by the evil Apollyon. The scaly fiend flung darts and knocked him to the ground over and again until he could not get up. Then the creature smothered Christian's meagre body until he lost his sword. He lay almost lifeless under the monster's body, ready to die. But at the last moment, he found strength, and his fumbling fingers reached out and grasped his sword and plunged it deep into the evil monster's belly and killed it.

But as the afternoon sun beat down on my head and my mind drifted, the umpire rescued me by signalling tea break. I filled my belly with pineapple juice and corned beef sandwiches. I closed my eyes and took deep breaths to relax until my spirit revived. Then I grabbed my bat and strode back onto the field. This time, I bruised the ball with my bat and removed its shine. I pushed it away from my body when threatened and left it alone when it tempted me into making mistakes. But when it made a mistake, I slammed it with brute force. And with the fury and focus of a matador driving his spear deep into a raging bull, until it was quiet and still, I danced into the misleading and subversive spin bowling and used my bat to crash the tired ball over the fence into four and six boundaries, until it was soft and its roundness beaten into flatness.

However, on graduation night, I sat in the dark, my memory ablaze with the past, but I could not see any farther than the brightly lit steeple of Kingsway Anglican Church on the hill and the uneven silhouettes of tombstones rising from the ground. I was about to walk back toward the grumbling bass of the reggae music when I heard a familiar voice whispering. It sounded like Hutch's father, the same baritone voice I had heard one year earlier. My ears cleared away the music and waited for my great-grandfather to speak.

Flinty, you will walk through life with the same determination you used to play the game you played here at 14. You will be invincible. No matter what obstacles you face or darts are flung at you, you will stand up. And when your mistakes like sharp-edged boulders cause you to stumble, you will get up and climb to new wisdom. Your character will be battered but unbent. And you will carry home your well-used blunt-edged sword on your shoulder, as you did your cricket bat four years ago—unconquered. Your strength is for good, not evil, for you are neither clever nor smart, but insightful.

The loud, clear voice suddenly went quiet. I closed my eyes to turn up my concentration, but I heard nothing more. I looked up at the full moon directly over my head and then at the gravestones on the hillside, but still heard nothing. I used my thoughts to search inside, to see if my great-grandfather's voice was really mine, but only felt the strength of the words he left inside me. I screwed up my face in astonishment before nodding my head, thanking him for his advice. I saluted the cricket field like a soldier grateful to the battlefield that had spared him and began walking in the direction of the music, where my friends waited for me.

As I walked along the brightly lit corridor of the administration building, I saw Mrs. Black leaving her office. She was elegantly dressed. She grabbed my right hand and squeezed it, and I began to walk beside her. "Mr. Magnum, I am so proud of you," she said. "Within one year you found your lost imagination and nourished it in time to pass your exams—you even won an award!"

"I just laid down my cricket bat, Mrs. Black."

She glanced at me and grinned. "Cynthia, Mr. Magnum. Call me Cynthia, but only for tonight. Tomorrow, I will be the same little half-pint tyrant—the name you gave me." She was smiling, but I was shocked and kept quiet. I had no idea she knew I had given her that name.

"I wish you the best," she continued.

"Thanks, Mrs. Black." I could not call her Cynthia.

She had a brown envelope in her right hand, which slapped her thigh as we walked toward the music. She was still working, even on graduation night, I thought.

"Oh, by the way, I kept one of your essays, *The Fall of Creative Thinking*", she said, almost shouting over the music, "for my new batch of students. Hope you don't mind."

"That's quite alright, Mrs. Black. Quite alright."

The music got louder as we got closer to the assembly hall. Mrs. Black shouted over the noise, "Mr. Magnum, I know your heart's in technology, but promise me you will write when you get a chance!"

I nodded, not sure if I really agreed or was simply caught up in the moment. She always complained that I had no respect for writing. But as I waved goodbye to her and walked toward my four waiting friends, a part from that final essay I wrote, the one Mrs. Black had mentioned, came back to me: "In this country, the bulk of the youth's free-flowing creative spring, their natural survival kit, endowed by God, at birth to be crafted into prosperity, is being dried up by the overheated climate of politics. Their minds hijacked by hard-core political alliances, polarized by blood. Much too early, their stream of youthful thoughts are being zigged and zagged, to the left and right, instead being guided by elders to create freely along the unbiased centre."

Even though Mrs. Black did not agree with many of my points, saying the essay was too abstract, she gave me a pass. A few days after I collected it, she asked for the essay again, and kept it.

I joined my friends (Myron Thompson) Mookie, (Michael Jones) Ziggy, (Samuel Jackson) Sam and (Stanley Chen) Stan-Chen in the foyer as we had planned, but for the last time. We have been with each other since our first day in Aunt Buckingstone's classroom. Mookie was now the new president of the Spring Valley Youth Club. His athletic six-foot frame, brownish face and straight nose and glossy eyes, under his wide afro, made him look like a police officer, not a Babylon. He lives with his mother and three brothers. His father died when he was only three years old. Ziggy's extreme dark face, bright smile, wide nose, short legs and stocky body gave him the distinct boyish air of an African. Ziggy lives with his mother and father, his older brother and two sisters. Sam's chiselled body and slim dark face with bright eyes gave him the look and air of a magazine model. Sam was leader for the Spring Valley's 4-H Club's Agricultural project, and lives with his grandparents, just down the road from his mother who is married to someone who is not his father. Except for Stan-Chen's dark complexion, which he got from his mother, he looked exactly like his Chinese father—a businessman. He owns two haberdashery stores, one in Spring Valley and another in Mandeville. Stan-Chen, who is an only child, would be always dispensing advice from his bag of Ancient Chinese Secrets to the four of us. And we could always bet on him having extra money for hot bread and cheese at Mr. Bennett's bakery in the evenings after school. But as I summed up my four childhood brethren, my mind felt at ease, as if a burden had rolled off it.

It felt as if we were Tommy, Johnny, David, Uriah, and Charlie, the five Maroon boys from V.S. Reid's *Young Warriors*, getting ready to start our first mission. What our duty was, none of us knew.

"Why are you always the last one to show up?" Sam asked.

"That's not true, Sam," I deflected.

"Flinty, where were you? We have been looking for you, man," Mookie interjected loudly. The light over his head helped me to see his mischievous grin, suggesting that I had drifted off with Deloris, with whom he had seen me dancing.

"Went for a final look at the cricket field."

"You are going to miss that cricket field, I just know it," Ziggy said. "There's only snow in Toronto."

I nodded. And for a few moments, there was silence except for the intoxicated beat of Hues Corporation's *Rock the Boat* in the background.

"Well, scouts, it's over!" shouted Stan-Chen. He thrust his right hand into the air with his palm opened. We all slapped it instinctively and shouted the Musketeer's pledge: "All for one, and one for all!" The pledge was our mantra for teambuilding during sports competitions, but our school games were over, and life's game was about to begin.

The music was still thumping, people were dancing, some cheering, as we left for a planned drink with Jah Spike at Blue Vail's. And for the last time, we walked—almost hustled—along the narrow road beneath pine trees up the steep hill, away from the school—the halls we had roamed for five years. At the top of the hill, I turned and glanced at the buildings in which books, pens, papers and sports had guided, nourished and moulded us into what we had become. A sliver of gratitude bubbled up in my belly as our feet tapped the asphalt. The moon shone its light on us, and our five shadows blended into one as we made haste, out from under the divine guidance of the school's brightly lit motto, "Preces et Opera Omnia Vincunt: Prayer and Work Conquer All," toward the house of alcohol.

We did not speak as we turned onto the quiet main street with our hands buried inside our pockets. Principal Black's warning that only poor people keep their hands inside their pockets came to mind, but I ignored it and sank my hands deeper. Stepping away from the principal's rules and regulations filled me with a sense of transcendence. I felt liberated. We moved swiftly along to the loud chirping of night creatures. Again, I thought about the five Maroon boys. They were Trelawney's boys, too.

Only a few lights were on in the town; most businesses were closed because of the graduation ball.

"This town is dead," said Stan-Chen.

"I have never seen it so quiet," Mookie agreed.

"Anyone heard why this morning was so dark?" Ziggy inquired, changing the subject.

"The radio announcer said a storm was on the way but turned back," answered Stan-Chen.

TA-TA, GRANDMA

"That was weird, man," commented Sam.

"Grandma said Barber Ipernot was warning the village," I chimed in.

"Yeah, right," Sam said.

Suddenly I heard Tomaso Albinoni's *Adagio*. Its haunting violins sounded as if they were streaming from the gentle swaying pine and eucalyptus trees. I had listened to the *Adagio* and other music from the baroque period in the school library when I skipped life skills classes and hung out with Marlon Anderson and his enlightened crew. Marlon said that some classical music can span the full spectrum of our emotions from birth to death, but our state of being determines how much of what—peace and war, happiness and sadness—is triggered by the music. So I was puzzled that after so much fun and dancing at graduation earlier, my mind had sifted such a haunting melody from the wind. But then I remembered Mr. Tabangi's warning after I argued with him that Napoleon had lost the battle at Waterloo because the Duke of Wellington knew how to set a good cricket field and Napoleon Bonaparte did not.

"Flinty," Mr. Tabangi had said, "it is true that Arthur Wellesley, The Duke, would have played cricket at Eton, but sometimes you amplify subtleties and fragments, ignoring the obvious."

"Mr. Tabangi, the obvious is empty of greatness, found only in fragments and subtleties," I argued.

"Yes, Flinty, but a person whose mind is fueled by subtleties alone either becomes great or is cut off and never heard from again."

I was not sure if Mr. Tabangi was correct, but after our debate, whenever I caught myself amplifying meagre undefined thoughts, I pulled back from making much ado about nothing. So I blocked out the sad symphony from my mind, withdrew from the wind and rejoined the thump of our feet pounding the pavement toward Blue Vail's.

CHAPTER 14:
For the Love of Country

Blue Vail's Bar was empty when we entered, and there was loud music blasting from the jukebox. Jah Spike was expecting us, and his grin brightened the dimly lit bar. "You idlers in monkey suits could pass for men!" he teased.

"Shut up, Spikey, and serve us some Red Stripe beer," Mookie ordered.

But Jah Spike would not let it go. "I got used to you idlers in school uniforms slinging Duke of Trelawny bags over your shoulders," he said. "What a difference some half-decent clothes make."

"Shut up," Stan-Chen shouted, "and serve the damn drinks, man!"

Jah Spike opened his palm and we high fived it—slapping it hard for teasing us. The five of us sat on swivel stools as Jah Spike slammed down the first round of ice-cold beer. The six of us clanked our bottles, spilling beer onto the acrylic counter. Jah Spike quickly wiped away the frothy puddles.

Sam proposed a toast: "To the five years in this town trying to escape from it!"

"And to leaving without any missing parts!" I chimed in.

Jah Spike grinned. "I miss you idlers already."

I thought about Jah Spike for a moment. He wore the latest and most expensive clothes, and rode new, shiny motorbikes but had no steady job. How lucky; living so lavishly off his father, who was a government official. He worked in Kingston at the Ministry of Local Government, but came home on weekends. Mr. Solomon Simpson was always on television, arguing politics, but I saw him once, maybe twice, in real life.

He was an intimidating fellow, who wore thick eyeglasses, his beard scraggy and moustache untidy, hair with ample grey spiking in all directions under his nose. His eyes were always red. Some say he drank white rum like water since his favourite son and Jah Spike's older brother Michael died in a car crash in the United States.

I remembered how, one Friday afternoon before class, in front of the Actor's Theatre, Jah Spike was updating the five of us about the latest cartoon episode of *Rude Boy Jammy* when Jah Spike's father drove up in his grey Peugeot. His son was imitating Jammy, jumping, kicking and slicing the air with karate chops. As soon as Jah Spike saw his father, he went quiet, bravado crumpling like a piece of paper and falling on the sidewalk. He bowed his head and hustled to the car window as his father barked at him, wagging his index finger. "The last time you drove the Land Rover you parked it without gas. Do not take any of my vehicles on the road until you find a job!"

Later that evening, we saw Jah Spike cruising along Spring Valley Town's main street in his father's green Land Rover with Angela Carter, one of his girlfriends, beside him. He was leaning back, his fingertips touching the steering wheel, a cigarette hanging from his lips. He honked, and we waved at him as he cruised past the roundabout, made a sudden left turn, and disappeared. But Jah Spike, our trusted friend who was four years older than us, had a youthful spirit to enjoy our company as much as we did his.

The music blaring from the jukebox forced us to talk loud. "So I hear you will be going to the College of Arts and Science in Kingston," Jah Spike shouted at Mookie.

"Yes."

"To do what?"

"Industrial engineering."

"I like that," Jah Spike said, nodding his head at Mookie sipping his beer.

Stan-Chen looked at Jah Spike. "You know I will be studying in Cuba, right?"

"Yes I heard, and I expect you to swim home on weekends!" Jah Spike joked.

"I heard about a man escaping from communism; swam the 90 miles from Cuba to Runaway Bay with his mother on his back. Stan-Chen, you can do the same," Sam shouted and slapped Stan-Chen's shoulder.

"Very funny, Sam," Stan-Chen said. "I see everyone's a comedian tonight."

We all burst out laughing. But Jah Spike refocused the conversation. "What will be your mission in Cuba?"

"Marine engineering."

"What use will marine engineering have in Spring Valley?"

"Who said I am coming back to Spring Valley?"

Jah Spike screwed up his face and glanced at Sam. "You, agricultural science?"

"Yes, at the School of Agriculture," Sam answered.

"At least you are not leaving the country."

"No, my grandfather has too much land. Somebody has to take care of it."

Jah Spike turned to me. "Flinty, Paulette Chambers told me you going to Canada, but never said why."

"Audio engineering."

A puzzled look came over Jah Spike's face. "What are you going to do with that?"

"You sound like my grandmother man!" I was the odd one out. No one seemed to know what an audio engineering education could be used for, so I lied. "I am going to build cool gadgets like those in James Bond movies."

"OK, Ian Fleming. I like that," said Jah Spike, nodding. Everyone understood James Bond movies.

"And you, Ziggy?"

"Working with the old man," Ziggy answered.

Ziggy's father was a respected architect who designed and built stately buildings all over the island. Ziggy, like his older brother, Mark, was going to join his father's business, but we joked that he would take it over because of his cocky sense of himself.

Jah Spike sipped his beer, scanned our faces, screwed up his face and said, "So except for Sam, all you idlers will be involved in some form of engineering."

"That's a good thing," I said.

"Why?" Jah Spike asked.

"We need more engineers on the island," I replied. "Prosperous countries are the ones that can build ships, planes and bridges."

"Too many paper pushers. We are the exception," Stan-Chen continued. "Almost sixteen years after independence and this nation is still hooked on every student using only pen and paper for a living."

"Didn't Mr. Tabangi say modern democracy was forged from the Battle of Stalingrad and from the Normandy landing, which was pure guts and engineering?" Mookie asked.

"He did," answered Stan-Chen.

"Technical education was the engine behind many great political achievements: President Roosevelt's determination to build the Panama Canal and Kennedy's challenge for America to be first on the moon, for example," I said.

"But Stan-Chen and Flinty will be studying abroad and will not come back," Jah Spike retorted. Before I could answer, Mookie held up his hand, looked Jah Spike in the eye and said, "I will never leave this island. But honestly, Jah Spike, with the political violence retarding the country's growth, I would not argue with Stan-Chen or Flinty if they decide not to come back."

"Guys, I will be coming back," I said. Stan-Chen said nothing. We listened to Bob Marley's *Talkin' Blues* blasting from the jukebox for a while.

Sam changed the subject. "Did you saw the big grin on Mr. Tabangi's face tonight when he gave Flinty his award?"

Mookie raised his Red Stripe bottle and shouted, "Let's drink to Tabbi!"

"To our oracle with red eyes and dashiki shirts!" toasted Sam.

Pension Green, one of Spring Valley's popular drunks, staggered into the bar with his stench close behind him. He begged Jah Spike for a drink. Jah Spike ordered him out, but Sam ordered a drink of white rum for him. Pension threw the rum down his throat, twisted his face, grunted loudly, pointed and shouted something unintelligible at us as if he was warning us about something, and tumbled out of the bar onto the street.

"Mook, Flinty and Ziggy, congratulations on winning awards," Jah Spike said.

"Mine's just a wooden plaque covered with fake gold. Should have been tuition money instead," I argued.

"Where is it?" Stan-Chen asked.

"With Lady Fisher."

Ziggy screwed up his face and asked, "Lady who?"

"Marilyn. I called her Lady Fisher because she looked so good tonight."

"All the girls looked good tonight," Stan-Chen said. "Jah Spike, you should have seen them."

Jah Spike nodded at Stan-Chen and took a swig from his beer.

"Doxie was the talk tonight," Stan-Chen continued, pointing at Sam. "That girl's parents special ordered her from God with extra spoonsful of sexy poured into every inch of her."

"How come you leave her?" Ziggy asked.

"Her uncle is driving her home," Sam answered.

"Her uncle still knows nothing about you two," Mookie said, shaking his head.

"Enough about me and Doxie." Sam tried to change the subject. "Ziggy, what about you and Claudette Powell?"

"She is off to Somerset Institute in England, I believe," Ziggy answered.

"So what?" I asked.

"You helped her with algebra, and said something nice developed between you two," Mookie reminded Ziggy.

Ziggy took a deep breath and leaned his head way back, looking at the ceiling, before answering. "Something is there, but whatever it is, I cannot bother with long-distance relationships."

"You are a loud clucking chicken, Ziggy," this from Sam.

"I am a mathematician and cannot bother with the letter writing," Ziggy repeated as he walked over to the jukebox and punched in a tune.

"Jah Spike, guess who Flinty danced with tonight?" Stan-Chen asked, and then before Jah Spike could answer, shouted, "Deloris Peckham!"

"Flinty, you dance with Deloris Peckham!?" Jah Spike asked. "Didn't I hear her calling you a beast of darkness, after you let her fall on the wet pavement?"

"She and I fixed up that little misunderstanding, long time," I answered.

"Flinty, where's that girl from Warville you walk home with sometimes?" Sam asked.

"In Kingston," I answered. "Why?"

"She's a furtive drizzle of evil," Stan-Chen interrupted, nodding and pointing at me. "Flinty, she's clandestine—a future poison tongue Gwendolyn you don't need in your life; leave her alone."

"How could you say something like that?"

"Because I'm your brethren since we were six years old," Stan-Chen answered. "Do like Ziggy. Forget about her, man."

I screwed up my face and swallowed the sudden lump of embarrassment in my throat. Then I scratched my head and gulped down a mouthful of beer to drown Stan-Chen's advice. But the soulful tune of Margie Joseph's *Words Are Impossible* in the background put my mind at ease.

Suddenly, Jah Spike threw both hands into the air as if surrendering to a gun pointed at him and shouted, "Enough with the gal talk. I am getting jealous!"

I slammed my empty beer bottle on the counter and asked Jah Spike for another round. "One thing for sure," I said, "I won't miss Principal Black. You all remember when that laminated core step-down transformer I was using as a power source for my full-wave rectifier I was designing, vibrated and punctured the insulation around the copper wire, and caused a short circuit. The transformer spewed reddish-blue flames, set fire to the table, burned my fingers and caused an electrical explosion."

"Speak English so Jah Spike can understand," Mookie said.

"Jah Spike, by accident, I caused an electrical fire in the lab some years ago."

"Flinty, you were one lucky rass," Stan-Chen interrupted. "I was standing beside you, remember? The whole area was in flames."

I sipped my beer and continued. "Principal Black asked if it was my intention to burn down the school, and if my grandparents had money to pay for the building. Said I was a troublemaker who got high on cricket and electrical gadgets, ignoring real school lessons, and he was about to ban me from the Industrial Arts Building. Then he handed me a book about Oliver Cromwell to read a few paragraphs and explain it. It was ironic that butchering the history of the violence that Cromwell's men used to capture the island from Spain in 1655 allowed me back into the electrical lab. While I sat in front of him, he kept sniffing and called Miss Chambers, you know, the chef, twice and asked if she was burning up the chicken in the canteen, not realizing he was smelling my burnt flesh; I held my hand under his desk for the whole half-hour."

"Flinty, why didn't you show him your burnt fingers?" Sam asked.

"You must be joking. If he had seen my burns, he would have panicked and instantly barred me from the building, because he would be worried whether the school's laboratory was up to Ministry of Education guidelines and things like that. When I got home, Grandma lit another fire under me 'cause Gwendolyn told her I almost burnt down the whole school. If you can believe that."

"Gwendolyn's lies stick like glue," Stan-Chen said. "Remember the one she told when the van crashed with us?"

"She said all five of us were burnt to a crisp and swore she saw five little piles of ash inside the van," Sam reminisced.

"Is the van still being repaired?" Mookie asked.

"Yes, should be ready next week. The mechanic and body people had to rebuild most of it," Stan-Chen answered.

"Enough of Gwendolyn," Stan-Chen said, letting out a sigh of relief. He slid his empty bottle along the counter toward Jah Spike and changed the subject.

"Look here," Stan-Chen continued. "Studying in Cuba could be a political hot rod when I return from Havana, especially if Michael Manley loses the 1980 election. For that reason, I am worried."

"Engineering education is not political," Mookie said. "You should have no concern about your Cuban education; a bridge is for all people to cross over no matter to which political party they belong. Is that too hard to understand?"

Ziggy scratched his head and sipped his beer. "You know how this country operates. It's all about politics. My old man knows, so I will have to work with that to help the business."

Mookie screwed up his face. "Ziggy, you know better than that. This nation is running on political gasoline to the edge of a steep cliff. That's why Mr. Tabangi's plea for us to use reason above passion every time is so important."

"Mook, my father's business is built on contracts. Many are political, so I have to work with that."

"Well, Ziggy, your job will be to lift your father's business out of the political mud-hole into principle," Sam advised.

Ziggy sipped his drink with a faraway look on his face, while Jah Spike served drinks to four noisy businessmen in suits at the far end of the bar. The Bee Gees tune *How Deep is Your Love?* came at us from the jukebox as Sam began to speak. "Fellows, I am worried you are all leaving and not coming back. This country can never develop its potential if you all go away, study and stay. What about those free books we used at school? We rented them. The government helped us out. It is only fair that you all come back and serve. Imagine what will happen in 20 years if all of you who studied abroad stay there? We know the answer: brain drain, from which the country is already suffering."

Sam sank his index finger into his thick afro, scratched his head and then sipped his drink before speaking again. "People like Claudette, Stan-Chen, Flinty, Marlon Anderson and the others who are leaving to study and stay abroad will invest time and effort in foreign countries and come back to retire, complaining about the broken-down country they all could have come back and fixed in their youth. I could have gone to United States, but chose the School of Agriculture in Kingston. Why? The solution for agriculture is not in the USA, Cuba or Canada, but here on the island. Not in foreign institutions, but in our will. Until we accept that our country and ourselves are just as good as others, our problems will spread like wildfire."

All eyes were now on Sam. "Our belief in ourselves is weak. Mr. Tabangi was right. We must find virtues in ourselves instead of politicians. Our patriotism is a puffy cloud. Manley's trying to sprout some pride in us. That's one of the reasons I chose to stay here. After that, I will cultivate some of my grandfather's land." He turned to me. "Flinty, when you come back from Toronto with your hungry belly, it's my sugar cane juice you are going to drink. We all know how much you love cane juice, and there's none in Canada."

Sam paused and grinned at us. But we were surprised by the seriousness of his words. He was known for cracking jokes, not making passionate speeches. We slapped his shoulder to cheer him, and Ziggy ordered another round. I tasted my fresh glass of white rum mixed with eggnog sprinkled thick with grated nutmeg with approval. A giggling bunch of girls from the graduation dance entered the bar, snapping their fingers to the music. I recognized Claudette Powell and Lavern Milton.

"How's the party?" Mookie asked.

"DJ Superman still mashing up the place," one answered.

"Serve a round of drinks for the girls!" Stan-Chen ordered.

Ziggy got up immediately and greeted Claudette, kissing her cheeks and holding both her hands. Their equally bright grin as they chatted suggested they had picked up exactly where they had left off after waltzing together at graduation three hours earlier. Lavern leaned on the edge of her stool, sipping Guinness from her glass, bobbing her head, her long, smooth, skinny legs exposed through the split in her gown. She never stopped teasing me since I told her my grandmother had burned the copy of *The Happy Hooker* she had given me as a present some time ago. "Flinty," she would say, "your granny read and knows what was in that book; that's why she burned it."

"Lavern Milton, leave my grandmother alone!" I would warn her.

Lavern winked at me; I winked back, and was thinking of joining her, but had learned the hard way never to mix girls into discussion with noisy friends.

A few months earlier, after a 4-H club meeting, I went for a walk with Janet Richardson—a real beauty. After weeks of pleading, Cupid arm-wrestled her beside me for a Sunday evening stroll, the best time to walk with a girl in Spring Valley. The streets were usually empty, everyone sleeping off their big after-church rice and chicken dinner. Janet and I strolled slowly, talking about anything that came to mind. As we meandered past Aunt Curry's stately home, I plucked a red hibiscus bloom hanging over the fence and gently inched its stem into Janet's soft black hair, on the left side, just above her ear. She was taken aback at first, and snapped her head back, but then she giggled and helped me adjust it to make it fit perfectly.

"How do I look?" she asked, grinning.

"You make the flower beautiful," I answered.

"But, Flinty, you full of lyrics," she said and burst into laughter.

I bought ice cream at Mrs. Codner's shop, and we competed to see which of us could eat the fast-melting ice cream without any of it touching our fingers. Her beauty distracted me, and she won. That was my excuse.

"I always liked you, Flinty, but my mother complained that the breed of Magnum think they know everything."

"Janet," I said, "your mother's wrong because all I know is that right now I feel good beside you."

She grinned and gently punched my shoulder. "It feels good with you, too."

We turned a corner and saw Stan-Chen and some school friends in the street. They were having a loud debate. I stopped. "What are you idlers arguing about?" I asked.

"About one of Mr. Tabangi's old assignments, about which idea is closer to God: beauty or truth," someone answered.

"Let's hear what Flinty has to say," Stan-Chen said.

I thought about the way I had answered that assignment: "Truth is closer to God," I'd said. "Truth: immutable and immovable, making it as eternal as God. Truth and God are one: finding truth is finding God. Truth is closer to God than beauty." An easy win, I thought, and started to walk away.

"Let's go, Flinty," Janet said, pulling my arm.

Flinty don't know what the hell he is talking 'bout," Cunchas argued. "Truth is the nucleus of all that which is beautiful. Therefore truth and beauty are equally close to God."

Maybe they were right and I was wrong. Maybe we were all wrong. But the debate fell over a cliff, into a raucous babble of disagreement. At times it felt like a fight was about to break out. Mr. Tabangi, who always reminded us of the eloquence of reason when debating in order to build respect for each other, would have been disappointed.

But Janet Richardson was most disappointed, disturbed by the noise as she waited across the street. After the debate, I walked over to her, grinning and apologizing for making her wait so long. She was furious, shook her fist at me for leaving her to fend off a swarm of guys trying to pick her up. "Flinty, you are an inconsiderate fool, leaving me alone for so long. How could you waste the whole evening chatting foolishness with your stupid friends? I was enjoying the evening until you spoiled it up."

I apologized again and tried to hold her hand, but she pulled away and grabbed the flower from her hair, flung it on the ground, and stomped on it. "My mother was right about the breed of Magnum; they think they know everything. I am going home," she shouted and sped off. Janet wanted nothing to do with me after that. I never forgot that lesson: When with noisy friends, leave girls alone; when with a girl, leave noisy friends alone. I was with noisy friends, so I smiled with Lavern but left her alone.

After finishing their drinks, Ziggy and Stan-Chen escorted the four ladies outside and into a crowded taxi sending them home.

"This one is for you idlers," Jah Spike said, walking over to the jukebox. Moments later, the poignant sound of The Main Ingredient's *Just Don't Want To Be Lonely*, wafted throughout the bar.

Jah Spike grinned, and then jokingly twisted up his face as if crying. Then he wrapped both his arm around his torso and danced slowly with himself. The five of us laughed loudly, took big gulps from our drinks, swiveled around on our bar stools. We tossed peanuts and bits of cookie crumb at our solo dancing brethren-to-the-bone, as the night's river of alcohol settled inside us and became part of our bloodstream. When the music was finished, the six of us chatted, until closing time; time to head home from school and Blue Vail's Bar for the last time. We high-fived Jah Spike and ordered a final round of drinks for the journey home.

"Finally, you idlers are leaving me for good," Jah Spike said. "No, Jah Spike, we are not leaving you at all. We are taking you with us," Sam assured him as the five of us—drinks in hand—staggered into the night to catch a taxi home.

CHAPTER 15:
Fallen Into Darkness

Surprisingly, after drinking so much alcohol, I did not feel drunk, just light on my feet—tipsy, as Hutch would say. Stan-Chen boasted that no matter how much alcohol he drank, he never got drunk. We yelled at cars going past; some drivers honked their horns.

We hopped into a taxicab—an old Austin Cambridge— its radio blaring loud music. The car creaked as we squeezed into it and our weight sank the vehicle. The driver fired up the engine and the muffler exploded like firecrackers. He drove briefly along the main street, past the Scotia Bank, circled the roundabout, turned left, and climbed a gently sloping hill heading home. The warm night breeze lashed our faces through the open windows, but I did not mind, as the wind also scrubbed away the car's frowsy smell. The loud music drummed my alcohol-soaked head like thunder and drowned our voices, so we kept quiet for most of the three miles to Spring Valley's square.

We paid the driver and skipped from the car. I gulped down a final mouthful of my white rum and eggnog and smashed the empty glass against the electric light pole from which a dim light hung over the square. The glass splintered in all directions; some scattered into the street. We yelled as if I had scored the winning goal in a soccer match. We had no concern about disturbing hard-working people long gone to bed. We hung around for a while, but the streets were empty, so we started to bid each other goodbyes, getting ready to go our separate ways.

Suddenly, I remembered my history award, but could not recall where it was, and I briefly wondered if I'd had too much to drink. My dazed mind returned to earlier that night and struggled with loud music and dancing until Marilyn Fisher's face came into my memory. I felt comforted knowing I had left the plaque with her.

As we began to slap each other's shoulders, bounce our fists together, and shout Irie, peace and love, we saw Blunter's old MG coming toward us. Mookie and Blunter had sat at the same desk at school for a year, but Blunter was transferred after a fight between them. He had graduated with us and was driving home. The car was sputtering, jerking and hesitating until it stopped on the other side of the Garden River Bridge. The vehicle's interior lights and its two bulging headlights brightened the area. I glanced at the sky. It was dark; a patch of cloud had covered up the moon.

People nicknamed Blunter's car "Hearse," and some refused to ride in it, but it was his pride and joy. His father had bought a new Lada and given him the MG for his 16th birthday. That gloomy looking hunchback car with toad-eye headlights was the only one of its kind in Spring Valley.

The other vehicles were rectangular shape—Leylands, Ladas, Chevrolets, Fiats and Austin Cambridges.

We were drifting toward Blunter's broken-down car when Rasta Binzy showed up. He was heading home with a bag of groceries. He looked at us, held up his right fist and shouted, "Congratulation, dreads." We bounced our fists against his and shouted, "Irie!" back at him.

"Blunter's death-trap broke down again," Binzy said, pointing to the car. He handed me his bag and quickly rolled a small ganja cigar, lit it, took a deep drag, leaned his head way back and released the smoke into the sky.

A warm, pleasant sheen of a smile coated his face as he pushed the cigar at Stan-Chen and said, "Stin-Man', now that you graduate, celebrate with a draw off the herb, no?" Stan-Chen squeezed his lips together, and stared at Binzy without blinking. Binzy understood and took his bag from me. He took a hungry man's drag from his cigar, released the cloud of smoke and said, "Dreads, guidance to you all; I have to go." We slapped Binzy's shoulder and watched him step away from us. For a while, we watched the moving, glowing fire of his cigar as he dragged smoke from it, until the darkness swallowed him and his cigar.

The five of us hugged each other, creating a line across the road, and staggered toward Blunter's old car. The red digits on my digital watch glowed a bright 1:10 as we crossed the Garden River Bridge into the stifling stench of gasoline from the sick vehicle. The usually noisy shop and bar facing the bridge where we bought bulla cake and cheese after our daily swim was closed, but there were loud, bubbling rhythms of frogs and toads gargling their throats in the shallow water trickling below the bridge. The water on the other side of the bridge—close to Blunter's car, where we swam daily—was quiet and deep.

The old MG's hood was open and the bright fidgety beam from Blunter's flashlight exposed the car's rusty, oil-soaked engine. He was holding a metal container close to the engine and collecting slow drips of gasoline from a hose leading from the gas tank. The fuel he collected was to prime the carburetor so he could start the vehicle. Sam, Ziggy and Stan-Chen were on the side of the road with a steep, vertical embankment, while Mookie and I were on the other side, which was flat and open to the riverbed, near the cricket playfield. We huddled over the exposed engine, our eyes snapping pictures of nested wires and metal parts. Like most vehicle owners in Spring Valley, Blunter doubled as a mechanic, though he was not sure what he was doing. The painfully slow drips of gasoline put him on edge, and he complained that it would be morning before he collected enough to prime the carburetor. He hissed his teeth, sighed and scratched his head with his greasy, blackened fingers, his thoughts wrinkling his face. Then he grumbled, "There's a faster way, but it's risky."

"How?" Sam asked.

"The fuel pump's not working, but I could rock a screwdriver back and forth between the two electrical contacts, like a switch to pump the gasoline."

"Do it, man!" we all said.

Blunter rocked his screwdriver back and forth, opening and closing the pump's electrical contact. It worked like magic; gasoline gushed into the container. We roared in laughter, slapping each other's shoulders, and took the credit for solving Blunter's problem. Blunter was quiet; he just kept rocking the screwdriver back and forth while our eyes were fixed on the gushing gas filling the plastic container. Suddenly a tiny spark burst from the screwdriver and fell into the container. The gas exploded into a fireball that engulfed the engine and scorched our faces. The night turned into daylight.

I ran as fast as I could, feeling the heat on my back and shoe heel. I stopped at a safe distance from the burning vehicle, Mookie beside me, breathing loudly, catching his breath. I could not see Stan-Chen and Sam. Blunter, at first motionless and grim, stood staring at the car. Then he ran swiftly, grabbed the fiery container of gasoline and tossed it into the air. As it fell, the area around the vehicle lit up the night like a B52 night-time bombing in a Vietnamese village of straw. Flames engulfed the entire road and the area around the vehicle, spreading outwards to the playfield, and rose about 10 feet up the vertical embankment on the other side of the road.

Mookie and I sped to a safer distance. The fire was so bright I could make out the green of the leaves and grass on the playground and the blue paint of the clubhouse close by. Blunter ran toward us, slapping flames on his pant legs. A jolt of excitement rushed through me like the times when the radio announcer said that a hurricane was coming. My heart skipped beats; I expected the car to explode into a massive fireball, like the ones that fall over cliffs and roast wicked villains to the crowd's delight at the end of a movie. But the car did not burst into flames. Blunter's tossing the burning container of gasoline from the vehicle had saved it. I was disappointed at the shrunken flames, until I saw other flames seeming to move about in the darkness.

At first, it seemed like a rolling barrel of flame, but after seeing Stan-Chen, Ziggy and Mookie standing beside me, but not Sam, I suddenly realized that the aimless wandering fireball was him. Mookie and I ran toward the drunken, staggering pillow of fire. I was still not sure and could not accept that it was Sam, but instinct forced Mookie and me to shout a loud grim refrain, until Stan-Chen and Ziggy joined in: "Run to the river! Run to the river! Run to the river... to the river run... to... river!"

As we got closer, it became clear that the drunken fireball was indeed Sam. His whole body, from head to shoes, was covered in flames. He struggled against the fighting flames that bound his legs, preventing them from moving freely. He seemed to be drifting toward the river, but I was not sure if his fire-engulfed body was moving on instinct to the water or if he had heard our shouts. But the travelling, human ball of fire was the night's only sick light. The prophetic moon had taken precaution and hid itself behind the clouds.

We ran behind him, guiding him to the river, and watched the flame jump into the water and sink, leaving cruel, stubborn lights burning on the water's surface—fire battling against water—until all brightness disappeared and left us in our darkest moment. We jumped into the water and swam toward Sam. He staggered toward us, dragging against the chest-high water resisting him. We hustled him from the black water and saw his brown skin hanging from his body, exposing a milky white skin that glowed in the dark, and we smelled his burnt flesh. We tried to remove what was left of his shirt, but his skin came off with it.

We stopped. All our senses collapsed. All sounds around us died. Nature's orchestra, so alive moments before, refused to play, halted in a silent tribute to our friend. We had carelessly unzipped that thin membrane in the night, and fallen into a fiery abyss that sealed us inside and trapped us. There was no way out. Time refused to move forward, and would not reverse as our legs mounted the steep riverbank with our friend, barbecue-smelling steam rising from his body. We slid backwards on the wet dirt, twice, maybe three times, trying to get to the top. But we rushed the stubborn hill one more time and made it over the top.

We laid Sam under the open sky on the soft grass. I smelled his burnt flesh on my hands, fell on my knees as if I was praying, and wiped my hands in the dirt, and then screamed at the black sky. Moments later, the moon peeked out from behind the cloud. The night brightened again. I saw pain and dread on my friends' faces, same as they saw on mine.

A few people who had seen the fire gathered around. One of them called the ambulance. "What happen?" Sam asked. His voice was weak.

"The car caught fire," Stan-Chen answered.

"It's okay, Sam," Ziggy said. "Ambulance's on the way."

"Tell my mother I am sorry," Sam whispered.

Sorry for what, we did not know—none of us asked. But we nodded. We stared at each other in the moonlight without talking. We did not know what to say, except to assure Sam the ambulance was on its way, and he would be all right. Stubborn steam was still rising from his thick afro. We gave him water to drink as he lay on his back; he pushed it away. We could not touch him, afraid his skin would fall off into our hands.

Suddenly, Priest Sanguinity's words from graduation hours earlier came to me: "In tough times, break that shell in which your final ounce of fortitude is concealed and wield it like a sword, to overcome." Here we were, neck deep in our first tough time without a sword to wield. Until that night, for us, trouble lived in books or was something we read about: shootings in Kingston, headlines about the Vietnam War; guerrilla warfare across Africa to unseat one colonial power or another, massacres of Black people demonstrating for rights in apartheid South Africa. The world's mayhem was far away. But on graduation night, that innocence was offended in the extreme.

Sam opened and closed his eyes, grimaced in pain, pulled up his feet, then stretched them out again. He asked for the time. Mookie glanced at his watch and said, "2:15." Though it was still night, a new day for us had begun. Overnight, new understanding of darkness had sprouted in our midst.

Suddenly, the wind, trickling river water, croaking frogs, toads, chirping insects, and the rest of nature's orchestra came alive again. And I heard the sad violin strains of the *Adagio* streaming with the same clarity I had heard while walking to Blue Vail's hours earlier. That's when I understood the warning message in the music, but it was too late. My eyes and mind stumbled around in shadows and silhouettes the moon's light had created, searching for meaning—anything that could explain what had happened—but nothing came, only the sound of trickling water, frogs and toads, and branches swaying under a detached moon, to that gloomy *Adagio* streaming from the wind.

The screaming ambulance bulleted down the hill, swung a sudden right around the corner, slowed and then stopped. Three paramedics jumped from the vehicle and raced toward us, carrying a stretcher. They squatted beside Sam, stuck a straw in his mouth for him to drink from a bottle. He sipped a few mouthfuls then pushed it away. They poured liquid on the burn areas to keep them moist, laid him on the stretcher and rushed him to the vehicle. The four of us followed and jumped into the ambulance. One of the paramedics held up his hand to bar us from getting too close.

"His wounds must be protected from infection," he said.

They tried to cut away his clothes as the van screamed its way to Spring Valley Hospital, but they stopped, as his skin fell from his body, hanging like pieces of wet brown towels.

When we arrived at the hospital, nurses ran toward the ambulance. They wheeled him away behind large wooden double doors, locking us out. We waited but were finally told that he had drifted off to sleep, so we left him in the care of those who were capable, and went home.

I got home after 6:00 and fell on the bed exhausted, still in my clothes that stank of burnt flesh. I lay on my back and watched the sun burst triumphantly over the mountain, brightening the room. But when I gazed at the ceiling, Sam's milky white face hidden under his brown outer skin appeared. Grandma, Hutch, Ma and my two brothers crowded into my room.

"What happened?" Grandma asked. I told them.

"Glad you are alive," Mother said. But then her anger burst out and her body shook as she yelled, "Jesus Christ. We were just at graduation, and now your friend is burnt up and in a hospital. Flinty, you are dancing with death, and soon it's going to kiss you or stomp on your toes!" She folded her hand across her belly and screamed. I lay with no energy to speak and continued to gaze at Sam's white face on the ceiling.

Later that day, the four of us visited Sam. He was all bandaged up, except for his eyes, mouth, and little holes for his nostrils so he could breathe. His bright spirit lit his eyes as he joked, "I look like King Tutankhamun in these bandages!"

We all chuckled.

"Man, we are planning a big party for when you come home," I told him.

He nodded. "Doxie came to visit this morning," he whispered, eyes sparkling.

"I am glad about that. Marry her when you leave this place," Ziggy said.

"Funny, Ziggy."

"I have your agricultural notebooks and will give them to your mother," I told him.

"Don't give her the brown-cover book," he advised.

"Why?" I asked.

"Some x-rated cartoon in it."

"What?"

"Flinty," he said, "make sure you keep the brown-cover book."

Mookie burst out laughing and Ziggy joined him. "What kind of cartoon?" Mookie asked.

"The one about Jammy and Margaret on his bike."

"That episode from one month ago?" Ziggy asked. Sam nodded.

"But that wasn't about sex," Stan-Chen said.

"I just redraw them without clothes, doing... you-know-what." We all laughed out loud again.

"Sam, you are crazy man," Stan-Chen told him.

"What page?" I inquired.

"A few pages. Well... almost half the book," he confessed. "I was trying to draw it perfect."

"Alright, then," I said. "The brown-cover book is mine until you come home." He nodded.

We updated him on Jammy's antics for that day and told him that Priest Sanguinity was praying at Kingsway Church for his quick recovery. We were about to say goodbye, but I remembered Grandma's rant at the dinner table almost a year earlier that *ta-ta* was the right way to bid leave of the ones we care about. I whispered to Stan-Chen, Mookie and Ziggy to say *ta-ta* instead of *goodbye*, and they did. We promised to see him the next day.

On the bus home, we kept looking out the window, not talking much, trying to find our own comfort groove. We just wanted to get home. I felt our friendship was ungluing. Then I remembered my father's warning after Stan-Chen's father's van had crashed, that I was pushing buttons to end my beginning. I went straight to bed again without dinner, even though Grandma told me she had made a special treat.

The second night of horror movies complete with the *Adagio* soundtrack playing in my head again: the single spark falling into the gas, explosive flames, running, drunken staggering ball of fire running to the river, shouting at the untidy bundle of fire to run to the river, Sam's skin falling off, the smell of burnt flesh, his white face printed on the wall, doors and ceiling. Then the questions: Did we give him the correct advice—to run to the river? Should we have told him to drop and roll as were taught at school? Would it have actually made any difference to drop and roll in monster flames wrapping him like a blanket? Were we drunk but did not know it? Why did we not go home instead of hanging out with Blunter's ugly old MG? All this, until the morning sun burst through the window and rescued me.

CHAPTER 16:
Waking Up

The sun came through the window and brightened the room. But I was foggy and tired from lack of sleep. I heard a voice in the living room. "He died in his sleep last night." It was Aunty Curry—Hutch and Grandma's trusted friend.

"What a sad piece of news, Aunty Curry."

I raised my head from the pillow, balancing my body on both elbows, and listened.

"It is better, Mrs. Griffin; his suffering is over."

There was a loud silence until Grandma spoke. "Thanks for coming all the way round here with the news. Miss Codling must be in bad shape."

I heard Mavis Codling had frozen in sadness since Sam's accident. He'd been her only child.

"I heard the doctor gave her medication to quiet her nerves."

"I will go and see her later."

"Where's Flinty?"

"He is sleeping. I will tell him when he wakes."

"Don't wake him, and only tell him after he put something into his stomach," Aunty Curry advised. "It will be hard on the four of them; been friends for so long."

My elbows would not sustain my shaking body, and I fell on my back, still listening to Grandma and Aunty Curry's voices, calmly thanking death for rescuing my friend from his suffering.

But I raged against death, and railed against its total victory, killing an only child. Death had snatched and carried him off like a night-time thief. Lying on my back, I made a promise to my friend's dead white face printed on the ceiling: *Don't worry, Sam; when I get up, I will grab Hutch's rifle, find that Angel of Death. Shoot it between its eyes, and wring its fucking neck. That chicken couldn't even face us in daylight. Then I will toss its dead carcass on the ground, shoot it again, and then kick it like a dirty piece of rag into Satan's eternal fire.... But I just, I just... I just need a few more minutes until I get the strength to get up....*

I punched and kicked the air and slammed both sides of my face into the pillow. I raised myself from the bed and growled at Satan and God—splitting the blame for Sam's death equally—before dropping my exhausted, trembling body into the bed, and finding Sam's white, lifeless face on the ceiling again. I hissed my teeth in defiance and defeat at the same time, for there was no strength left in me to hunt down and kill death's angel—that shadowy companion that had travelled beside us on that unseen parallel plane of destruction on graduation night and had snatched Sam from across that invisible curtain between life and death. That beguiling angel of death recoiled in quiet and confidently waited to seize its next victim, and I was useless to do anything about it. Death had triumphed. I could no longer delay getting up out of bed.

Aunty Curry's voice found me again. "The family is sending his body to Miss Allen's funeral home."

"Such a nice boy. Never gave anyone an ounce of trouble," Grandma mumbled. "You know, Aunty Curry," she continued. "Flinty is in shock since the accident. He's not eaten a thing."

There was a brief silence until Aunty Curry spoke. "Flinty will be alright. He is tough. I see that boy hobbling home on crutches from getting hit by cricket ball and bats so many times, but his smile still bright."

"Blossom is worried 'bout him."

"I cannot blame his mother. As soon as these boys reach teenage, trouble circle them," Aunty Curry said.

"Since Blossom came back from Canada, she started to see how hard it is, raising teenage boys."

"Where is Blossom now?"

"She went to Kiwanis Club meeting in Falmouth."

Both women were quiet for a while. "Mrs. Griffin, I am going to leave you," said Aunty Curry. "I will see you at Miss Codling's house later."

"Yes, Aunty Curry, walk good."

I heard her boots on the steps. "Your garden's beautiful, and the pink dahlias are sunny and bright this morning," she called out.

"Thanks, Aunty Curry. The dahlias are from my nephew's garden in Kingston."

"Goodbye, Mrs. Griffin."

"Ta-ta, Aunty Curry. Watch your step."

Grandma muttered to herself for a while before mutilating a few stanzas from one of her favourite hymns, and, for the first time, her singing sounded good. But then her voice went silent. Suddenly it was quiet, and in that peace Hutch's father spoke to me for the third time. But there was no mystery or excitement this time. I was numbed as he spoke: *Flinty, nothing prepared you for what you are getting up to face, but you are waking up to exactly what your life has prepared you for. Wake up. It's time.*

I staggered out of bed, my knees gave way and I fell on the floor, where I sat for a while. I watched a buzzing housefly repeatedly slamming itself against the window, trying to escape from the room. I struggled to my feet.

During the six days between Sam's death and his funeral, I sat on my grandparents' verandah and stared at the mountains. But all I saw were slow motion, frame-by-frame pictures of the accident, like ugly blotches—patches of virus soiling the lush green mountains. Our short walk from the graduation dance; our fun debate at Blue Vail's Bar; the old car bursting into flames; Sam's fiery body running to the river; the stench of burnt flesh, skin falling off; finding hope in the ambulance's siren and flashing lights; his white face on walls and ceiling, windows and doors; and finally, waking up to Aunty Curry's news of his death.

Sam's funeral was held at Kingsway Anglican Church, the same church where our graduation had been held one week earlier. All his friends were there, and the school's Coronation Choir did a special tribute to him. Ziggy, Mookie, Stan-Chen and I, with gloomy faces, huddled close to his casket, like honour guards ready to defend our fallen companion's honour. We felt proud of the way everyone talked about the way he had lived.

A grim-faced Principal Black told the sad crowd, "Sam wanted to use agriculture to solve the world's problems. There was no reason for him to die so young."

"Sam was Spring Valley's first comedian," Mookie said.

"He loved this country and wanted to stay when we wanted to leave," Stan-Chen said.

Ziggy told the mourners, "Sam laughed at everything around him. But I am amazed at the speed and amount of hot bread and cheese he could put away, and stay so slim and trim." There was scattered laughter as Ziggy returned to his seat beside us.

Priest Sanguinity's face was red and puffy; with the ardent gaze of a soldier, he began to speak. "Lift up your hearts; be not afraid; the Lord is with you."

He paused and gazed at the gloomy faces. A starving crowd—hungry for reinforcement in the form of words to mend our wrecked spirits. "Young people," he began. "Evil, like a virus, ignores the withered and dead, to feed on life. Sam was life. Young people, be ever mindful of that aimless, drifting, wind of evil that slithers into cracks in your spiritual armour and latches onto your youthful sprouts to retard them before they bear fruit."

The priest looked directly at the four of us, with a half-smile upon his face, and closed his eyes. His chest rose and fell as he took a deep breath. Then he said, "Stanley, Myron, Flinty, and Michael. You young men celebrating with your friend knew sorrow in your morning, but always remember God is with you."

Priest Sanguinity closed the service with a hymn. The four of us stood in that crowd and gazed at our friend's casket dressed in flowers and ribbons of many colours. I heard our voices loud and clear, thrusting every word with vigour, like daggers slaying the dark cloud of grief death had brought. Our fearless voices lifted our companion and carried him onward to dwell with his God forevermore.

After the service, the mourners gathered outside the church's green grassy hillside. I stood with my friends, looking at the slow-moving crowd of people in black clothes. Some sought comfort in clusters of friends and families, hugging and squeezing each other's hands. Many of the students, who, like me, had graduated a week earlier, were dressed in the same clothes they had worn to graduation. But the elegant Doxie Chambers, Sam's secret girlfriend, wore a conservative full-suit black dress with a slim white trim around her collar. Her tears had soaked into her brown cheeks and puffed them up. Her hair was out of place because her head kept snapping back and forth from the spasmodic rhythm of her crying, as her uncle, grandmother and friends consoled her. She would settle down and stay quiet for a short while, until tears flowed and her head made sudden snapping jerks again. The well-kept secret that Doxie and Sam were sweethearts burst into the open for both families to witness. Perhaps Sam's death had finally healed the feud that had lasted between them for generations.

Ziggy, Mookie, Jah Spike, Stan-Chen, and I calmly raised our hands in salute and whispered, "All for one and one for all," as the gloomy black vehicle inched away with what was left of our friend, to be buried in his grandparents' garden.

The hearse drove slowly down the steep hill, away from the church, made a sudden right turn, and vanished, taking the funniest of the five musketeers.

I drifted from my friends to gaze at the rolling mountains of the Cockpit Country in the distance, to find comfort in the sun, sinking behind the mountain, sprinkling golden rays onto the lush blue-green forest skyline to end a sad day. I saw Marilyn Fisher walking toward me with my Marcus Garvey award, her smile as bright as a new morning. Seeing her forced me to grin as she carefully selected level spots among gravel and stones to place her feet, making sure not to twist her ankles that were strapped down on top of her black, extra-tall high-heel shoes. She was wearing a plain black dress fit for the occasion, but as she got closer and my smile widened, for a brief moment, I saw her wearing her beautiful mauve-and-white gown, floating gracefully in andante tempo across the dance floor on graduation night a week earlier, her sparkling eyes and warm dimpled cheeks brushing against mine as she smiled, our feet barely touching the floor.

Her loud whisper brought me back to her. "Flinty! Flinty! I have been looking all over for you, to give you your award." She handed me my history award. I took it, inspected it briefly, and gave it back to her, whispering, "To Lady Fisher, my dance partner and Spring Valley's best history student." She took it and curtsied with a mischievous smile, and then burst into a fit of laughter that jerked her heavy chest. Her dimples put two craters on her cheeks. She quickly slapped her hand over her mouth and covered it in embarrassment, leaving her sparkling eyes exposed. "Something to remember me by," I said, confused by her laughter.

She continued to laugh.

"What... what are you laughing at!?"

"Are you crazy?" she whispered, "You know how much I hated history."

She was right. Marilyn Fisher hated history. I helped her through most of Mr. Tabangi's history assignments. She was one of many who believed history had no use.

"Flinty, whatever happened, happened, and there is nothing anyone can do to change it. The faster we forget about it, the better," she would argue. And when I argued that history is a guide to help choose a better path to the future, she would shout, "Flinty, the reason why you love history so much is because you cannot forgive and forget." And if I continued to explain that knowing history could prevent another Adolf Hitler from becoming president or prime minister of a country, she would put her hands over her ears and shout, "Blah blah, blah..." until I shut up. However, when I finished an assignment, she would grab it and copy all I had written down. Sometimes she screwed up her face and asked if that was all, but she would also correct my punctuation, so our relationship was complementary.

She examined the plaque and stepped toward me, a residue of laughter still lighting her face. "Flinty, I would feel guilty taking an award you worked so hard for."

I stepped closer and looked into her eyes without blinking. "It's yours. Keep it. Let it remind you of that Homer's Iliad assignment we struggled with."

"You did most of the work." She examined the plaque again and said, "Okay, Flinty, I will keep it."

"I am glad."

She threw both her arms around my body and nipped a small piece of my cheek with her lips, like a bird with a sharp beak, and laid her head on my shoulder. My arms circled around her waist and I leaned my head into her cheek. We stayed that way, listening to each other's breathing, and watched the crowd scatter slowly back to their lives. Then she asked; "Flinty, how are you getting home?"

"Stan-Chen's driving us."

"Aren't you afraid Stan-Chen will drive you over a gully again?"

"No. He's a good driver. The accident was just carelessness."

Still leaning against my shoulder she whispered, "Paulus drove my mother's van. Come with us."

"But I live in the other direction."

She pulled her head from my shoulder and looked into my eyes. "Stop at my house for a while. Paulus will drop you home afterwards."

"Wouldn't your mother get into a fit?"

"Yes, she would. She heard that Angie's father found you in her bedroom and almost chopped you in two, and because you were my dancing partner at graduation, she warned me to stay far from you. But she is in Kingston, and won't be back until tomorrow. Only me and Dimples, my big sister, are at home."

"Angie's father's machete would have bounced off my steel frame."

"Flinty, your frame is flesh and blood," she said. "We danced together, remember?"

"Marilyn. I was young and foolish. I don't do that sort of thing anymore."

It was after 7:00 when we got to Marilyn's house. Her sister was not home. Her mother was a successful and respected businesswoman. Her house was large and well decorated. There were no pictures on the wall of Queen Elizabeth or of state funerals of important historians and politicians like at Grandma's. There were pictures of Marilyn's family at the beach and of family reunions. Her father, who had died when she was small, her mother and big sister Dimples were all smiling.

"Make yourself at home. I'll be right back."

I sat on the couch. It felt like a vacation from the last few days. Marilyn returned, wearing white shorts and a pink top. My eyes popped as she dropped herself on the soft leather sofa beside me, smiling. Suddenly, I felt cheerful.

"So, Flinty, I have alcohol-spiked Chaney root, sorrel, Irish mash and Red Stripe beer in the fridge. Pick your choice," she said.

"Tea—mint tea—please."

She lifted her eyebrows. "Mint tea?"

I nodded yes.

She turned on the television and left for the kitchen. I watched a news commentary on the large number of people leaving the island for United States, Canada and England. The announcer said that people were still leaving because of Michael Manley's comment a few years earlier that there were five flights a day to Miami for those who wanted to leave. I thought about Sam's passionate speech at Blue Vail's Bar on graduation night against people leaving and not returning, and let out a loud sigh.

Marilyn returned with two steaming cups of tea and sat on the couch beside me.

"Turn off the television," I said. She did.

The tea freshened my spirit—each sip added a layer of calm. I gazed at Marilyn's sparkling eyes and grinned as we chatted, until it felt as if we were on vacation, on a beach in another country.

"Marilyn, thanks. If I was with Stan-Chen and the crew, I would end up at Berti's or Blue Vail's, drinking and talking about Sam. Nothing's wrong with that, but I am enjoying this."

Marilyn got up. "Come, Flinty."

I followed her to her room. It was neat. Books were arranged in order of topic, and the bed was spread without any wrinkles in the sheet, just like Grandma's. She took my cup of tea, put it on her desk, and sat on the bed.

"Sit," she said and patted the space beside her.

I sat and gazed at a framed picture of her standing beside the Prime Minister, hanging above her desk. "Impressive," I said loudly. "How did you get a picture with Joshua?"

"Remember when he came to Spring Valley almost two years ago? I was part of the school's dance group."

Still gazing at the picture, I said, "Oh yeah, I was there. His visit was really something." I sighed loudly and fell backwards across the bed, lying on my back, feet hanging over the bed's edge. "Marilyn Fisher, I am dead tired."

Still sitting beside me, Marilyn looked down at my face for a while, perhaps studying it. Then she dropped her body beside mine, both of us on our backs gazing at the yellowish cotton of light inside the light bulb on the ceiling.

"So much has happened: almost got killed by Angie's father, a cricket ball almost killed Shampoo Grill, Stan-Chen's father's van crashed with us, and now Sam's death. What's next?" I asked.

"Only good things, Flinty."

"Name one!"

"Well, let's see. Tonight you are here where it's safe, instead of with your crazy friends."

"I am serious!" I replied. "Did you know how calming our graduation dance practices were, for the last few weeks?" I asked.

"Really?"

"Yes."

"You mean you enjoyed dancing for an hour every day for five weeks with me and you did not tell me?"

"Thought you knew."

"Just joking. I felt you," she said, whispering into my right ear.

"My mother thinks me and my friends are dancing with death."

"Flinty, it's not only your mother. People are whispering that recklessness caused your friend's death."

"I heard; saying that we were drunk. Why don't they say it to our faces? Fisher, please, can we change the subject?"

She did. "Flinty you are leaving soon..."

"About the first week of September," I answered. "And I heard you are leaving as well."

"Yes. To work at a bank in Kingston."

"Congratulations."

"Thanks."

"You'll be the first hibiscus to bloom."

"Stop that, Flinty. It sounds stupid."

"Maybe there is some truth in Nadia's waltz."

"Maybe," Fisher said, nodding and smiling without showing any of her teeth.

There was quiet for a moment until she remarked, "Flinty, I am going to hang your... I mean my history award next to the prime minister."

"Joshua will be happy to have Black Moses beside him."

"Who is Black Moses?"

"Marcus Garvey."

"I did not know that."

"He was."

We lay on our backs and gazed at the lonely light bulb on the white ceiling for a while. I felt relief that I had not seen Sam's face.

"Flinty, you used to look so nice in your uniform."

"You never told me."

"No, Flinty, you should have noticed me noticing you."

"Why is it always the guy who must make the first move? If you like me you should have said so."

"I did not say I like you. I said you looked nice in your uniform."

"What's this, an exercise in primitive logic?"

"No, Flinty, you need to pay more attention to subtleties."

"Stop it right there! Mr. Tabangi thinks I pay too much; you think too little."

"I selected you for my dance partner; did you know that?"

"You did, really? I thought Mrs. Simpson paired us off," I said with a trickle of embarrassment. "That was nice. It was nice dancing with you, Marilyn."

"I enjoyed dancing with you as well."

Still gazing at the ceiling I said, "Marilyn, I read somewhere that dancing is the vertical expression of a horizontal desire, and we have already done the vertical expression. Here we are horizontally."

She snapped her face toward my cheek; I turned my face to meet her sparkling eyes. She chuckled, her chest jerked, and she said, "Smooth, Flinty, real smooth. I bet you made it all up."

"I did not. I swear!"

"I like it."

We laughed and glanced at each other's eyes for a few moments, until I began gazing at the ceiling, making sure Sam's face was not there. As Marilyn's chest and belly rose and fell softly beside me in the quietness of her bedroom, I realized that this moment was my calmest since the accident that took my friend's life. I relished the calmness, and instead of letting the moment melt into sex with Marilyn, even though I was tempted, I lay beside her and soaked up the peace for a while, until it was time to go.

"Marilyn, it was nice of you to invite me," I told her. "Good luck on your new job." We embraced.

"Flinty, if I don't see you before you leave, have a safe flight and write to me."

"I will," I whispered. I kissed one of her dimpled cheeks and then walked down the steps. We waved at each other as Paulus drove off into the dark.

TA-TA, GRANDMA

The next morning, Mother woke me up early. "Flinty, after Sam's funeral, I did not sleep a wink last night thinking about you. I have some money in the bank and will use it for your first tuition payment. If I have to work my ass off to pay the balance, I will. I am going to book a flight back to Canada." She stormed out of the house and through the gate as though she was being dragged by an unseen force.

CHAPTER 17:
A Tranquil Afternoon

The last Wednesday afternoon in August was warm. The wind slept and the leaves were still. I took an armful of books to the verandah, dropped them on the floor in front of the chair, and sat. I leaned back for comfort and raised my feet, resting them on the wall in front of me. The pile of books between my legs was from the mobile library, and Mr. Tabangi's, and included Fyodor Dostoyevsky's *Crime and Punishment*, Plato's *Republic*, Erich Fromm's *Marx's Concept of Man*, Jackson's *Introduction to Electric Circuits*, James Baldwin's *Nobody Knows My Name*, V.S. Reid's *The Young Warriors*, Thoreau's *Walden Pond* and a copy of my *Student Companion*.

I thought about how Mr. Tabangi would grin mischievously and pull his beard as he paced the floor and told us, "Your books are made, not of words, but of sleeping actions, waiting for you to wake them up and put them to use." Then he would point to the row of fidgety boys and ask, "Anything you read lately you want to share with the class? Stanley, Myron, Flinty, Samuel, Michael, Mr. Harold,

Mr. Dules, anything to share today?" If we impressed him, he would take us deeper by lending us a relevant book on the subject after class. He always wanted us to go deep.

Once I handed him an assignment about the life of Albert Speer, Adolf Hitler's architect, who designed imposing swastika-draped architectural monuments, those colossal platforms from which Hitler made his fire-and-brimstone speeches. He later became the efficient Minister of Armaments for the Third Reich. The next day, while Mr. Tabangi reviewed the assignment with the class, without warning, he dropped a monster book on my desk, patted my shoulder gently, but said nothing, just continued his lecture. The book was William Shirer's *The Rise and Fall of the Third Reich*. After class, I walked toward his desk. He glanced at me and waved me on. "Just read the book and explain it to me in a month," he said.

I also borrowed books every other Wednesday from the bookmobile. I would swap one armful of books for another and read them as quickly. But after Sam's accident, I could not read for a long time. I just randomly scanned books, taking bite-sized pieces of information from random pages. My mind had lost its appetite for big chunks of anything, so I snacked from different books, as if sampling foods at an intellectual buffet.

Thoreau was a favourite of mine, ever since Mr. Tabangi had us read his essay defending American abolitionist John Brown, who raided Harper's Ferry Armory to procure weapons for his 1859 rebellion against slavery. In the essay, Thoreau called John Brown, who dared to risk his life for the liberation of slaves, "transcendentalist above all, a man of ideas and principles." When John Brown was hanged for his actions, Thoreau wrote, "Some 1800 years ago, Christ was crucified. This morning, Captain Brown was hung. He is not Old Brown any longer; he is an angel of light."

But Thoreau's book, *Walden Pond*, I enjoyed; it always transported me to the deep woods of the Cockpit Country to find peace among tall rocks, steep valleys, and trickling waters. I was disappointed that there were no books about the rugged beauty of the Cockpit Country but hoped someone would write one someday. So on that quiet afternoon, as Grandma's stout body disturbed shrubs and plants in her garden, ruffling branches and leaves, I opened Thoreau's *Walden Pond* to "Solitude," and began to read: "This is a delicious evening, when the whole body is one sense, and imbibes delight through every pore. I go and come with a strange liberty in Nature, a part of herself..."

I could not go on. Grandma's movements and the snipping of her scissors gingerly clipping and pruning excesses from her garden intruded on my solitude. I put away the book and watched her body bend at the waist, moving nimbly under her wide straw hat protecting her from the sun. Her agile brown arms extended from her crimson short-sleeve blouse, and her long green skirt pulled up above her tightly laced-up black shoes, exposing blue socks up to her knees. Her fingers delicately cupped lilies and forget-me-not blooms as she smelled them. Sometimes she smiled and whispered to them as if she was telling them her secrets, or thanking them for their company. A bee hidden inside one of her African violet blooms buzzed, flew out, and slammed into Grandma's nose and frightened her. She dropped her scissors, jumped, laughed, and frantically slapped her hair and blouse to get rid of the bee. "A little winged devil!" she shouted at the buzzing insect.

Soon she regained her tranquility and continued to tend her garden. The care with which Grandma's nimble fingers slithered between and around the delicate beauty of her flowers had no equal. It did not matter how far her nomadic pain travelled around inside her body at night, or how much her arthritis caused her finger joints to swell and stiffen, next morning in her garden, those rigid fingers effortlessly cupped her roses so she could smell them. Her plants and flowers calmed her spirit.

Whenever she was in the garden, I knew I could argue for more lunch money, or extra pocket money for school trips, and win. I also knew I had to be careful. Grandma could be tough, like the time she came and carted me back home from the Spring Valley Hospital when I was only three, lying sick for many weeks without getting better. She practically kidnapped me out of the building, but not before wagging her index finger at the head nurse and scolding her after she challenged Grandma about the risk of taking a sick baby from a hospital without proper facilities to care for him at home. "I will stand up to any of you, but I am taking Flinty home today. Better he die at home than in this dead house you people call a hospital."

Within a week, all traces of my sickness had disappeared. According to Grandma, she knew exactly what was wrong when she saw me stretching for the pint of acidic pineapple drink in the car on the way home. It was the same type of drink the doctors warned her I should not drink, so she gave the bottle to me. I drank it all, burped loudly, and cried for more. "You were starving, boy! That's all was wrong with you! All I did was gave you food when we got home," she told me. "It was on God's grace that I took you out of that dead house."

Every time she told me that story a satisfied smile came over her face, but usually she told it to remind me of how lucky I was to have her around. I realized that her good deed was a trade-off for me not causing her any troubles as I grew older. "Flinty, you must listen when I talk to you. If it was not for me you would not be here," she would warn. But Grandma, deaf in one ear and afraid of lizards, was easy to tease. So as I watched her on that peaceful afternoon in her garden tending her plants, an ugly thought slid into me like the Grinch who stole Christmas—that I should shout, "Lizard, Grandma! Lizard!" and watch her run and scream in a breathless panic, allowing me to enjoy a cheap laugh at dear old Grandma's expense. But I disobeyed that Grinch inside me. Instead, I called out, "Hey, Grandma, do you need any help?"

She raised her head under the wide-brimmed hat so she could see me. "What?" she answered.

"Do you need my help in the garden?"

"Yes, Flinty, I know. It's going to rain; close all the windows." Then she bent her head down and continued to dig out pebbles and pull weeds from the soil, healing her arthritis and finding happiness among her African Violets, Joseph's Coats of many colours, dahlias, tulips, orchids, hibiscuses, forget-me-nots and many other beautiful plants and flowers.

A chirping flock of grassquits landed around her, the fidgety brown birds hopping about, eating bugs and worms, and sucking juices from the flowers, enjoying their meal before the rain came. Grandma grabbed after one of the fidgety birds but missed, and her hat fell off, exposing her red head wrap. She laughed loudly and collected her hat from the ground, adjusting it on her head, and went back to working again.

The whole neighbourhood was proud of Grandma's garden, but she had the same love for her plants that she had for her five grandchildren. The lizards had no chance, especially the large green ones that changed their colours to grey and black when agitated, like chameleons. "Those lizards changing colours are devils, you know, Flinty," she said. And if the branch of one of her lilies swayed without any breeze blowing, she instantly blamed a fat lizard and would yell for us to drive it off before it broke the stem.

In summer, when we were on holidays from school, she would pay us to shoot lizards with slingshots. Grandma, who never missed a church service, had no problem putting hits on lizards like a mafia boss. The going rate was 10¢ per lizard, but my cousins and I only pretended to shoot them, collected and saved the money and bought bulla cake and cheese on Saturday evenings. Grandma would complain to Hutch, "The lizard population gets bigger the more money I pay to get rid of them." Hutch knew we were not shooting the lizards, but stayed quiet.

After Grandma finished in her garden, her bent frame hobbled up the steps to the verandah with a beautiful bouquet. "Smell them," she commanded as she thrust the flowers at me.

"Smells nice, Grandma!" I shouted, to make sure she heard me.

Her face flushed with satisfaction and she shuffled into the living room to fill her three vases. She returned several minutes later to the verandah and sat in the chair to my right. "Flinty, aren't you tired of reading? You will have a lot of time to read in Canada; you won't be doing much else."

I felt a gap open between us when she mentioned Canada. I was to leave in a few days. "I am not reading, Grandma; just scanning the pages."

Grandma stared across to the bluish-green mountain range she and Hutch had named "Bush Corner." "Did you close the windows? A rainstorm is coming," she confidently predicted. I instantly agreed; both she and Hutch were more accurate than the weatherman, and all they did was look at Bush Corner. They'd look at the colour of the mountain range that changed from extreme blue to extreme green throughout the day. As the sun travelled across the sky, they would match the mountain's colours with the colour of the sky and accurately predict the weather. After many years of sitting on the verandah and watching afternoons change into nights, they had become experts.

"I will close the windows soon."

"Do you have all your travel documents ready?"

"I need one more and will get it in Kingston tomorrow."

"Why did you not tell me you were going to Kingston?"

"I forgot."

"Say hello to Fitzbright and Kaz."

I nodded.

Still gazing at the mountain, and rattling her bundle of house keys in her hand, she complained, "If you had told me you were going to Kingston, I would send Fitzbright some yams and bananas."

I kept quiet.

"Have you finished packing?"

"No, but I don't have much to pack. I won't be taking most of my clothes."

"Why?"

"It will be autumn and then winter," I answered. "My clothes are only good for summer."

She turned and looked at me. "I just want to see you get on that plane. Death is following you and your friends. Every time you leave this house my blood pressure goes up and only come down when you return."

"Your blood pressure will be normal soon after I leave."

She stretched out her hands and examined her finger joints, touching them. "Swelling gone down," she said. "Last night I had to wake up three times and sop them with eucalyptus oil."

"Spending time in your garden helps you. You should never stop."

"My garden gives me strength, but my knees are weak." Then she changed the subject. "Flinty, when you get to Canada, study your lessons and stay out of trouble." I nodded yes. "Are all your friends gone already?"

"Mookie's leaving tomorrow, Stan-Chen the day after, and Ziggy, next week. We are having a quick drink this evening at Berti's Bar," I added.

"Jesus Christ! Tell me you are not going back to another bar!" Grandma shouted, lifting both hands above her head in a plea. "You are really going to another rum bar, so soon after your friend's funeral?"

"Just Berti's, Grandma, to wish each other good luck over a Red Stripe. Only one beer."

She tried to stop me by using her full ammunition. "Isn't that what you were doing when the car caught fire and burned your friend to death?"

I kept quiet and gazed at the mountains; removing the fuel from her fire she was about to light.

"Okay, Flinty. Go if you must, but come home early. I will wait up."

"Be back before bedtime, Grandma. I promise."

We sat quietly until she said, "Your grandfather will be home soon. I am going to start dinner."

As she shuffled toward the door, I pulled at her skirt. "Grandma Catherine?"

"What?"

"I am going to miss you," I said, grinning.

"Yes, of course, who else would put up with you for so long!" she retorted and burst into loud laughter that ended in her singing one of her favourite hymns. Her voice was like a dull machete chopping the song, splattering the notes all over the house and into the yard, causing lizards to scurry into hiding, and birds to cover their ears with their wings before hastily flying away. But I was not so lucky. I had to listen.

CHAPTER 18:
Oh, Hello, Mr. Tabangi!

I was about to get ready for Berti's Bar when Mr. Tabangi's blue Lada drove up and his tall, athletic frame skipped over the steps and onto the verandah. He looked relaxed, wearing white baggy shorts just above the knees, a blue bush jacket, and black leather slippers and was smiling widely. I jumped from the chair, grasped and pumped his hand hard. He handed me a light, skinny book. I thanked him, glancing at the title, *Phaedo*, by Plato, before dropping it onto the pile of books on the floor. I was glad to see him more than to receive another book. So I stared at his face and continued to pump his hand fast and with a tight grip until he pulled it away, wiggling his fingers to restart the blood circulation.

"You should read Plato's *Phaedo*," he advised me and sank into the chair that Grandma had sat in earlier.

His car engine had alerted Grandma, who was in the kitchen. "Who is it, Flinty?" she asked, shouting.

"Mr. Tabangi!" I shouted back.

"Mr. Who? Mr. Franklyn? Good!" she shouted. "The fish van's early today. Tell Mr. Franklyn I want two pounds of parrot fish and two pounds red snapper!"

"Grandma, it's Mr. Tabangi!" I interrupted. "And tell him the piece of Jack fish he sold me last week had worms in it. I had to throw it away. Tell him I want my money back. Don't let him leave. I have to give him a piece of my mind!" she shouted.

"Grandma! GRANDMA! It's Mr. Tabangi. Not Mr. Franklyn!" I shouted. Grandma still did not hear and came to see for herself.

"Oh! Hello, Mr. Tabangi! Flinty, why didn't you tell me Mr. Tabangi is here?" she demanded, smiling innocently and drying her hands quickly on her red-and-white plaid apron. She grabbed and shook Mr. Tabangi's large outstretched right hand.

"Flinty said 'Mr. Franklyn,' so I thought the fish van came early."

"Grandma, I said Mr. Tabangi. Your hearing is getting worse." She paid me no attention, but kept talking to the man who had caused her grandson to put away his cricket bat and start reading books. Grandma respected him, even though sometimes she yelled at me to put away Mr. Tabangi's old books and find something worthwhile to do around the yard.

"Mr. Tabangi, I am so glad you came to see my grandson. Sit and talk with him. Stay for dinner—curried goat and rice 'n peas," said Grandma.

"I have an appointment—"

Grandma did not let him finish. "Would you like a glass of lemonade?" she asked as she hustled back into the kitchen.

"Yes, thanks, Mrs. Griffin," he replied, and then stretched out his long frame in the chair and stared at the mountains, the same way my father did the night after Stan-Chen drove his father's Volkswagen van over the gully with me and my four friends.

"Sam would have been good for this country, but death has no logic; that's why we are so fearful of it," he said, still looking across the valley to the mountain. "Someone said the fear of God is the beginning of wisdom, but I believe the fear of death is the mother of religion. If we were to live forever, religion would be useless."

"Atheists should live without fear, then?" I asked.

"In theory, they should, but I don't believe there is any true atheist. When death knocks, fear of the unknown enters and causes their lifelong belief to waffle."

I stayed quiet. Finally, I said, "There are rumours that people saw Sam's ghost walking to school as if he were alive. What do you think?"

"It's not him, Flinty. Sam is gone. That's why I brought you the *Phaedo*. It's about Socrates' discussion with close friends before drinking hemlock—the poison that killed him after he was found guilty in Athens for corrupting the youths. You studied some of it in class, but the whole thing is in the book. Read it. It's the same as Christ's discussion with his disciples the day before his crucifixion."

"I will read *Phaedo* on the plane," I replied.

"No, Flinty. Read it only when you mean to, deliberately," he said. "You will get more out of it."

"Alright, then, I will read it when I am relaxed," I said.

"Flinty, you will be a good student, but you need discipline. Brush up on that, and you will be good at anything," he advised, and gulped down the last mouthful of his lemonade.

"Thanks, but this you must have told me a thousand times."

"I know, and I'm telling you again. It's your biggest problem."

I nodded, thinking about how far I had come from where I'd been one year earlier, when cricket, and technology were my only passion.

He leaned forward and looked at me directly. "I will be leaving Spring Valley in October to work for the Ministry of Education in Kingston," he confided.

I was shocked. "No, you just got here, and the students love you. Why?" I demanded.

"Teachers like me are becoming obsolete," he said. "Teaching is becoming a female thing, Flinty. Years from now there will be none of us men with a strong presence in the island's classrooms. Simply put, we will be fossils, like the dinosaurs."

"Before you came, me and my friends took the whole school thing for a joke, and look how you helped us."

"Teaching and learning are becoming training in sensitivity, a balancing act between public relations and nurturing. Females are caregivers, and education boards are confusing teaching and learning with nurturing."

"But you are going to the Ministry of Education to stop this, aren't you?" I asked.

"No, Flinty. I will be writing proposals for one thing or another. I later plan to write a book about the physics of cricket, and then retire to farming." He stood up and stretched. His joints creaked, but not as loud as my father's. He was ready to go.

"Mr. Tabangi, thanks for the books."

"Make sure you read them more than once," he advised and walked down the steps. "Tell Mrs. Griffin I am late for a meeting, and that I will stay for dinner next time." He turned and waved. "Flinty, goodbye and have a safe flight!"

"Goodbye, Mr. Tabangi." He waved once more and drove off.

I entered the kitchen, where the stove's flames were burning red instead of blue. Grandma complained its burners were flooded with kerosene oil. "I have to keep my eyes on the stove. That is why I did not come back to the verandah," she informed me.

"Mr. Tabangi had to leave for a meeting," I told her.

"At least he could have come and say goodbye."

"He said he was running late. Next time."

"I was hoping you changed your mind about going to Berti's Bar."

"No, Grandma. I am leaving now, but will be home early, as promised."

"Be careful. I will wait up for you."

"See you later, Grandma." I long-jumped over the steps and onto the street.

But as I walked towards the bar, I could not help but think how much more grit was in Grandma's advice. Before Sam's death, I would not have even listened to her tell me about the dangers of life. Now, I had started to pay close attention to her dinner stories. I would do everything I could to be home early, as promised; I knew Grandma would not sleep until I got home.

CHAPTER 19:
Musketeers' Farewell

Stan-Chen, Mookie and Ziggy were already waiting when I arrived at Berti's Bar. The four of us greeted each other in a somber mood but still managed to grin widely and pat each other's back a few times, though the loud, festive, noisy slapping and high-fiving was gone. It was our first time together since the funeral. Since Sam's burial, we'd made excuses that kept us apart. I stayed away from 4-H Club and Youth Club meetings and just hung out on my grandparents' verandah, flipping through the pages of books instead of reading. When I got bored, I went for long walks on the edge of the Cockpit Country's wilderness.

As we clinked our four Red Stripe bottles together and toasted our dead friend's spirit, I could swear I heard Sam's voice, as usual the loudest and funniest of the bunch. He always kept our conversations light, but at Blue Vail's Bar on graduation night, he'd been eloquent. His points were serious, even patriotic, and for a moment, I drifted back, while struggling to be present with my remaining three friends.

"To Sam!" Ziggy shouted.

"And to the funniest of the crew!" Stan-Chen shouted.

"To the man whose knife left its mark on my left arm!" I shouted.

Everyone laughed as we recalled the time when the five of us used our pocketknives to see who could slice the fastest and closest to each other's body without cutting. Sam's knife blade sank into my arm. I grinned as I recalled how I had chased after him with a sureness of burying my knife deep somewhere inside his body. But I could not keep up with his long, skinny legs and gave up the chase. That evening, we poured generous amounts of beer on the floor, and as the beer crackled into froth and rose up off the floor, we shouted, "Jah guide you, Sam!"

Suddenly, all was quiet, and I listened for that killer *Adagio* anthem of death, but heard only drizzling rain and a soft wind entering the bar through an open window. I smiled. Everything was fine.

"I am packed and ready. Leaving at 5:00 tomorrow morning," Mookie said, grinning.

"Hail to da man!" Stan-Chen shouted. Then we clanked our beer bottles against Mookie's.

"Guidance!" we all said.

Then the sudden noise of a motorbike filled the bar.

"Hey! It's Jah Spike! Where did you come from?" Stan-Chen shouted. We rushed to the door and watched his tall, athletic frame, without an ounce of fat, drag his father's red Suzuki 200 motorbike onto its stand before entering the bar.

"I was heading to Warville to see Danny Peart and heard you idlers were here. How come no one invited me?" he demanded, rolling his eyes at us suspiciously.

"It was a last-minute plan for a final send-off drink. Nothing big," I assured him with a gentle slap on his shoulder.

Familiar sparkles appeared in his eyes again.

"Daliah, give Jah Spike a drink," Stan-Chen called out. Jah Spike grabbed his beer, punched the air with the bottle, and then poured some on the ground.

"Long live Sam," he shouted.

We did the same, echoing Jah Spike.

"Stan-Chen, you ready for Cuba?" Mookie asked.

"Yeah I am ready; all packed," he answered. "Leaving Friday."

"Irie," Ziggy responded, and then turned to me. "How about you, Flinty?"

"Almost ready; collecting my student visa Friday and leaving Tuesday."

"Well, brethrens, looks like we are all ready," Stan-Chen said.

"Hold it. What about me? Because I am not leaving the country, no one remember me?" Ziggy gave us a derisive look.

"I am not leaving the island," Mookie shouted. "But we all know you are going to take over your old man business," Mookie joked.

We laughed loudly and slapped Ziggy's body. For a moment I felt the fun fuzz around us just like when Sam was alive.

"So, after all our rudeness, twists and turns, bumps and bruises, here we are, ready to fly straight!" Stan-Chen said.

"Jah guide us all!" Ziggy exclaimed, hoisting his right hand into the air for our final musketeer salute. We slapped his wide open palm against ours as we had done so many times before. "All for one and one for all!"

The evening was fun, but we stuck to our schedule. I gazed out the window and heard my father's warning about pushing buttons to end my beginning. Sensible advice makes no sense until clear and present danger. Sam's death was clear. We were careful. We finished our beer and left Berti's Bar for the last time. I walked home in the dark with both hands in my pockets. The road was still wet. I felt Sam's spirit walking behind me. He was cheering me on loudly. Flinty, pack your bag and go, but don't stay. Come back. I glanced behind me and for a brief moment saw his pink face and smelled his burnt flesh. "Sam, is that you?" I whispered. The darkness did not answer me, so I screwed up my face and felt an apprehensive grin sneak over it as I hastened my steps.

CHAPTER 20:
Mr. Magnum, Sit Down

Hutch was reading the day's newspaper in the living room when I got home. As I entered, he looked up and said, "The political violence in Kingston is getting worse."

He waited to hear my opinion, but I was hungry and kept quiet. Grandma sat at the old, Victorian, dark, wooden dining table and gave me a bright smile, showing all her gold teeth. "You are home before my bedtime as you promised," she said. The twinkle in her eyes and big smile meant I'd been a good boy.

"Yeah, Grandma. I am hungry."

"But you must be hungry; you had nothing to eat all day."

"What's for dinner?" I asked, looking around.

Hutch put the newspaper in his lap and spoke. "So you boys... I mean, you young men, are ready to go your separate ways?"

"We are all ready," I answered.

Grandma got up and headed for the kitchen. "I am glad you are hungry, Flinty," she called out. "I made rice 'n peas and curry goat."

"Mr. Magnum, sit down," Hutch said. I sat down at the dining table, looking at Hutch. "I am proud of you," he said.

"Thanks, Hutch."

"Maybe we can put in a final hunting trip before you leave."

"I am going to Kingston tomorrow, back on Friday," I said. "How about Sunday?"

"Yes! I look forward to it," Hutch replied.

My nose followed the aroma into the kitchen. Grandma made the best curry goat. She would wash the ram goat meat with lime and then marinate it overnight in curry, onion, garlic, scallion, allspice, chopped scotch bonnet pepper, thyme, coconut milk, cloves and lime juice. Then the next day, she'd cook the meat for about three hours until tender.

"I gave you a big plate for coming home early," she said as she carefully placed the steaming meal on the table.

Hutch looked up from his newspaper again. "You put down your cricket bat for only a year and passed all your exams. In only one year! Imagine how much better you could have done had you done that two years ago."

I spooned in the food as Hutch continued to speak. "You hide great potential behind your smile, Flinty. I mean, you are blessed to do many things. But you squeeze out all the enjoyment from the one thing you like until there is no more fun in it, before you move to the next."

I swallowed a mouthful. "Mr. Tabangi really helps. I still have some of his old books," I answered.

"Make sure you tell him thanks before you leave."

"He was here today," Grandma said, "but him left just before dinner."

"Nice man," Hutch said, "giving Flinty so many of his books. I have something to tell you in private, on our hunting trip. Make sure you remind me," Hutch said.

I nodded yes, my mouth full. Hutch turned the newspaper page and wrinkled his face as he continued reading.

Grandma's dinner story was about Alvin, Gwendolyn's new sweetheart from Clarendon. "Alvin's nothing like Brownie; he is tall and stout and serious," Grandma said.

"Good. Gwendolyn will finally start minding her own business," I told Grandma.

"Flinty, leave Gwen alone."

After dinner, I collected my books from the verandah. Max had been kind enough to push them under the chair I had sat in earlier and saved them from the rain. I lay on my back in bed, reading *Crime and Punishment*. Ever since Mr. Tabangi had lent me a copy of *Notes from the Underground*, I tried to read whatever I could by Dostoyevsky. In the time and land of powerful Tsars, I liked the way he wove average people's lives into his stories, the same way Marley's lyrics never leave out society's downtrodden.

I fell asleep with the open book on my chest and drifted into a dream. I walked toward the Garden River Bridge. I could hear trickling underneath as I approached the centre of the bridge. The day was a foggy grey, but I could see Sam on the other side, dressed in his school uniform. I was happy to see him and waved to him as he walked toward me. We met in the middle of the bridge and walked over to the rail and sat.

"We have been looking for you, Sam."
"I am busy making an agricultural farm, Flinty."
"Where are you farming?"

"*Behind my grandparent's house. Where are the others? Are they coming to school today?*" he asked.

"*Yes. They are on their way. Let's wait for them.*"

Sam looked at my chest and said, "*Power is of more use to poor people than freedom.*"

"*But power comes from freedom,*" I responded.

"*Yes, from mental freedom. Most difficult one; comes always before physical freedom.*"

"*I agree,*" I said, nodding.

Sam continued. "*But it's really about justice, that balancing act between freedom and power. Justice must be from bottom up, to first protect little people's rights, but trickle-down justice, where the rich scatter crumbs under tables and whistle for the less fortunate to grab them like dogs, is often the case.*"

"*I agree,*" I answered again, puzzled at Sam's lecture.

"*That's the real reason why Raskolnikov killed that pawnbroker in St. Petersburg,*" he said. "*In a weird way—like our hero, Jammy—he was trying to help.*"

"*What are you talking about?*" I asked.

"*You know, the killer in* Crime and Punishment*—the book on your chest,*" Sam replied.

He walked away quickly and was swallowed up by the fog on the other side of the bridge. I grabbed my chest, but there was no book on it. I was wearing my Duke of Trelawny khaki school uniform. I kept my eyes on the fog that Sam had disappeared into and waited for him to return. I wanted to tell him that there was no book on my chest, but he did not return. I did not see Stan-Chen, Mookie or Ziggy, either. I was alone.

Suddenly, a bright bundle of fire rolled out of the fog toward me. I jumped off the bridge's rail and strode into the middle of the road. The charging fire picked up speed, and I could not get out of its way. I closed my eyes and waited for it to engulf me, but it stopped in front of me—really close. The heat burned my body. I opened my eyes and dropped my school bag on the ground, but the fire rolled toward the edge of the bridge. It hovered over the rail for a moment, and then jumped into the water below. I heard it splash into the river. I ran and looked over and saw the flame on the water's surface below. Sam... Sam... Sam! I called out. There was no answer. The flame burned until it disappeared, leaving me in a dreadful darkness. I ran in the direction from where Ziggy, Stan-Chen and Mookie should be coming. I fell on the floor and woke up shouting, Sam! and saw Mr. Tabangi's *Crime and Punishment* on the floor beside me.

"Only a dream, thank God," I whispered, breathing hard. I tossed the book on top of the others and sat on the floor for a while, clearing my head before getting up and getting ready for bed. It was after midnight.

I went back to bed, half asleep, and again I dreamt I was on the bridge, wearing the same clothes, but this time I stuck both hands in my pants pockets and walked across the bridge, almost bumping into a beautiful woman. She appeared suddenly in front of me as if she had sprung up from the ground. She was wearing a full-length black dress, and was younger than me, with a shawl loosely wrapped over her head. She had short brown hair neatly tucked under her shawl, which hung loosely under her chin. Her smile was perfect, her face warm and friendly. The sparkle in her eyes pulled me closer to her, and immediately the sun came out. I could see tall buildings around me.

The street seemed wider, and the silent river underneath the bridge was enormous. I was not in Spring Valley anymore but did not know where I was. She grabbed my right hand and shouted, *"Flinty—I have been waiting for you. Let's go."* She walked quickly, pulling me along.

"What's your name?" I asked her, but before she could answer, I heard, "Flinty, wake up. You need to get ready for your trip to Kingston." It was Grandma's raspy morning voice. She was shaking me.

"Who were you talking to in your sleep?"

"A girl, Grandma." I answered, rubbing my eyes.

"Was she beautiful?" asked Grandma.

"Yes, and she was about to tell me her name."

"Flinty, that's the only place you will meet beautiful girls. So hurry up with that dream machine you promised me so I can see them with you." She burst out laughing as she walked to the kitchen to make breakfast, leaving me in a groggy state, trying to guess who it was that had grabbed my hand in my dream, as if trying to rescue me from some unknown danger.

CHAPTER 21:
Detective Fitzbright

I took the 6:00 o'clock bus to Kingston and got to Aunt Kaz's house only at midday, as the bus stopped many times, to pick up passengers along the way. Aunt Kaz—a JOS bus conductor—stayed home that day. She made me sandwiches, which I washed down with ice-cold artificial pineapple juice. Kingston was hot and humid, as usual. Even the picturesque Blue Mountains, Jamaica's tallest mountains, hovering majestically over the capital, did not draw enough rain to cool the city. The heat generated a river of sweat that ran off my skin, soaking my short-sleeve, striped arrow shirt and brown, gun-mouth-style, gabardine pants.

That evening at dinner, I updated Aunt Kaz and her husband, Fitzbright—Grandma's nephew—with news from the country. Fitzbright listened with a half-smile, but Aunt Kaz's face was pensive, and a colony of little sweat beads sprung up on her pointed little nose. Her mouth gaped slightly, a few white teeth peeking out from behind her half-opened lips, as if she expected bad news. Except for Sam's death, however, which she had already heard about,

Hutch's on-and-off sickness, and Grandma's worsening arthritis, the news was good. At the end of my update, she simply said, "Tell them I will write soon."

Next morning, I went with Uncle Fitzbright, a detective in the Central Investigation Division, to the Canadian High Commission in New Kingston to collect my visa. As he drove his blue Vauxhall, the police radio crackled constantly, which he ignored while he asked me all kinds of questions about his old girlfriends. As I entered the High Commission, I saw the red maple leaf once again. But this time, instead of the flimsy leaf I'd seen on Mother's luggage one year earlier, it was like a three-pronged star with a stem made of steel, because it was fast representing my new home, at least while I attended school. There was a coloured picture of Pierre Trudeau, Canada's prime minister, hanging on the wall beside that of Queen Elizabeth II.

I took a number, sat down and waited to be called for my interview. I scanned an old copy of the *Toronto Star*. The front-page article was about President Jimmy Carter brokering peace between Egypt and Israel. Mr. Tabangi always asked us to read and interpret current events. We were encouraged to form our own opinions using a wide range of information. "Never arrive at a conclusion from only one source of information," he would tell us. He advised us to seek information from many sources, stitch it together, and, like solving mathematical equations, cancel out likeness, disregard spurious noise and ignore distractions, until the entire bulk is reduced to a strong, simple argument girded by reason. "It's like taking a fat person to the gym, to get rid of the fluff," he would say. We were advised to ensure that we could defend our conclusion in front of the class or anywhere else for that matter.

Once, I felt the force of his tenet when I told the class that the many guns in Kingston were the reason for so many deaths, and that laws should be passed in parliament to create a gun-free zone for the city. Mr. Tabangi fired back, saying that Remington, Winchester, and Smith and Wesson, the gun makers, were not Jamaicans, so the law I was proposing would be useless unless I was prepared to stop gun importation into the country all together. "Strive for the problem's root cause, young Magnum," he advised me, as I stood in front of my fellow students, befuddled.

All attention switched to the tall, broad-shouldered oracle's voice. "When your conclusions are based on narrow information streams, like young Magnum, standing there not knowing what to do, gaps are open around you for others to sneak in and snatch the flimsy platform on which you stand. Furthermore, to Mr. Magnum's argument, there are more machetes in rural areas than guns in Kingston, and farmers are not chopping up people, so it's more than the availability of guns causing the killings. Also consider that there are more churches in Kingston than anywhere else in Jamaica, so in theory there should be less violence. Always turn the information around and examine it in different ways before reaching a conclusion. Take your seat, Magnum. Give him a hand," he told the class. They clapped as I scurried back to my seat, feeling whipped.

"Mr. Magnum, I see you will be studying audio engineering at The Northern Institute of Technology?" the blue-eyed blonde lady said as she scanned my face.

"Yes," I answered.

"What will you do after that?"

"I'm coming back to Jamaica." She stamped the letter of acceptance and sent me to another lady to collect my visa.

On the way home, Fitzbright planned to visit his electrician friend, who was rebuilding a compressor for his refrigerator. Fitzbright was tall, about six feet and more, and had a dark complexion with a long face and straight nose. His trimmed beard gave him a boyish but serious look to conceal his easy smile. He carried a revolver in the centre of his back and pulled his shirt over it to cover it up, but when driving he put the pistol on the seat between his thighs. There was also a Remington shotgun in the trunk; he took no chances. He constantly glanced around like an anxious bird sitting in a clearing, aware that hungry sharp-eyed eagles were circling overhead.

"One of my best friends was killed in a shootout on Spanish Town Road last month," he said. "He left three young children and a wife behind." My mind tried to see the gun battle, but only the 6:00 O'clock news on Aunt Blanche's television came to mind. The scratchy police radio crackled. An urgent sounding male voice burst out of it, yelling codes that Fitzbright alone could understand. He slammed the brake and shouted, "Hold on! There've been multiple shootings!"

"Three of dem dead," the radio crackled.

"Flinty, I will drop you home," he shouted as he made a U-turn, causing the wheels to scream with his frantic hand-over-hand steering. The radio continued to call all units in the area.

"The 1980 election will be dread. You lucky you are leaving," Fitzbright said as we sped home with the radio crackling and the car gliding around and through traffic. Fitzbright was referring to the mounting feud between supporters of the ruling People's National Party and the opposition Jamaica Labour Party. He dropped me off and I left for the safety of Spring Valley that evening, while he made sense of senseless political killings in the city.

CHAPTER 22:
Hutch's Secret

Hutch was sick in bed when I got home. We had to cancel our hunting trip. It was our last chance before I left, so I was in a sombre mode, but the old man was groaning from the pain. One of the things I was sure of was that if Hutch was groaning, he was really sick. His voice weakened, almost to a whisper. His face was thin, his eyes sunken and his gaze far away. He apologized for not being able to keep his promise, but I deflected his excuse, telling him that we would go hunting on my first return from Toronto. As I told him, my mind leaped into the future, where Hutch and I headed into the wild, meandering quietly, among swift rushing streams, under a dense canopy of century-old trees and a great wall of rocks pointing to the skies.

But then suddenly, my mind's eye came home from the future to Mahalia Jackson's big voice filling the house with song: *His Eye is on the Sparrow*. I sat on a chair beside Hutch's bed. He was lying on his side and raised his head. His attention was split, one half on me and the other on his singing diva, whose melody switched on the smile that lit up his face. "Ummm... that woman can sing," he whispered.

"She's the best," I told him. And I recalled how on Sabbath mornings, Hutch and Grandma would beam when they listened to Mahalia sing. Sometimes, Grandma enjoyed her singing so much she patted Hutch on his behind as he passed by. Hutch would smile and pat hers in return—romantic resuscitation moments, all thanks to the strong voice of their soprano. Mahalia would start her songs quietly, to draw us in, serenade us, and put us at ease. Her voice would hug us, relaxing us almost into a dreamy state, where we lingered. Then suddenly, her voice would rise to Herculean strength and shake us loose with an exploding note and wake us up, pushing us away from her bosom, telling us to stand up, be vigilant and not fall asleep, for we know not when Christ the saviour would part the cloud and come down from heaven.

Hutch changed the subject. "How was Kingston?" he asked, wrinkling his face in discomfort, with eyes squinted tight behind his glasses.

"Alright. Spent some time with Fitzbright. He is worried about violence in the coming election. Said many will die."

"I don't need Fitzy to tell me that; I am sure of it. The Americans don't want Man-lie back in power," Hutch responded.

I changed the subject to avoid starting any debate. "Do you want me to shave you?" I asked him. He rubbed his stubbly chin with his shaking right hand. "No, I will do it later on," he answered. "Have you finished packing?"

"Yes, I am ready. Think you will make it to the airport?" He did not answer.

"I have been meaning to tell you something," I told him, "but never got the chance. Last year, the day after Mother's return from Canada, I felt hands lifting me off the ground. I actually saw my feet dangling in the air and heard a man's voice counselling me; he said he was your father."

"My father... You mean your great-grandfather! Where?"

"Behind the house... in Bluefield's area."

"What did he say?"

"That I have a tough job ahead, but will be alright..."

"I know that."

"Why?"

"Too many options to choose from," he said. "Your head's everywhere."

"Shouldn't that be a good thing?"

"Not always," he said. "A one-option person has no choice but to focus... understand?"

"Mr. Tabangi always said I should fix up my focus."

"My father's spirit will guide you," Hutch said, nodding in assurance. "One of my ancestors appeared to me and told me to cultivate the whole 100 acres of land. It took many years, but I am happy to have worked every inch of the land." He turned fully onto his left side and tilted his head upwards so I could see his eyes. "Flinty, we are always doing our ancestors' business. I feel satisfy that I did my share and hope they agree. Except my father, that slave driver never satisfied, always demanding more from me when I dream him."

I chuckled but said nothing.

Hutch spoke again. "But it makes sense my father's spirit visited you," he continued. "You are his first great-grandson, and you spent much time hunting alone on the land. My advice is to just pick one or two things from your head, focus, work hard, and whatever you are supposed to become will appear, through hard work."

"Well, Hutch... I ..."

A cup fell off the table and bounced around on the floor, interrupting me. Hutch cleared his throat as I put the blue plastic cup where it was before. Then he took a long, deep breath and said, "Flinty, here's something you should know. It might help you. When you were only three years old, and your grandmother took you home from the hospital, one night I dreamt of a tall, slim, athletic man. Even though he was wearing a long white cloak, I could tell he was strong. I could not see his face, only muscular hands sticking out from his long-sleeved shirt, placing a large black book on your little forehead as you lay sick in the room next to ours. The book was so large it covered up your whole face and stomach. I jumped in front of him and began to fight him, kicking and throwing fists; you know how I fight in my sleep. But he just slapped me, sending me flying through the air. I struggled, got up, and demanded he leave you alone. I shouted, 'Who the hell are you?' but he paid me no mind. He just calmly bent over you and adjusted the book on your tiny forehead to make sure you could breathe. Then he straightened your feet and put his head close to your heart as if he was listening to it.

Then he kissed the thick book, touched it one last time, stood up, looked at me, pointed at my face, and warned, 'That's Flinty's book. Whoever removes it carries a burden 10 times their weight.' Finally he turned his back, walked a few paces, and disappeared as if he was never there."

I gazed at my grandfather's wrinkled face and nodded to make sure the words from his raspy voice sank into me.

"I thought the heavy book on top of you was suffocating you, so I grabbed it and tried to pull it off. Flinty, I could not lift the book, even with all my strength. The harder I pulled it, the heaver it became, until it started to sink into your face, forehead, neck and chest. I panicked and pulled with all my might, but it disappeared into your little body. Gone! I mean the heavy book sank inside your little body. I bawled out and jumped off the bed, washed in a cold sweat, yelling as I rushed into your room. But there you were, on your back, playing happily."

"Flinty, ever since that night, I knew there were things about you that were beyond my understanding. That black book weighed a ton. It must have been a thousand pages and had no title on it. Whatever was written on those pages is inside you. When you were a little boy and you would tell your stories but refuse to study your lessons, I would think about that dream and leave you alone. I kept my mouth shut about what you choose to do with your life, because you can understand anything you care to. But while I have no idea what's in that book, I know the flip side of every good book is equally bad, just like the Bible. So let no one anger you so much to awake the wrong chapter of that book, because there will be no further peace for you and them. Find that book living inside you and live your life so as to wake up only what's good in it, one chapter at a time, and you will be fine."

"It's the most frightening thing I ever heard, Hutch, but have you ever thought the book was actually empty and I am supposed to fill up the pages?" I responded. "Maybe that's why Mr. Tabangi came, so I would learn how to write, in order to fill up the book's pages!"

"No, Flinty, that man in my dream was guarding that book like it was a prize—things he wanted only you to know. That's why he knocked me out of the way, sending me tumbling."

I took a deep breath and my head tilted so I could gaze at the ceiling, as Mahalia Jackson's song *You Never Walk Alone* framed the secret Hutch had revealed to me after so many years. We listened together for a while. I pocketed the song's message for my trip which was only four days away.

"Have you heard from your mother?" Hutch asked; his feeble voice forcing Mahalia's singing into the background. Mother had left for Canada earlier.

"Yes, she has set up everything, and got me an apartment, in the city's west end. All I have to do is show up."

"She believes in you. Don't let her down," Hutch advised.

"I won't," I answered. "I still hope you come to the airport."

Hutch did not answer, but he mustered up some strength and sat up in the bed, resting his back against his pillow and adjusting his glasses to see and talk to me directly. "Look, Flinty, when you come back from Canada, it will be on a quiet day when the sun's light sprinkles the forest floor through the trees, and dry, brittle twigs explode when stepped on. I want you to grab the old Winchester rifle and walk to the same place you saw my father last year. That's where you will feel my smile upon you, smell my sweat, and know for sure, there will never be any goodbye between us," he said.

As I looked at him, trying to make sense of his words, he asked, "Do you understand?"

"Yes. I understand, Hutch," I answered him. But I really did not fully understand, because like most of what I learned from him, it took a second processing cycle of my thought. As I left the room, however, it came clear that for all the years I had known him, those words were the most from him to me at one time. And I got a foreboding feeling that he was forced to empty himself upon me because he was sure that, in this world, we were never to see each other again.

CHAPTER 23:
On the Edge of a Hurricane

Two days before I was to leave, Hurricane Carol, a dreadful category-four storm, suddenly sped toward the island, scheduled to make landfall the day after I was supposed to leave. The sky turned to darkness, and nonstop strong wind and heavy rain battered houses and trees. My face brightened and I kept my ears glued to the constant weather news, begging nature to unleash Hurricane Carol with vengeance and wreck the island. I wanted swift-moving rivers to wash away houses and farms and trap people for days in the darkness. Not because I was leaving, but because I had been waiting to fight my way through a deadly hurricane all my life, but none had ever made it to the island. Almost every August, since I was a little boy, the radio would announce a terrible hurricane coming, and I would get excited, but the furious wind softened into a tropical storm by the time it reached the island, toppling trees and causing rivers to swell over into the streets. Except once in a while, three or four people drowned when the odd bridge or a car washed away.

But Grandma, who never forgot Hurricane Flora's destruction, would be disgusted that the five of us joyously celebrated when hurricanes approached the island. It felt like Christmas, and we would run around the yard, shouting with our shirts open to feel the breeze on our bare chests. It was as if we were using our naked chests to give the wind a boost. Watching this spectacle from the verandah, Grandma would shout, "If you boys knew what a hurricane can do, the five of you would be on your knees praying to turn it back, instead of gallivanting like when dry red-pea soup almost cook."

We, however, would pay her no attention. Grandma would continue, "Flinty, you the oldest should know better and be setting a good example, instead of encouraging such nonsense." We would continue ignoring her; running around the house. However, when we reached the verandah again, Grandma's salvo of warning would put dread in us. "Boys, any of you ever seen a flying sheet of zinc slice someone's head clean off, blood spewing into the sky?" That image would force the five of us to sit on the verandah steps and listen to Grandma's Hurricane Flora story again.

She would begin, "It was September 1963 when Flora came. It killed everyone and washed people's houses into the sea." After Grandma's stormy hurricane history lesson, we would drop our heads, our bodies drooped, as if Grandma's words had sucked the air from our lungs. And we would walk slowly back to whatever we were doing, with images of wholesale destruction and death on our minds.

But on that final evening in the fury of that island, preparing to trade tropical hurricanes for winter blizzards, the rain poured, lightning ripped clouds, and thunder exploded, causing a dread to come over the house. I was calm because I had walked away from Angie's father's machete; witnessed a cricket ball slam into Shampoo Grill's chest, almost killing him; survived the crash of Stan-Chen's father's van; and lived through the fire that had killed Sam.

That night, before bed, I prayed for Hurricane Carol to attack that same night, so I could leave with honour after facing my own fury—feel death's embrace like a soldier who had survived a blitzkrieg battlefield; feel the heat from exploding bombs that rained from above; watch slow-spinning canisters packed with metal shrapnel from grenade launchers floating toward my face, explode and kiss me goodbye. The pieces of metal burrowing deep into my body would build a monument of my own intimate embrace with death upon my memory. Then I would be worthy of my dear brave friend, Sam, a hero-soldier who had died on that fiery battlefield on graduation night.

Instead, I woke up to calm. Many trees had fallen, but most of the wind-battered untidy trees were still there. Green fields and meadows where monarch and yellow-winged butterflies fluttered idly were covered in reddish-brown dirty water. The usual bright September sun climbed over the Cockpit Country's mountain range, burned away the bluish-grey fog, and lit up Spring Valley as if it was a normal day. Hurricane Carol—that tempest of scorn and rage—had ignored my prayers. I was angry with her. It was as if she had turned around and headed back out to sea.

There was a hush over Spring Valley as people's eyes stared, with a slim, singular mission of survival imprinted upon their faces: herding home weaker animals from farms; tapping hammers to batten down windows and nail up doors; collecting food, batteries and flashlights; buying gasoline cylinders, kerosene oil and candles to flicker in the dark for lovers to gaze across tables at frightened faces over dinner, while Hurricane Carol raged her fury outside. Oh, how I envied them.

The car wheels rolled slowly as Uncle Terrence carefully steered the sluggish vehicle through reddish water that swelled over Garden River's bank. The main road was flooded, and we had to leave early for my 3 p.m. flight. Grandma was with me. Hutch, still sick, had forced himself from his bed, clad in blue pajamas, onto the verandah. His face strained a smile as his right hand waved a long and lively ta-ta. I reversed through the gate into the vehicle, my left hand still hanging out the window, waving back as the car drove away, until Grandfather's body and face disappeared behind the thick leafy-green and colourful blossoms of Grandma's garden.

The car manoeuvred around potholes and wind-tossed debris, fallen utility poles, overflowing ponds and springs. Gushing torrents of water washed away large chunks of the road. Uncle Terrence had to drive slowly as he carefully mapped a path for the vehicle. He would speed up, only to be slowed down by the next obstacle in his way. The midday sun directly overhead followed the car along a narrow winding road that snaked around and down the lush mountainsides of the Cockpit Country to a flat postcard coastline. There, the choppy sea curled its bulky waves and raced them one after the other to crash into retaining walls, and splashed salty water onto the street. Port Duncans was a lake, and vehicles had to crawl slowly through. Frantic drivers with urgent faces, gathering essentials they needed to battle Hurricane Carol's oncoming fury, impatiently honked their horns, long and frequently. The car radio announced that Carol had marched around the tip of Florida, sparing it, but was rattling the western tip of Cuba. It said that Carol was on schedule to storm my goodbye island's lush coastline, coves, hills and valleys the next day. I felt like a soldier who had prepared for a battle and was pulled from the battlefield a day before the big fight.

The car slowly crawled out of Falmouth toward Montego Bay, along the narrow scenic road that trailed along the sea's edge. Grandma, in the back seat, gazed at the rough sea. "Flinty, it's not good to let a hurricane blow you out of your country," she advised.

"I wanted to fight Carol, Grandma," I told her. "But people sometimes escape battlefield until the rage is over."

"What are you talking about, Flinty?"

"Dostoyevsky was uprooted from St. Petersburg, his execution commuted in Siberia. Bob Marley rushed to England after they tried to kill him, but they both returned to do good work," I told her.

"Which one of Mr. Tabangi's books you twist that from?" Grandma quipped.

"Not twisting anything, Grandma; many people don't know that Marley and Dostoyevsky agreed with each other about life. Bob Marley said, 'If I was educated, I'd be a damn fool.' Dostoyevsky believed that an educated man, a man of character, gets nothing done; it takes a man with circumscribed imagination to take action, not the overly educated. So you see, Grandma, both men think the same way, but teachers of arts and literature would panic that

I mentioned Marley and Dostoyevsky together. At school, we had to read *Crime and Punishment* and explain the two murders that took place more than a hundred years ago, way over in St. Petersburg, Russia, to Mrs. Black. But not a single line as to why Bob Marley was so heartbroken over Johnny, who was shot down and died in the streets of Kingston, from a stray bullet only a year ago, even though he was a good man and never did a thing wrong."

"My know-it-all grandson," Grandma said sarcastically. "Tell me how you are going to use what you learned from Mr. Tabangi's old books when you are going to Canada to burn up your fingers with electricity like you did at school some years ago?" Her words landed in a sore spot. Grandma still could not accept me travelling to another country and paying all that money to learn how to build audio amplifiers, so she had to put in her final punch to the gut.

"Uncle, I am going to learn how to build spy gadgets like those in movies. I told Grandma many times," I appealed to my uncle, trying to build an alliance against Grandma. Uncle Terrence just nodded and said nothing. He kept his face with bushy moustache forward, eyes on the road, as his nimble hands manoeuvred the car around potholes, some as wide as the car.

Grandma continued. "You know, Terrence, Flinty could have done something that makes sense— become an accountant, a teacher, even a writer—if he put his head to it. All those stories inside him. One morning when he was only five, he told Hutch about a man who got his hand stuck in the post office concrete mailbox, stealing letters. That when the strong men grabbed the thief's body to yank him out, his right hand broke from his shoulder, spewing blood all over the road. Uncle Terrence, that story had me crying all day. He even told me how the hand was still twitching while on the ground, and said all five fingernails on the hand were long and dirty," Grandma continued. "I gave him all kind of food and drink, worrying about him, and the more food I gave him, the more terrifying his story got until there was no more food left to give him. I was so concerned about the awful violence my little five-year-old grandson had seen that I called his father in the room when he came to get him that evening and asked him about it. His father just smiled and said Flinty had made up the whole thing. 'That little boy scares me with his stories sometimes,' his father told me."

"Grandma, I don't remember the story you're talking about."

Grandma just continued appealing to Uncle Terrence like he was an umpire in a cricket match. "Uncle, from that day, I know Flinty has a special kind of brain in his head, so when he and I were alone, sometimes I read my old *Beowulf* and Homer's *Iliad* stories to him, but him gambled off his brain in cricket matches, and now want me to agree with him going all the way to Canada to study what the hell, I don't know, Terrence."

Uncle still said nothing, concentrating on keeping the car on the left side of the narrow road, where shrubs and bushes hung from the vertical rock face and swooshed the vehicle's windows. He was avoiding accidents from the mad rush of fast oncoming vehicles.

"But really, Flinty, you should have waited until after the hurricane, when it was safe," she advised quietly. Then she tapped my right shoulder and gave me a handful of icy mints.

"Grandma, the plane ticket is not insured, so it would cost extra money to change the flight date."

I tossed one of the mints into my mouth and gazed at the clear blue sky over the choppy sea, stirred up by the approaching hurricane. Uncle Terrence briefly took his eyes off the wet road and looked at me. "I don't think your flight will be over Cuba because that would be directly into the hurricane."

"I want the plane to fly me head-on into it, and see what I am made of, Uncle," I told him.

"Well, then, don't leave your wind breaker... I mean your sword," he said, and smiled.

"Why?"

"Because you are a fighter, Flinty; don't ever leave your weapon."

Grandma sat comfortably in the back seat with a satisfied face. It was her time once again to hand her grandson back to her daughter. Once again, she could reflect that there were near misses and many close calls, but no flesh wounds.

"Grandma, one day I will make sure there is a 'Grandmother's Day' on this island, like in Poland."

"That's a good idea, Flinty," Uncle Terrence said. "A lot of children on this island are raised by grandparents, who receive not even a thank you for taking on second parenthood after growing up their own."

Grandma said nothing; she just gazed at the sea as the car turned right and circled the roundabout, made a left, and drove between swaying palm trees and red hibiscus blooms hanging over both sides of the road, toward three horizontal two-storey white buildings—the airport complex. I handed Grandma the comic book I had thumbed through when conversation lulled in the car.

"Give the comic book to one of my brothers," I told her.

She bowed her head and dropped the thin book into her handbag. I enjoyed comic books, even though my father said they are junk food, same as fatty meals, clogging the mind and short-circuiting the imagination. To me, however, comic books like the one I handed Grandma cut to the heart of the story. The one I handed her was a Second World War story about two Americans whose fighter planes were shot down over the Ardennes Forest. They were captured but escaped and dressed themselves in German army uniforms. They hijacked and killed a German tank commander and gunner, and rode along in the German formation. Then they strangled the battalion commanding officer and led the whole German tank battalion into an ambush, where all of them surrendered to an army officer resembling General Blood and Guts.

My mission in Canada would be just as slim as that of those two air force pilots. I would get off the plane and kiss my mother's cheek. Next morning, one of her friends would drive me to the Northern Institute of Technology, without a cricket field, where I would meet young men from around the world with slide rules sticking out of their pockets. I would be shocked and disappointed that none of my island's brethren would have been to Spring Valley, and would call it "bush," and only one would admit he had driven through my beloved village on his way to Montego Bay.

But that would all be just fine with me because, like an electron zipping around the nucleus of an atom, I would stabilize my mind with the same equilibrium of centrifugal and centripetal forces to stay on track. I would stay focused and use calculus instead of history and literature to work out the rise and fall, and the rate at which things and time will change. After only three winters I would graduate and build Grandma's dream machine, wasting no time in the freezing cold. Instead, I would be back in St. Ann's Bay, home of Marcus Garvey and Burning Spear. I would set up Magnum Engineering in bright flashing lights on a steep hillside so I could gaze at the sea while I designed and built the silkiest sounding, earthquake-jolting series of Magnum Audio Amplifiers and export them to music lovers around the world. Yes, sir, my mission felt simple and clear, just like the comic book I handed Grandma as Uncle Terrence parked the car and turned off the engine in the airport's parking lot. It had been a long journey from Spring Valley to where I stood and gazed at new dark clouds gathering in the sky over my head.

CHAPTER 24:
Ta-ta, Grandma

The airport was not as busy as it had been one month earlier, when I'd seen Mother off to Canada. Many flights were cancelled; mine was not. Stan-Chen, Mookie and Ziggy had already gone, to craft or be crafted by the world; it was my turn to go—even in a hurricane.

I grabbed my heavy suitcase from the car trunk, careful not to let it soil my Kariba suit. I had worn it only twice: once to graduation and once to Sam's funeral. But as I walked toward the airport, I felt troubled, on edge. I gazed at the moving crowd but did not see them; only my thoughts were drifting—searching for a final boost of courage. Suddenly, I remembered a moonlit night when I was 14, while walking home late and alone from the Actor's Theatre. A tall, terrifying, wide-shouldered ghost stood in my way, taking up the whole road, leaving no room for me. The spirit's angry, red eyes observed my every move. I stopped and was about to turn back but found the little firmness I had left inside me. The hair on my head and neck stood up, and I felt my fists clench without my effort.

I moved slowly, putting one foot in front of the other, toward the entity. As I got closer, my heart drummed to a nervous rhythm and, fists raised, poised to punch holes into the seven-foot tall demon dressed in a black suit and a Stetson hat, with a bulky nose and thick red lips with a long pipe between them. But then I realized the scary spirit was only the silhouette of tree branches reflecting on a vertical slab of rock by the side of the road, lit by the moonlight. Both the ghost and my worry were entirely my creation. I exhaled, and my heart's drumbeats softened. I smiled and melted away the anxiety my mind had created and lowered my fists and went home to bed. Even though flying into a hurricane is no phantom but a real danger, I could not turn back.

My legs carried me along, Grandma beside me. Her right arm dropped heavily on my shoulder. It was unusual for her to let her hand linger on me like that; I could think of only two other times: once when she found out Hutch had to spend a few extra days in the hospital, and once when her friend Aunt Millicent told her that her face was bony because cancer was feeding on her body.

It was clear Grandma was not ready to part company with me, even though she had knelt down, closed her eyes many times, and begged her Lord to remove me and her other four grandsons from her sight, so she and her husband could enjoy the peace they had worked so hard for. Now, in the moment God was finally answering her prayers, the burden was heavier than she could bear. Grandma gazed at my face, but her sad eyes were searching inside her mind as we entered the cool, air-conditioned building. Her hand and shoulders shook, and her fingers squeezed mine tight as the baggage handler heaved my suitcase onto the scale. It had few clothes, but was heavy with Mr. Tabangi's old books and some from the Spring Valley Library—books I'd had all honest intention of returning when I'd borrowed them.

My baggage was checked and tagged, my passport stamped, and my aircraft window seat confirmed. In less than an hour, an Air Canada jet would bullet down the wet tarmac and slice through the air, hovering over the angry turquoise sea for a while. It would then slowly turn and point north, climbing to high altitude, and fly me into a hurricane.

"All is checked, Grandma. I am ready to go."

"I forgot to bring my Dodd's pressure pills," Grandma confessed.

Grandma took her pressure pills prescribed monthly by her earthly god, Dr. Hector Goodwin, when nervous. She swallowed them religiously every day.

"You don't need those pills." I squeezed her fingers to still their trembling. Tears sprung up in her eyes, and I thought for a moment that after all the troubles I had heaped upon her and Hutch for so many years, she could not let go. Uncle Terrence went to chat with one of his boyhood friends, returning from England, whom he had not seen for thirty years. Grandma and I sat at a small square Formica table in the airport's cafeteria. "Flinty, I am going to miss you," she said and pulled out her white handkerchief with little blue flowers around its edge from her green handbag and wiped her face. Then she took an envelope from her handbag and handed it to me. It read: "To: Flinty; From: Hutch."

I put the thin letter into my jacket pocket, and Grandma used her index finger to sink the envelope deeper into it. "It's from your grandfather. Open it only when you get there. He said you should read it after your first week," she said.

I nodded. "Okay, Grandma."

A pleasant female voice came out of the airport's public address system: "Flight 067 to Philadelphia is delayed until further notice." I tuned out the rest of her announcement, but heard loud grumblings from a bunch of dissatisfied tourists sitting at the next table. Meanwhile, others behind us yelled with excitement, happy that Hurricane Carol was giving them another night or two on the island.

I gazed at Grandma's half white head of hair, and recalled that, when I was eight years old, it was my job to use a tiny pair of scissors to hunt down and cut the few strands of white hair that were sprinkled about her head. My mission was to prevent white thorns from overrunning Grandma's lush head of black pearl. My patrol through her head took place every Sunday, after the rice 'n peas and chicken dinner was digested. She would lie on her back across Uncle Terrence's bed with her full head of hair hanging over the bed's edge with a small round mirror in her hand, directing my fingers armed with the sharp scissors. She would collect every strand of hair the scissors snipped and examine them to make sure they were all white. She would beg me every minute, "Flinty, make sure you cut out only the white ones."

When my mission of cutting only white strands of hair was accomplished, she would give me a large square of pink and white grater cake, which I would eat slowly. Then I'd lick my fingers to savour the taste before running off to catch the end of the Sunday evening cricket match. But sometimes, when my hand got tired, I would cut a few strands of her precious black hair. She would examine her fallen black pearls, sliding them between her fingers, and eulogize their untimely death in a sad voice like they were brave heroes. "Look how stout and long they are, and you cut them out," she would say. "Flinty, do you know how long these take to grow?"

I would agree that those stout strands of black hair were heroes that died in the struggle my father often talked about with his friends —heroes like Paul Bogle and Patrice Lumumba—martyrs in the fight to prevent dangerous white invaders from taking over Grandma's healthy black community of hair. But sometimes it came to my mind that Grandma's head was the village of Umuofia, a place in Chinua Achebe's book, *Things Fall Apart* that Aunt Buckingstone read to us at school.

She said no one paid any attention to the few white-haired people who showed up until they changed the way the people had lived for many years and then used debt to trap and dishonour the village's proud and respected leader, Okonkwo. Okonkwo hung himself in disgrace, and then the white-haired people ruled the village. I was determined not to have any of that foolishness happen to my Grandma's head, so I would squint my eyes to see and cut only white hair from her head.

But sometimes I was confused, because those in banks, those who owned supermarkets and businesses, and those living in big houses with gardens much larger than Grandma's, with maids with black hair, all had white hair. Also, at school, the prettiest people in my reading books had long, white hair. So I was shocked that my grandmother wanted me to cut all white hair from her head. Until one day I asked her, "Why do you cut only white hair from your head, Grandma?"

"They make me look and feel old, Flinty."

"But they should make you pretty, Grandma."

Grandma laughed and said, "Flinty, when you reach my age, you will find out."

Then she used her little mirror and pointed to another strand like it was a fugitive from the law. "Flinty, see a nice fat white one here? Snip it out. Make sure you cut it close to the root."

After that, I thought my Grandma was a rebel, a freedom fighter like Captain Cudjo and his sister Nanny—Maroon warriors who had fought the Redcoats in the Cockpit Country's jungle, heroes Aunt Buckingstone told us to be proud of. And when I heard news on the radio about Nelson Mandela and Stephen Biko who was in jail, I would feel happy the soldiers did not know where Grandma lived. So I never told anyone I cut white hair from Grandma's head, even though I was not sure if my cousins had told anyone. That was Grandma Catherine's little secret I kept for her for many years.

One afternoon, during Independence Day—a national holiday—I wanted to attend a special cricket match. I had heard Uncle Manny talking about the visiting team from Westmoreland, bringing pretty girls wearing shorts for the party at Berti's Bar afterwards. And that Aunty Berta would be selling pink ice cream, coconut drops, and syrup-drenched-snow cones. So I hurried the scissor and crunched out thick clusters of grandma's black hair. She panicked, a look of terror flashing across her eyes, and her face washed in cold sweat as she leaped from the bed and bawled out, "Boy, you trimming all the hair off my head like those mad people from Bellevue!"

She galloped to her bedroom and dropped her butt on her wooden stool in front the large mirror hanging over her mahogany bureau to assess the damage. Then she complained bitterly to Hutch, looking down at the woolly clump of hair in her hand. After counting every black strand of hair I had slaughtered, she shouted, "The bowy is cutting them out on purpose!" Then, before I could mount a defence, she screamed, "Flinty, you cut out over 50 strands of black hair from my head!"

"Sorry, Grandma," I said, feeling like a soldier in the South African security forces, firing into a crowd of innocent Black people demonstrating for their rights. She continued quarrelling, so I tried to cheer her up. "But Grandma, I only kill 50! Aunt Buckingstone said soldiers killed 69 in the Sharpeville massacre."

Grandma stamped the floor so hard the whole house jerked. Then she shouted, "Bowy, are you damn mad? Flinty, go trim Aunt Buckingstone's head, then, you wicked brute! Next time I see that woman at church, I have to find out what the hell she is teaching you at school."

I bolted from the room, out the front door, down the steps and onto the street. But all my guilt vanished when I joined Stan-Chen, Mookie, Sam and Ziggy at the game, grinning at each other, and cheering on the Spring Valley team.

But as we sat in the airport, I noticed Grandma's few black hairs, her remaining youthfulness flickering like candles in a hurricane's strong wind. Soon, all of her head would be overrun by the invasion force of white hair and would impose new rules of old age upon her. But my Grandma would still begin each day just as daylight overpowered the tired moonlight. She would spread her bed without any creases in the sheets. Then she would sit on the edge of her bed, slip her feet into soft warm, pink slippers, and put on her blue sweater with little red roses on the front, to protect her from the morning chill.

She would light a candle and shuffle to the kitchen to make a strong cup of black coffee. Sitting by the kitchen table, she would sip from the steaming cup and gaze out the window at the brightening of a new day, but that noisy Methuselah family of woodpeckers that had drummed that hollow cedar tree trunk behind the house forever would grab her attention. Those noisy, bombastic birds would take her back to when her daughters, sons and grandsons were just as noisy.

That's when she'd push the play button on the dream machine I built for her. Her dream begins on a bright sunny morning, with many cars parked in front of the old house. There is loud music and chattering from dozens of her family members scattered around the yard, all stemmed from her, from near and far, all come to wish her a happy 90th birthday. Grandma watches her happy self, carried around by her nimble feet, smiling and greeting everyone. She greets Uncle Manny, with his three girls, Suzan, Julia and Charlene, who teaches literature in Kingston.

"Do you read *Beowulf* to your students?" Grandma asks her.

TA-TA, GRANDMA

"Of course, Grandma. I read it to them in the same scary voice that you read it to me when I was little," Charlene answers, letting her right arm relax gently on Grandma's shoulder.

Grandma squeezes Charlene's hand and whispers, "Always remind your students that the scare births the hero. Villains and disasters are mothers of heroes, so make sure Grendel gets his credit for creating Beowulf."

Reggae-Slim, now tall and slim, came from St. Elizabeth with his wife, Carmen, and tells her, "This house used to be so big; now it's so small."

"House's the same size, Reggae-Slim; you are the one who got bigger," Carmen answers.

Grandma scurries past me with a drink in her hand. "Grandma, what's that you drinking?" I ask.

"A little brandy, Flinty; good for the digestion, you know," she answers, patting her belly.

"Never see you drink alcohol before, Grandma. Not even Hutch's Tonic wine."

"It's my birthday, and I intend to enjoy all of it. And Napoleon's helping!"

Her police nephew, Fitzbright, adds more rum punch to his glass, and Grandma grabs his shoulders from behind. He turns around. "Fitz, I prayed for you every night while you were patrolling Kingston, especially during election time. The Lord sure taking good care of you."

Fitzbright laughs and throws his long, slim, dark right arm around Grandma and squeezes her to him, like the protector his aunt believes him to be, and shouts, "People, it's because of this beautiful lady's prayer that I made it to police superintendent. Thanks, Aunt Griffin!"

Some of the people laugh and clap. "Don't you think the music is too loud for you, Grandma?" Brenton shouts at her.

"Brenton, leave the music! Let me enjoy what I can from my one good ear."

Grandma then walks across the lawn to Terri, Uncle Terrence's son, and listens to her grandson talk with pride about his research project in Africa. Terri, who works at the United Nations, is developing seeds that can grow in the desert without water. "Hi, Grandma! I was explaining my project," says Terri. "Even the slimmest success will save millions of lives."

Grandma, however, is more interested in how much the tall, handsome young man resembles his father. "Terri, I would have mistaken you for Terrence if I saw you on the street," she tells him.

"No, Grandma, it's my father who resembles me!" Terri replies.

"Terri, your swift mouth reminds me of Flinty."

Grandma walks over to her niece and shouts, "Sharon, you look fat and pretty. Me glad to see you all the way from Brooklyn!"

"Grandma Catherine, I could not have missed your 90th birthday!" Sharon answers and hugs her.

"I saw Aunt Olga one morning last week on Flinty's dream machine," Grandma tells her chubby, fair-skinned niece. "She was wearing a beautiful white dress, looking happy, and was in a beautiful place, just like heaven." Aunt Olga was Grandma's youngest sister and Sharon's mother. She was killed and buried in New York when her apartment was robbed.

"I miss her very much, Aunty Griffin," Sharon confesses. "The case is still in court, but that will not bring her back, so I don't pay much attention to it."

Grandma consoles her. "Sharon, win or lose won't bring her back, but I am glad they catch the killer. The good Lord will take care of it; don't worry yourself."

Hutch, smiling, walks slowly from Grandma's garden toward me with a glass of clear liquid. White rum, I think. He looks at my eyes and lays his hands on my shoulder. Glad to see you come back safe, Flinty, he says and cracks a big laugh.

"Hutch, I am so glad to see you again," I reply. "But you look real tired."

"Yes, I was up all night. I have to go and catch a nap, but will come back and see you later," he assures me. He walks over to Grandma, holds her hand, and whispers something in her good ear that makes her smile. Then he drifts toward the old cotton tree.

Many of the family members gone before, including Hutch's older brother, PVT Uriah Griffin, who died in the Great War in 1914, were buried under that old fat-trunk methuselah cotton tree. Cousin Bernie Griffin, who died from too much white rum, finally found rest in the shade of that tree. Grandma's first born, Cynthia, who died at two months, was also buried there. Great-Grandma Eva, whom I remember walking around with bent back, the lit portion of a cigarette inside her mouth—the butt hanging out—was also buried there.

A familiar voice shouts, and I feel a gentle tap on my shoulders. "Flinty!"

I turn around to see the wide, tall frame of Mr. Tabangi, with a big grin. He is wearing his trademark dashiki blouse and Bermuda shorts, holding a Red Stripe beer in his hand.

"Mr. Tabangi!"

"I heard you came, so I dropped in to see you."

I grab his right hand and pump it with excitement. He pulls it away and wiggles his fingers to re-start the circulation. "You still shake my hand like you want to drag it from my shoulder," he protests.

"Man, I am so glad to see you. I came back for Grandma's 90th birthday. I figure there won't be many left."

"So many..."

"It turned into a family reunion," I tell him. "There are many I don't know."

"Didn't know your family was so big," Mr. Tabangi says. "How do you know who is who?"

"I don't; I just ask their fathers' and mothers' names to get clues and act like I know their younger ones," I confess.

"How long has it been since you left?"

"Twenty-five years."

"That's a long time, Flinty."

"Congratulations on being a Deputy Minister of Education; I read it in the newspapers."

"Thanks, Flinty, but I'm retiring in a few months."

Grandma, come here, I call out. "You remember Mr. Tabangi?"

"Yes, of course. It was so nice of you to come and see Flinty after his friend's death many years ago. That was beyond your duty as his teacher, but you came. I always remembered you for that," she tells him.

"Hi, Dad." It's Ohmsie, Peter, and Luana, my two sons and their sister, full of excitement and breathing hard, as if they had just completed a marathon.

"I've been searching for you kids all morning."

"Just getting to know where you grew up, Dad," Ohmsie answers.

"Meet Mr. Tabangi, my old teacher. He taught me the little I know."

"Hi, Mr. Tabangi," says Peter. "My dad talks about you all the time."

Peter, then Ohmsie, shakes Mr. Tabangi's hand.

"Your sons' grips are as strong as yours, Flinty!" Mr. Tabangi says, pulling his hand from Peter and wiggling his fingers.

"Grandpa Hutch went to take a nap. Don't go too far. When he wakes up, I want you children to meet him," I tell them.

"Grandpa Hutch... is... " Grandma did not finish.

"I am writing a book, Grandma, and the last chapter is about you," I say, interrupting her. "I will send you a copy as soon as it's finished."

Her face flushes with satisfaction, and she flashes me her widest smile. "Flinty, it will be a sensible book. I can't wait to read it. You see, Flinty, I had no doubt you would write one day."

"Thank you, Grandma."

"Your sons are handsome, Flinty. And Luana, oh my, she's a sunflower bloom!"

"The fun in them is all yours, Grandma," I say.

She kisses their foreheads but quickly changes the subject. "Flinty, you should give up being a vegetarian for today and try the curry goat; it tastes just like I used to make it."

"Grandma, it's been 22 years since I ate animal flesh; my stomach will get sick if I eat meat!"

"Your letters about becoming a vegetarian frightened me," she tells me. "But you look strong and healthy."

Grandma looks over to the crowd of women on the steps. "Flinty, Mr. Tabangi, excuse me a minute. I need to get news from Gwendolyn about Aunty Curry's husband. He had a stomach operation yesterday for the 'evil C,' you know," she whispers, patting my shoulder, and walking off.

After everyone eats and sings a few songs, and Terri says a word of prayer for the family, the women cut fat bundles of flowers from Grandma's garden before leaving. Dozens of family members embrace and kiss cheeks. Many wave and shout loud ta-tas at Grandma, who waves and smiles back at tooting car horns with heads and arms hanging from windows of slow-moving vehicles until the video screen turn black to end Grandma's dream. She turns off her precious dream machine.

After another sip from her coffee, she will smile, and then take a deep breath. Thank you, Flinty, for the dream machine. Now I see all my dreams as soon as I wake up, without wasting time trying to remember them. That strange name education of yours was good for something after all, she will say. Then she will get up from her chair and walk to the verandah, holding on to the table and wall for support.

Later that morning, when the sun has burned the dew from her garden, Grandma will drag herself from her verandah chair and down those cold concrete steps, using her walking stick for support. She will shuffle herself into her garden and pull her forget-me-nots and sunflower blooms to her face and whisper a new set of secrets to them before using her scissors to snip their stems to decorate her vases. After cutting her flowers, she will pray quietly to her God for strength to climb up those Mount Everest steps. She will stop and rest after every footstep, until she makes it onto the verandah, breathing heavily. After collapsing her tired self into her chair, and gently laying the bouquet of flowers on the cold concrete floor in front of her, she will gaze at the mountains across the valley. She will whisper to the stoic mountains about the pain in her legs, neck, hands and knees, as her chest rise and fall rapidly; every breath she hauls from her world slipping from her grasp will be like pulling on a tug-of-war rope against Goliath.

After telling her husband that a shower of rain is coming, she will examine every joint on her fingers and ankles—tap, jiggle and pinch her swollen feet to hasten the blood circulation. She will then remove her red-and-white plaid head wrap to let the warm afternoon wind ruffle her white hair before she summons a new truckload of will to shuffle her tired ninety-five year old body into the living room. She will divide her flowers into three vases, making sure there is one sunflower in each vase, before fluffing and patting the flowers gently and arranging them into neat symmetry. She will whisper to them, thanking them for brightening her day. She will promise to water them every day until next Wednesday, when she will cut a new bunch.

Then, sitting by the table, she will talk to her husband beside his radio, saying, "No change in my arthritis. Weeds are killing my garden. I can hardly climb up those steps anymore. My blood pressure is up; my right ear is pounding like a drum. And I heard Aunty Curry funeral was bigger than Gwendolyn's."

Grandma will wait for her husband's voice, but hearing nothing, she will begin talking again. "Miss Nicey cooks and brings lunch and dinner, and she always late, but I cannot complain; she is doing her best. Lizards have taken over my garden, but I have not seen the crocodile monster-lizard since Blanche replaced my Dennis Watson eyeglasses. I got a letter from Flinty yesterday, with pictures of him and his children on vacation in Cuba. Don't know why he went to that communist country; better him did just come home for the two weeks."

After a few moments, her lone voice bouncing off the wall and back to her will remind her that her husband died only six months after Flinty left. She will sigh and stare at the faded, old, black-and-white pictures on the wall, when she was fresh in her spring and summertime of only 20, with Hutch grinning beside her. Her fingers linger in the memories of the tired picture for a while. *Where did the time go?* she will ask.

Finally, she will exhale deeply to squeeze the past out of her, and inhale the fresh aroma of flowers around her, for new strength, to take a stem of red roses from one of her vases, grab her walking stick and hobble down those steps again, turn right past her garden and place the rose on her husband's tomb under the old fat-trunk cotton tree, and whisper a new secret to him...

"Flinty! Flinty! Wake up. You fell asleep! Are you tired?"

"No, Grandma, not tired. Just dozed off and had a dream."

"Flinty, wrong time to be dozing off! The plane will leave you and your dream behind."

"I am okay now, Grandma," I said, stretching my arms to the air conditioning fans in the ceiling.

"You looked drowsy," she said. "Have one of the icy mints to freshen you up."

"Grandma?"

"Yes?"

"Do you think we will see each other again?"

Grandma smiled mischievously. "Oh yes, of course. One day while in my garden petting my African violets and whispering to my forget-me-not blooms, you will come back with that dream machine you promised. Then I will sit on my old Victorian bed, listening to your stories, same as when your mother used to come home from Toronto. And when you ready to leave, I will wave long ta-tas at you, even when you can't see me."

"You cannot hide from me, Grandma," I replied, trying to understand what she meant. "Grandma, Mrs. Black—my English teacher—"

I did not finish speaking before Grandma asked quickly, "You mean the little half-pint tyrant?" She was smiling, with her eyes wide open.

"Yes. How do you know I called her that?" I asked.

"I know all your secrets, Flinty, even about the little red-skin gal from Warville. You used to visit her on Thursday nights when her grandmother went to market," Grandma said.

I screwed up my face and chuckled before talking again. "Mrs. Black told me I should write whenever I get a chance.

And you always believed I could write. Hutch even said there's a book inside me."

"Hutch said that?"

"He did."

"But he always said you should do whatever you want."

"It's a long story, Grandma; ask him when you get home."

The aluminum chair I sat in screeched on the concrete floor as I leaned back. "I don't know if I can write or not, but if I were to write a book, you would be in it," I assured her.

"Flinty, you will write one day. I know for sure. And if you don't while I am alive, my spirit will put a pen in your hand and compel you to write after I am dead. Just watch and see."

"Grandma, your ghost will be too busy with your garden."

Grandma chucked at first, but suddenly, a serious look came across her face. "Flinty, you may be right about my garden. It pains me to think what will happen to it when I am gone."

"Grandma, your garden will be alright."

The squeaking air conditioning blades overhead spun slowly and sliced the air to provide cool comfort while plane engines roared and whistled outside as they landed and departed. Grandma sipped the last of her B&G pineapple drink and dabbed her mouth with her kerchief. I touched the spot on my belly where anxiety pangs pulsated inside me. She gazed over her left shoulder at the line-up for my flight, and then snapped her eyes back on mine.

"Flinty, I believe I have told you everything," she said. "Write as soon as you reach— Oh! One more thing. Don't forget, pray before going to bed at night."

I nodded yes.

"I am serious about that," she snapped. "My nightly prayers got you this far."

"Okay, I will pray before bed."

"Good!"

As Grandma and I stood up, a little girl dressed in a bright, frilly, yellow, knee-length dress, black shoes, white socks and two red ribbons hanging from two long locks of her hair, ran toward us and smiled. She squatted, picked up her red ball from the grey concrete floor, and handed it to Grandma. Grandma took the ball and smiled widely at the little girl, smiling as if at herself when she was young, playing rounders with her friends on Sunday afternoons on Mission Hill under the Bell Tower, above Spring Valley's Baptist Church. That's when I recognized dear old Grandma's childish spirit, ready for me to pack and carry.

I whispered into her ear that still listens to the world, "Ta-ta, Grandma!"

"Ta-ta, Flinty!" she whispered.

I kissed her cheeks, patted her left shoulder, turned and strode into the open, under the cloudy sky and stormy wind stirred up by the afternoon sea—now a roaring monster. I grabbed the handrails, mounted and sprinted to the top of the aircraft's steps, turned around, and waved at Uncle Terrence and my two Grandmas: the young, girlish spirit in the sunny yellow dress with ribbons in her hair, and the older one I was more familiar with, waving her handkerchief swiftly. I waved and shouted a final "Ta-ta, Grandma!"

and entered the red-and-white Air Canada aircraft with its red maple leaf of steel on the tail.

I strapped myself into my seat and waited to slip from sure family ties. The aircraft engines whistled a high-pitched squeal like a howling vengeful wind battering down windowpanes on a dark, stormy night. Suddenly, all was quiet. And I heard the crystal clear violin peals of Albinoni's *Adagio* streaming in from the aircraft's engines. It was as if the screaming noise of all four engines had transformed into a full-size orchestra performing a forceful rendition of that familiar but lethal prelude—alerting me to the angel of death's arrival. I was trapped. There was no escape. I closed my eyes and leaned back into my seat.

A mischievous grin crossed my face and masked the twitching inside my belly, as the pilot manoeuvred the jumbo jet, readying it to slice into the vexed air, above the raging sea, and fly me head-on into Hurricane Carol.

The End

GLOSSARY

Ackee Jamaica's national fruit

Anancy Stories Folk tales of a trickster and a culture hero, told in Jamaica and the Caribbean; originally from Africa

Babylon Any system or politicians deemed to be corrupt

Baldheads Slang for leaders with greedy and corrupt intensions (used commonly in 1970s Jamaica)

Black Moses Nickname for the Rt. Hon. Marcus Mosiah Garvey (Jamaica's national hero)

Blitzkrieg A German term for attacking the enemy with everything available

Bookmobile A library on wheels

Bulla cake A popular Jamaican cake that looks almost like a doughnut

Bush Jacket Type of jacket worn in the Caribbean during the 1970s

Callaloo A vegetable that resembles and tastes like spinach

Chaney root A scruffy root believed to be an aphrodisiac, found in Jamaica's Cockpit Country region

Coco bread A bread often eaten with beef patty

Cockpit Country A rugged interior wilderness region of Jamaica

Deep fine leg A leg-side position on the cricket field

Dem Them

Duke of Trelawny A tailor who designed Flinty's and his friends' clothing with bling

Duppy Ghost or bad spirit

Evil C Cancer

Forward short leg A cricket fielding position close to batsman's on the left

Fried dumpling A dumpling made from flour

Ganja Local name for marijuana

Grassquit A small brown bird that hops about on grass

Grater cake A sweet cake made from coconut

Hibiscus A plant grown in warm climates for its large brightly colored flowers.

Icy mint A popular Jamaican mint

IMF International Monetary Fund

Irie To be at total peace with your current state of being; the way you feel when you have no worries

Jah Short name for Jehovah

Jah Rastafari A spontaneous praise and salutation to Haile Selassie I of Ethiopia

JOS bus Jamaica Omnibus Service

Kariba suit A formal bush jacket suit worn by men in the Caribbean during the 1970s

Lignum vitae Jamaica's national tree, whose wood is dark and as tough as mahogany

Lion of the tribe of Judah Rasta believed to be Haile Selassie of Ethiopia

Manners Strict discipline

Obeah-man Voodoo practitioner

Patois A non-standard language; in Jamaica, the form of English mixed with African spoken in the Caribbean

Pimento Allspice tree

Pot-soup The water in which food is cooked

Rass A popular Jamaican swear word

Purple Label wine A popular local Jamaican wine

Rounders A game played by girls with a soft ball

Shitstym Slang for broken and corrupt system

Silly point A cricket fielding position close to the batter on a cricket field

Sour-sop A fruit squeezed into juice

Sorrel A popular drink served at Christmas in the Caribbean

Spring Valley A fictional village located in the Cockpit Country Region

Student Companion A student reference book with information about almost any subject

Tripe Intestine

Walk good A salutation that wishes another person the very best in his endeavors/journey; to travel with good spirits, peace, love and affection towards others

About the Author
Jeffery Wright

Jeffery Wright was born in the Parish of Trelawny, Jamaica, but now is a writer living in Pickering, Ontario. He divides his time into writing, spending time with his two sons in Canada, his daughter in St. Petersburg, Russia, and his family in Jamaica. He studied Creative Writing at the University of Toronto and at The School for Writers at Humber College. Ta-Ta, Grandma is his first novel.

Email contact: Jeffery.wright@live.ca

Acknowledgements

Horatio, my father, whose natural storytelling mastery I tried to copy with only a slim margin of success in my attempt to write this book.

Myra, my mother, a kind and gentle soul, who always had a hot meal ready after returning home from libraries on dark winter nights in Toronto.

Lucille, my grandmother, whose spirit forces me to begin writing.

My uncles, Reuel, Joe, Euwin, Guy and Phillip; men whose stories kept my mind buzzing with excitement when I was a boy.

Mrs. Wright, my aunt, who flooded my three, four, five, six and seven-year-old ears with the most riveting stories, while hanging out on her verandah.

Aunt Teslyn, my aunt, who meticulously inspected my school uniform for sugar cane stains on my way home.

Omar, Pierre and Caroline, this novel is for you all.

Monique Mueller, for your enduring friendship and support for my writing.

Roksana, for your warm support throughout the writing of this book.

Mr. Morris Stewart, my History and Social Studies teacher who got me thinking.

Mr. Morris, my Electrical Technology Instructor. Thanks for your confidence.

Mr. A. Levy, for your positive encouragement on and off the cricket field.

Paul Smith, Captain of Southern Trelawny's under nineteen Sports Development Division cricket team. One of the coolest Rastaman to ever trod upon this planet.

Mr. Dennis Shepherd, for those evenings of enlightened conversations, in between the penning of this novel.

Pastor H. Johnson, of Agape Temple Seventh-day Adventist Church, whose prayers continue to do exactly what they are supposed to do.

Olive Senior, for her mentoring and support.

Mr. McCurdy, my Semiconductor Physics Professor who introduced me to a calm and logical problem-solving method.